LOGIC,
LANGUAGE,
and
COMPOSITION

LOGIC, LANGUAGE, and COMPOSITION

Hulon Willis
Bakersfield College

Winthrop Publishers, Inc., Cambridge, Massachusetts

Library of Congress Cataloging in Publication Data

Willis, Hulon.
    Logic, language, and composition.

    1. English language — Rhetoric.   2. Logic
3. Language and languages.   I. Title.
PE1408.W613   808'.042   75-1422
ISBN 0-87626-504-2

Copyright © 1975 by Winthrop Publishers, Inc.
17 Dunster Street, Cambridge, Massachusetts 02138

ISBN 0-87626-504-2

10   9   8   7   6   5   4   3   2   1

for BRUCE

CONTENTS

PART I
LOGIC

PART II
LANGUAGE

PART III
COMPOSITION

PREFACE

This text is predicated on two assumptions: first, that an elementary study of logic and language, as well as a study of usage and composition, can greatly enhance a student's verbal skills and ability to think rationally; and second, that for freshman — especially for the so-called "new generation" of entering college students — variety in one class period's assignment is desirable. Therefore each of the thirty-six short chapters in this text contains both a lesson in logic, language, or composition and a lesson in usage, both accompanied by exercises.

My suggested plan for use of the book is to assign the chapters on logic and language in the sequence presented but to intersperse throughout the term (or even in the first half of it) the chapters on composition. The main point is that I do not intend the parts on logic and language to be completed before the chapters on composition are assigned. The three-part organization is designed to let each instructor decide for himself when to assign a chapter on composition. Also I have not myself provided writing assignments to accompany the chapters on logic and language, leaving it to each teacher to decide how he wants to combine those chapters with writing assignments.

The chapters on logic rigorously avoid all difficult technical aspects of formal and symbolic logic and deal only with simple ideas — not symbols or abstractions — that the students can understand. Yet this simple presentation shows student how their minds establish generalizations and come to specific conclusions, and it also provides them with a basic understanding of the chief logical fallacies. The chapters in Part II deal with a variety of simple aspects of language study likely to be of interest to the students and likely to increase their awareness of and skill in using language.

Most teachers recognize that nowadays most entering college students need instruction in usage, but there is no consensus as to how usage can best be taught. Perhaps the most common method bases instruction in usage on a study of elementary grammatical analysis. Though this approach cannot be called completely a failure, most realists recognize that its success is minimal. My experience leads me to believe that usage can best be taught on a practical basis: "Do this; don't do that." Therefore in the sections on usage that accompany each chapter (they are discrete units and need no be taught in sequence) I have used the minimum possible grammatical terms. I have also found that usage can best be taught in small doses; thus the practical lessons in usage are short. This spreading out of the teaching of usage into short lessons that will each occupy just a part of one day's assignment will, in my experience, provide the student with more lasting and usable knowledge than do most other approaches to the subject. Still, it is a truism that no teacher is fully satisfied with anybody else's text, and thus I have tried to prepare this text so that different teachers can use it in somewhat different ways.

Inside the front cover is a simple chart of correction symbols, with chapter references to the lessons in usage. Inside the back cover is a list of the 100 words most frequently misspelled by several thousand of my students over many years.

A free instructor's manual provides a key to the exercises.

Hulon Willis

PART ONE

LOGIC

CHAPTER 1
DEFINITIONS OF LOGIC AND RELATED TERMS

Experimental psychologists have recently learned that a normal infant begins to use logical processes at about the age of nine months — usually before he can walk or talk. After that early beginning, the normal individual uses logic constantly until he dies or loses his mind. But the logic he uses may be faulty rather than sound and thus may cause harm (to him or others) rather than good. Therefore, it is worthwhile for human beings to understand what logic is and how they can reduce their faulty use of it. Also, an understanding of logic helps one write better, for clear thinking leads to clear writing.

First we will define the term *logic* and other terms used in connection with it[1]; then for a number of short chapters we will consider both sound and unsound logic. The word *logic* comes from a Greek word meaning "reason," and logic may be defined as "the science of reasoning." **Reasoning** is the process of drawing a conclusion from evidence or what one takes to be evidence. The **conclusion** is the fact, judgment, or opinion produced by reasoning. For example, if you see a girl with black eyebrows and blond hair with black roots, you have evidence to conclude that she has dyed her hair. You have reasoned, in that you have drawn a conclusion (in this case a fact and not just an opinion) from sound evidence. However, logic does not always lead to a factual conclusion. For example, if you saw a student come out of a restroom walking erratically and acting abnormally, you

---

[1] The very important terms *induction* and *deduction* will be introduced later at the **appropriate places.**

might use logic to conclude that he has taken drugs. But it might be that he is just sick. You would have used evidence to reach a conclusion, but the conclusion would (unless you investigated further) be an opinion rather than a fact. Logic, then, is the whole process of reaching a conclusion through the use of reasoning.

Another important term in discussing logic is **assumption.** An assumption is a judgment or opinion which a reasoner takes to be true even though he is not certain — and perhaps can never be certain — that it is true. For example a professor might assume (i.e., take as an assumption) that a term paper is not the student's own work because its quality is much higher than any of the student's other work. The professor, unless he investigates thoroughly, has no proof of his assumption; indeed, he may be completely wrong in thinking the student cheated. But he may act on the assumption and lower the student's grade. Many assumptions are not even based on as much evidence as the professor had. For example, "God punishes the wicked" is an assumption some people hold, but it is not based on evidence; it is just a belief. We constantly use assumptions of all sorts in our logical thinking, and we need to carefully avoid false assumptions that may hurt others.

Another important term in the study of logic is **premise,** which is a statement phrased so that it affirms or denies that something is true or false. A premise may be an assumption or it may be a fact. It serves as the basis for argument or for drawing a conclusion. For example, "arsenic is poisonous" is a premise, and one can reason from this premise to the conclusion that "I should not eat this food, which has arsenic in it." But "arsenic is not poisonous" is also a premise, and one might harm himself if he drew a conclusion from that premise, since it is false. Problems in logic are often complicated because we might not ever be able to know whether a premise is true or false. For example, many educators reason from the premise that "heredity does more than environment to determine one's intelligence." Other educators draw conclusions from a completely opposite premise. So far, no one knows for certain which premise is true. We all frequently are forced to draw conclusions on the basis of premises that we cannot know are true.

Two other important terms in the study of logic are **generalization** and **specific.** A generalization is a statement that covers many specific cases, such as "many industrial wastes kill fish," which applies to countless different instances. A specific applies to just one case, such as "At 10:00 AM on January 29, acid dumped from the AGC plant killed three fish." Some statements, such as "free enterprise is desirable," can seem to be generalizations from one point of view and specifics from another. The conclusions we reach through reasoning are sometimes generalizations and sometimes specifics.

In connection with generalizations, the term **qualification** is important. Many generalizations are stated in such a sweeping way that they become over-broad and thus unsound. For example, some people have said that "smoking marijuana leads to taking heroin." That generalization is so sweeping or over-broad that intelligent people will reject it. But a generalization may be **qualified,** which means that it is stated so that not all specifics that it could cover are included. Qualification is achieved by the use of such words as *many, a few, under certain circumstances, sometimes, a certain percentage of,* and so on. For example, the qualified generalization "smoking marijuana seems occasionally to lead to taking heroin" is acceptable.

The final term we will define in this introductory chapter is **refutation,** which is the process of destroying the logical basis of someone else's argument. For example, prior to our Revolutionary War, many Tory colonists said we should continue to be colonies of England, since as colonies we had prospered. To refute this argument, Tom Paine said you might as well say that since an infant thrives on its mother's milk for its first year, it should eat nothing but its mother's milk for its next twenty years. Paine, in effect, destroyed the premise of the Tory colonists, which was "what has caused us to prosper in the past will cause us to prosper in the future" — a premise which cannot be true for every situation. Or for another example, suppose that in a presidential election a supporter of the president should assert that since the country is in a crisis it should not change presidents. Then he clinches his argument by saying, "you shouldn't change horses in the middle of a stream." You might refute the argument by retorting that "you *should* change horses if yours is too weak to cross the stream or if you can get onto a better horse without danger." You would have smothered the premise that "one president cannot adequately handle a crisis that began under a former president." To refute an argument, you need to know what premises your opponent is basing his argument on.

A LESSON IN THINKING

Some people argue that possession or use of marijuana should be illegal because, though the drug is not addictive, a user may become psychologically dependent on it. After deciding what premises those people base their argument on, refute their argument if you can. Or, if you agree with their argument, tell why you think your premises are sound and thus also your conclusion (i.e., the conclusion that possession or use of marijuana should be illegal).

EXERCISE

1. What premise or premises do you believe led to the following conclusions? Would you accept any of the premises as true?
    a. The best candidate always wins.

b. Medical doctors should be our highest-paid professionals.

c. Participating in sports builds good character.

d. Any drug — prescribed or not — is harmful.

e. Students learn most from likable teachers.

2. Distinguish between specifics and generalizations in the following statements:

a. Drinking alcoholic beverages is wrong.

b. Social drinking of alcohol is not wrong.

c. My cat See-See died.

d. Every cat deserves a balanced diet.

e. Cat Chow contains more protein than any other cat food.

f. Competition for grades in college promotes better education.

g. I did not deserve the low grade I got in calculus.

h. High grades impress prospective employers.

i. Teachers often grade arbitrarily.

j. Julius cheated to get his high grades.

3. Would you qualify any of the following statements, and if so, how?

a. Undergraduates are not mature enough to engage in independent study.

b. Unmarried lovers harm no one.

c. Trade unions are necessary if workers are to be properly paid.

d. The brightest college graduates make the best teachers.

e. Regular church attendance builds good character.

USAGE
LESSON
1

A
SPELLING
RULE

The Doubling-of-the-Final-Consonant Spelling Rule
When adding a suffix beginning with a vowel to a word that is accented on the last syllable and ends in one consonant preceded by one vowel, double the final consonant.

   This is the most complicated and probably the most important of the spelling rules. It is based on a very important phonetic principle in English spelling, called the "long-vowel, short-vowel principle." The principle is this: *In a vowel-consonant-vowel sequence the first vowel, IF ACCENTED, is long; in a vowel-consonant-consonant or a vowel-consonant-end of word sequence, the vowel is short.* In the following examples the vowels in the accented syllables in the first column of words are long and the vowels in the second column are short:

Long	Short
rate	rat
interfere	refer
bite	bitten
rote	rot
cured	occurred

Made-up words will have the same pronunciations:

yate	yat
zete	zet
pibe	pib
tove	tov
dure	dur

Even a third- or fourth-grader would know what pronunciations to give these made-up words.

The vowel sounds in the first column are long because of the vowel-consonant-vowel sequence. The vowel sounds in the second column are short because the vowel is followed by two consonants or by one consonant and the end of the word. This phonetic principle accounts for the doubling-of-the-final-consonant rule.

The rule is complicated. You should get all of its parts in mind. These conditions must be present:

1. You must be adding a suffix beginning with a vowel, such as *ing, ed, er, est,* and so on.
2. The word must be of one syllable or be accented on the last syllable, such as *refér, compél, occúr,* and so on. The accented syllable is the one spoken loudest.
3. The word must end in one consonant preceded by one vowel, such as *admit, debar,* and *slap.* (*Equip* and *quit* are exceptions.)

When these three conditions are present, you double the final consonant.

Here are some examples:

occur + ed = occurred	brag + ing = bragging
refer + ing = referring	quit + ing = quitting
stop + ed = stopped	begin +ing = beginning
omit + ing = omitting	compel + ed = compelled
red + est = reddest	admit + ed = admitted

Note what the pronunciation of these words would be if the final consonant were not doubled. For example, if there were only one *r* in *occurred,* it would rhyme with *cured.* Or if there were only one *r* in *referring,* it would rhyme with *interfering.*

If the last syllable of a word is not accented, the consonant is not doubled. Examples:

BANter + ing = bantering	proHIBit + ed = prohibited
HAPpen + ed = happened	BENefit + ed = benefited

Similarly, the final consonant is never doubled when a suffix beginning with a consonant is added. Examples:

glad + ness = gladness	sin + ful = sinful

Do not confuse doubling-of-the-final-consonant words with silent *e* words. You must not double the consonant in such words as these:

dine + ing = dining	interfere + ed = interfered
write + ing = writing	come + ing = coming

Note that doubling the consonants would give such pronunciations as *din + ning* and *writ + ting,* with short *i* rather than long *i* sounds.

EXERCISE 1. Build the following words as indicated. In some cases you should double the final consonant and in some cases you shouldn't.

1. occur + ed = _____
2. interfer + ed = _____
3. refer + ed = _____
4. honor + able = _____
5. omit + ing = _____
6. debar + ed = _____
7. hinder + ed = _____
8. begin + ing = _____
9. com + ing = _____
10. din + ing = _____
11. dine + ing = _____
12. bid + ing = _____
13. bide + ing = _____
14. benefit + ed = _____
15. equip + ing = _____
16. concur + ed = _____
17. note + ing = _____
18. rot + ing = _____
19. confer + ed = _____
20. sin + ful = _____

21. sin + er = _____
22. big + est = _____
23. big + ness = _____
24. drop + ed = _____
25. droop + ed = _____
26. red + en = _____
27. red + ness = _____
28. abandon + ed = _____
29. firm + er = _____
30. war + ing = _____
31. war + fare = _____
32. bite + ing = _____
33. bit + en = _____
34. fog + y = _____
35. submit + ing = _____
36. differ + ing = _____
37. transfer + ed = _____
38. suffer + ed = _____
39. regret + able = _____
40. offer + ed = _____

41. hate + ing = _____   51. drag + ed = _____

42. bat + ing = _____   52. repel + ing = _____

43. stop + ed = _____   53. defer + ed = _____

44. stoop + ed = _____   54. shin + ed = _____

45. unforget + able = ____   55. blot + ing = _____

46. shine + ing = _____   56. lop + ed = _____

47. recur + ed = _____   57. rap + ed = _____

48. excel + ed = _____   58. drip + ing = _____

49. hop + ed = _____   59. bid + able = _____

50. hope + ed = _____   60. glad + en = _____

CHAPTER
2

INDUCTION,
OR
ESTABLISHING
GENERALIZATIONS

In the preceding chapter you were introduced to important terms used in the study of logic and were generally introduced to the idea that using logic means reasoning from evidence to reach a conclusion. Now here and in Chapter 6 you will learn about the two major kinds of reasoning — **induction** and **deduction.**

Inductive logic is usually defined as "reasoning from the specific to the general," but that definition needs explanation. With induction, the conclusion reached is *always* a generalization. As you learned in the last chapter, a generalization, such as "college subjects require more weekly study than high school subjects," covers many specific cases. Any inductive generalization is reached only after a few or many occurrences end with the same result, leading the observer to believe that in the future a similar occurrence will also end with the same result. Sometimes a person sets out deliberately to prove (or disprove) an inductive generalization. Often in our daily lives we just accidentally stumble on such generalizations.

Here is an example of how you might accidentally establish an inductive generalization. Suppose you have enrolled in a course called Great Novels and learn at the outset that for the course you are to read ten novels and have a test on each. Being a busy college student, you decide for the first novel just to read a short summary of its plot and one of the commentaries that are sold in college bookstores. You fail your first test. Saying, "Well, the next test will be a different kind," you try the same tactic. And you fail again. With your third consecutive failure after not reading the assigned novel, you are ready to believe the inductive generalization that "I can't pass Professor Blank's tests on novels by just reading plot summaries and commentaries." It may be too late for the generalization to do you any good, but you can pass it on to others, for whom the generalization would also probably be true. The above is a very simple example, but it in effect explains how inductive logic works: On the basis of observed specifics, one draws a generalization that he thinks will apply to all similar specifics in the future (though we must note here than an established generalization may last for only a certain period of time because conditions change).

The number of specifics needed to establish a sound, unqualified inductive generalization varies, of course. Sometimes even one specific is enough to establish a sound generalization. For example, someone (never mind who) once decided to use a solution of chromic acid to try to cure a case of athlete's foot. That one specific (which led to the use of crutches) was enough for him to draw a permanent, sound inductive generalization about the use of chromic acid to cure athlete's foot.

Sometimes just a few specifics are enough to establish sound generalizations. For example, suppose you switch to a new kind of low-lead gasoline for your car. On the first tankful your car runs smoothly, but on the second tankful your car engine knocks. You nevertheless try a third tankful and get good results, but on the fourth your engine knocks badly again. You now have enough evidence to draw the generalization that "This station's low-lead pump does not always carry the same quality of gasoline." In simple, uncomplex matters, a very few specifics often suffice to establish a sound inductive generalization, though, as we said, many such generalizations have a short life.

Sometimes you must observe a large number of specifics before you can reach a true inductive generalization. For example, a college textbook company would have to undertake an extensive study of specifics to draw an acceptable generalization whether their use of airmail postage to speed examination copies of their books to college professors over the long run brings more profit than using slow fourth-class mail. A half-dozen specifics in such a case just could not be trusted to establish a general truth that would hold in the future.

Sometimes no reasonable number of specifics is sufficient to establish an unqualified inductive generalization. For example, in the nineteenth century most Americans believed that all American Indians were cruel. But such a generalization about a trait of character within an entire race is simply not acceptable on the basis of just a few dozen or so specifics. Instead a *qualified* generalization would have to be established (see Chapter 5).

Inductive logic, then, is one of the two primary modes of reasoning. Whenever a person forms a generalization (knowingly or unknowingly) after observing specifics, he has used induction. His inductive generalization may be true, like some of those cited above. It might need qualification, such as observing that *some* students will cheat if given a chance. Or, because of misinterpretation of evidence, a generalization may be entirely false, such as the near-universal belief in the seventeenth century that witches existed.

A LESSON IN THINKING

Avoiding generalizations that you already believe, think of one sound generalization that you think could be established on the basis of just one observed specific, another that could be established on the basis of just a few specifics, and a third that would require many specifics before it could be accepted as true.

EXERCISE

As you will discover later in the course, if you haven't already, many paragraphs in student themes are developed inductively. That is, the topic sentence is a generalization and then the paragraph is developed with specifics which are supposed to make the generalization of the topic sentence believable. Here is an example from a student theme:

> Furthermore, the recreational facilities in this town are in disrepair and often are unsafe. In Washington Park the children's swings are not hung level nor high enough, with the result that many children skin their knees when they try to swing. The public swimming pool in Jefferson Park does not have adequate life guards; its water is not kept in the proper chemical balance; and stucco is peeling off its sides. The baseball field in Jefferson Park is just too small for the use of strong teenagers, who knock the ball out of the park every time. The pool tables, ping pong tables, and other equipment in the City Recreation Hall are warped and provide no fun for skilled players. These are just a few of the reasons why young people in this town are unhappy with the means provided for them to entertain themselves.

The writer stated his generalization as a topic sentence and then gave specifics to justify his statement.

Choosing one of the following three topic sentences, or a topic sentence of your own, write such an inductive paragraph yourself.

1. The money spent on space exploration is not wasted.
2. Teachers can be deceived as to the actual amount of work a student does.
3. Teenagers are more idealistic than members of their parents' generation.

USAGE
LESSON
2

TWO
SPELLING
RULES

Rules for Dropping and Retaining Silent e's: The First Rule

When adding a suffix beginning with a vowel to a word ending in a silent e, drop the silent e (exceptions noted in the next rule). This rule, like the doubling-of-the-final-consonant rule, is based on the long-vowel, short-vowel principle, which says that in an ACCENTED syllable a vowel-consonant-vowel sequence makes the first vowel long. For example,

dine	write
shine	cite

are all pronounced with a long *i* because of the vowel-consonant-vowel sequence. The *e*, though not pronounced, is doing the work of making the *i* long. To understand that this is true, just drop the silent *e* and see what pronunciations you would have.

Now it is not a silent *e* alone that will produce such long-vowel sounds; *any* vowel will do the work of the silent *e*. Therefore, when we add a suffix beginning with a vowel to such a word, we don't need the silent *e* any longer and thus we drop it. Examples:

dine + ing = dining	imagine + ative = imaginative
write + ing = writing	mange + y = mangy
mate + ed = mated	use + age = usage
create + ive = creative	mere + est = merest

Because each suffix begins with a vowel, the long-vowel sounds are preserved even though the silent *e* is dropped. (Never double a consonant in a silent *e* word, for that would make the vowel short and give an entirely different pronunciation, such as *din-ning* instead of *dine-ing*.)

The silent *e* is not dropped when the added suffix begins with a consonant.

Examples:

like + ness = likeness	safe + ty = safety
fate + ful = fateful	late + ly = lately

Note that if the silent *e* is dropped in such cases, wrong pronunciations, such as *lik-ness* and *fat-ful,* result. The following words are exceptions to this part of the rule; the silent *e* is dropped even though the added suffix begins with a consonant:

whole + ly = wholly	argue + ment = argument
true + ly = truly	awe + ful = awful
judge + ment = judgment	

The Second Rule

When adding able, ous or ance to a word ending in a silent e preceded by a c or g, retain the silent e. The reason for this rule is that *c*'s and *g*'s in English have two sounds. First, the **soft** *c* is pronounced as an *s,* as in *city* and *nice.* The **hard** *c* is pronounced as a *k,* as in *cable* and *recount.* A *c* is almost always soft (*s*) when followed by *e, i,* or *y.* It is almost always hard (*k*) when followed by *a, o,* or *u.* Thus in words ending in a silent *e* preceded by a *c,* the *c* is soft, as in *service.* When we add *able* to such a word, we must retain the silent *e,* for if we drop it, the *c* is then followed by an *a* and would thus become hard (*k*). For example, in *servic-able* the *c* would be hard and the pronunciation would be *servikable.* Here are examples of the rule being applied:

service + able = serviceable	peace + able = peaceable
notice + able = noticeable	replace + able = replaceable

The silent *e* must be retained to prevent the *c* from being pronounced as a *k.*

There is also another minor matter in English spelling concerning the hard *c.* A *c* is hard when it is the last letter in a word, as in *tic* and *Bic* pens. Thus when a suffix beginning with *e, i,* or *y* is added to a word ending in *c,* a *k* must be added to retain the hard *c* sound. For example, *panic-ed* would be pronounced with a soft *c,* as in *pan-iced.* Here are the most common words affected by this rule:

panic + y = panicky	politic + ing = politicking
picnic + er = picnicker	traffic + ed = trafficked

We also have a **soft** *g,* pronounced as the *j* in *Jill,* as in *gin* and *gyp,* and a **hard** *g,* pronounced *guh,* as in *begin* and *got.* The hard and soft *g*'s are not nearly as regular as the hard and soft *c*'s, but these regularities almost always hold: (1) a *g* followed by a silent *e* is always soft, as in *rage;* (2) a *g* followed by an *a* or *o* is always hard, as in *gat* and *gone.* Thus when we add *able, ous,* or *ance* to a word that ends in a silent *e* preceded by a *g,* we must keep the silent *e* to retain the soft *g* sound and prevent a hard *g*. For example, *courage-ous* retains the soft *g* sound, but *courag-ous* would have a hard *g* with the last syllable being *gous*. Here are examples of the rule's being applied:

advantage + ous = advantageous   arrange + able = arrangeable
outrage + ous = outrageous   change + able = changeable
venge + ance = vengeance   manage + able = manageable

The silent *e* must be retained to prevent the *g* from being pronounced as *guh*.

EXERCISE 2. Build the following words as indicated. In some cases you will drop the final *e* and in some cases you will keep it.

1. write + ing = _____
2. change + able = _____
3. service + able = _____
4. dine + ing = _____
5. come + ing = _____
6. shine + ing = _____
7. arrange + able = _____
8. condole + ence = _____
9. peeve + ish = _____
10. love + able = _____
11. whole + ly = _____
12. argue + ment = _____
13. safe + ly = _____
14. use + ful = _____
15. care + less = _____
16. pursue + ing = _____
17. complete + ly = _____
18. use + ing = _____
19. love + ly = _____
20. guide + ance = _____
21. improve + ment = _____
22. sincerely + ly = _____
23. sure + ly = _____
24. trace + able = _____
25. outrage + ous = _____
26. venge + ance = _____
27. argue + ing = _____
28. charge + able = _____
29. fame + ous = _____
30. shine + y = _____
31. scare + ed = _____
32. dine + ed = _____
33. late + ly = _____
34. immediate + ly = _____
35. approximate + ly = _____
36. true + ly = _____
37. awe + ful = _____
38. interfere + ing = _____
39. rage + ing = _____
40. confuse + ed = _____

41. ice + ing = _____   46. revere + ed = _____

42. courage + ous = _____   47. sole + ly = _____

43. suppose + ed = _____   48. bite + ing = _____

44. place + able = _____   49. merge + able = _____

45. appropriate + ly = _____   50. cure + ed = _____

CHAPTER
3
SCIENTIFIC INDUCTIONS

Inductive reasoning is used by everybody; any time a person (knowingly or unknowingly) establishes a generalization on the basis of observed specifics, he has used induction. But induction is most closely associated with the **scientific method.** Scientific observation of specifics leads both to facts and to *theories* and *hypotheses* (which are assumptions), all being inductive generalizations. For example, it is a fact that penicillin will cure some venereal diseases. But it is only a hypothesis that heavy doses of vitamin C will lessen one's susceptibility to colds (no factual generalization has yet been established, and may never be).

It took mankind a long time to come to an understanding of the value of inductive experimentation. The great Greek civilization, particularly in its last days at Alexandria, Egypt, produced some remarkable scientific inductions through experimentation, but throughout the Dark Ages and Middle Ages in Europe it seldom occurred to anyone to test widely held generalizations through observation of specifics or to establish new generalizations through experimentation. Instead, thinkers and common people alike in those times simply accepted the ideas of ancient "authorities," especially Aristotle. No matter how much everyday experience contradicted authoritarian ideas, most people believe the authorities and ignored their own experience. For example, millions of people bought or touched pieces of the "original" cross in the belief that such touching would cure their diseases. It made no difference that their diseases usually remained uncured; they still believed the authoritarian ideas and did not think of trying inductive experimentation. As late as 1725 in England it was believed that scrofula (a form of tuberculosis) could be cured by the touch of the king. It is not recorded that any cases were cured, but it seldom occurred to anyone before that time to disbelieve the authoritarian generalization.

In the thirteenth century, a little inductive science was practiced by Roger Bacon; and early alchemists, whose chief goal was to change base metals into gold, used induction (unknowingly) in that they discarded methods that didn't work. However, it was not until the late sixteenth century that the great Englishman Sir Francis Bacon proclaimed induction as the road to an understanding and control of nature and thus a means to man's salvation on this earth. Since that time man has gradually increased his respect for and command of induction as the way to knowledge. But even today the mass of mankind has little understanding of scientific induction and its successes.

Scientists use induction in both **applied** and **pure research.** In applied research scientists set out to solve a specific problem. For example, after the atom bomb was invented and exploded, applied researchers set out to find a method to control the fission of the atoms so that energy could be slowly released and used to produce electricity. They achieved their goal through inductive experimentation — that is, by accumulating specifics until they had enough to base a generalization on. For a time, all the generalizations they established were negative so far as achieving their goal was concerned. But eventually they got positive generalizations, and we now have atomic power plants.

Or for another example of applied research, consider the search that thousands of medical scientists make for medicines that will either cure diseases or reduce their symptoms. These researchers synthesize new compounds and try them first on test animals, observing the effects to establish generalizations. Perhaps one out of fifty new compounds shows promising results of some sort. Eventually the researcher may test the compound on human beings with a certain malady. With careful observation of specific cases a researcher may, after months or years of work, be able to form such a generalization as "Fifteen milligrams of X compound four times per day will significantly reduce depression in 80 percent of patients who suffer clinical depression." Such results of scientific induction have so altered the death rate of human beings that the earth is now in serious danger of overpopulation.

Scientists engaged in pure research also depend on induction, the difference between them and applied researchers being that they are not looking for a useful product or process but just for almost anything that might turn up. For example, in the mid-nineteenth century, an obscure monk named Gregor Johann Mendel experimented with cross-breeding peas of different colors. He was not trying to breed a better pea or to establish useful knowledge, but just to find out what would happen. His inductive experiments established the generalization that hereditary traits are transmitted in discrete units, though the importance of his discovery was not recognized for thirty-five years. Pure inductive research on hereditary transmission continues. Eventually there will be applied research on hereditary transmission, and one day it may be that some deformities that occur naturally in some human infants will be removed from hereditary transmission. Inductive generalizations will make these marvels occur.

But it should be noted that many scientific problems are so complex, particularly those relating to human physical and mental illnesses and social problems, that it is often very difficult, if not impossible, for scientists to arrive at usable inductive generalizations. For example, the blood of schizophrenics has a component not found in the blood of nonschizophrenics, but researchers have not yet been able to establish conclusively whether the blood component *causes* schizophrenia or is the *result* of it. And as for such social problems as child abuse, social scientists are far from being able to establish sound inductive generalizations which will predict which parents will be child abusers.

We should also note that **pseudosciences** exist, with the practitioners claiming inductive generalizations for which there is very little reliable evidence. For example, astrologists claim to base their generalizations on observed specifics, but of course they do not. Even if the planets and stars do have some influence on our lives — which is possible (consider the moon's effect on the tides) — it is certain that no one has any valid inductive evidence as to what that influence might be.

Such fakery has always been with us. For example, in the nineteenth century virtually everybody believed in phrenology — the "science" of determining one's character and personality (and thus to a degree forecasting his life) by analyzing the shape of his head. No valid inductive evidence was ever produced to show that phrenologists had any true generalizations, and yet many millions of people paid good money for "head readings." Even today many palmists — those who claim to read your future in the creases of your palms — bilk millions of gullible people. Palmists too, of course, have no sound inductive generalizations, though they claim to. Just as real science thrives on induction, pseudoscience thrives on pretended induction, most of its victims not even being aware of what induction is.

A LESSON IN THINKING

In the seventeenth century virtually everyone, including the most learned, believed in witches. During that century in Germany alone there were over 100,000 recorded instances of witches being burned at the stake. Learned and common people in America also believed in witchcraft. From a good encyclopedia, find out what kind of evidence was used to convict and hang nineteen witches in Salem, Massachusetts in 1692 and show how scientific induction might have overturned that faulty evidence.

EXERCISES

1. Suppose a hog farmer is not satisfied with the rate of growth of his pigs and hogs. How might he use scientific induction to reach a generalization about increasing the growth rate of his animals?
2. Explain how a teacher might form an inductive generalization about which method of teaching spelling is most successful.
3. Explain in detail any experience you have had in a school laboratory in which you used induction (observation of specifics) to arrive at a generalization that you assumed would hold true for all future specifics of the same kind.

USAGE
LESSON
3

TWO
SPELLING
RULES

The *ie*, *ei* Spelling Rule

Place i before e when pronounced as ee except after c; place e before i when pronounced as a long a.

In using this rule you must know everything about a word except whether it has an *ie* or *ei* combination; the rule tells you which. For example, the rule will not help you spell *receipt* correctly unless you know it has a silent *p;* but it will tell you that *receipt* has an *ei,* not an *ie,* combination.

The rule works only when the *ie* or *ei* combination is pronounced as a single long vowel: a long *e* or *a.* For example, the *i* and *e* are pronounced separately in *science,* and thus the rule does not apply to that word. And in *foreign* the rule does not apply because the *ei* has the vowel sound of *run,* not a long *e* or *a.*

Here are examples of long *e* words covered by the rule:

ei *after* c	ie *after other letters*
receive	believe
deceive	niece
deceit	chief
conceive	achieve
receipt	priest
ceiling	thief

And here are examples of long *a* words covered by the rule:

freight	neighbor
veil	vein
weight	reign
reins	heir (in some dialects)
surveillance	their (in some dialects)

Five troublesome exceptions to the rule can be learned by memorizing this nonsense sentence:

Neither sheik seized weird leisure.

All three are *ei* words even though the combination does not follow *c*. A few other exceptions, such as *either*, give no trouble.

The *y-to-i* Spelling Rule

When adding a suffix to a word ending in y preceded by a consonant, change the y to i.

When this rule is used to make nouns plural or verbs third person singular, present tense, an *es* follows the *i*. Examples:

ally — allies   deny — denies
baby — babies   fry — fries
lady — ladies   try — tries

The rule also operates with other suffixes. Examples:

busy — business   easy — easily
cry — crier   lonely — loneliness
dry — driest   necessary — necessarily

The rules does not apply when the suffix is *ing* or *ist*. Examples:

copy + ist = copyist   study + ing = studying
deny + ing = denying   worry + ing = worrying

The *y* is *never* just dropped. For example, *studing* is a very common misspelling.

There are a few exceptions to the rule:

shyness   dryness
dryer (the machine) slyly

Also the rule does not apply in spelling the plural of proper nouns:

Bradys   Kennedys
Crowlys   Moselys

When a final *y* is preceded by a vowel, the *y* is NOT changed when a suffix is added. Examples:

alley + s = alleys   coy + ness = coyness
annoy + s = annoys   donkey + s = donkeys
boy + hood = boyhood   employ + er = employer
convey + ed = conveyed   stay + ed = stayed

There are a few common exceptions to this part of the rule:

day + ly = daily   pay + ed = paid
gay + ly = gally   say + ed = said
lay + ed = laid

EXERCISE 3A. Following the *i-e* spelling rule and exceptions, fill in the missing letters in the following words.

1. ach ____ ve
2. bel ____ ve
3. br ____ f
4. c ____ ling
5. ch ____ f
6. conc ____ t
7. conc ____ ve
8. dec ____ t
9. dec ____ ve
10. f ____ ld
11. fr ____ ght
12. gr ____ f
13. l ____ n
14. l ____ sure
15. n ____ gh
16. n ____ ghbor

17. n ____ ce
18. perc ____ ve
19. pr ____ st
20. rec ____ ve
21. rec ____ pt
22. r ____ ns
23. rel ____ f
24. rel ____ ve
25. s ____ ze
26. sh ____ ld
27. s ____ ge
28. th ____ f
29. w ____ ght
30. w ____ ld
31. w ____ rd
32. y ____ ld

EXERCISE 3B. Following the *y-to-i* spelling rule and exceptions, build the following words as indicated.

1. deny + al = _____
2. mercy + ful = _____
3. carry + er = _____
4. carry + ing = _____
5. play + ed = _____
6. rely + ance = _____
7. copy + ed = _____
8. copy + ist = _____

9. try + al = _____
10. modify + er = _____
11. defy + s = _____
12. defy + ing = _____
13. kindly + ness = _____
14. enjoy + s = _____
15. fly + s = _____
16. study + ous = _____

17. delay + ed = _____   29. day + ly = _____
18. employ + s = _____   30. stray + ing = _____
19. lonely + ness = _____   31. try + s = _____
20. busy + est = _____   32. busy + ness = _____
21. study + ing = _____   33. ready + ness = _____
22. happy + ness = _____   34. alley + s = _____
23. greedy + er = _____   35. ally + s = _____
24. lovely + ness = _____   36. holy + ness = _____
25. pay + s = _____   37. harry + ed = _____
26. pay + ed = _____   38. shy + ness = _____
27. beauty + ful = _____   39. Grady + s = _____
28. hurry + ed = _____   40. Kennedy + s = _____

CHAPTER
4

PUBLIC
AND
PRIVATE
INDUCTIONS

Induction — the forming of a generalization on the basis of observing specifics — is the foundation of the scientific method, and in the past few centuries the world has repeatedly been profoundly changed by the scientific method. In only the last couple of decades, for example, the dramatic rise of the giant computers has significantly altered our ways of conducting many of our affairs and even our ways of looking at ourselves — of understanding what kind of beings we are. But induction is by no means limited to the scientific method.

Induction is not even exclusively human. There is hardly an animal species of much complexity that does not use induction and modify its behavior on the basis of acquired inductive generalizations. Insects, for example, are notoriously instinct-bound. A praying mantis will placidly continue to devour a victim while its lower part is itself being devoured by some other predator. Yet even insects will occasionally modify their behavior after a few specifics has etched an inductive generalization into their tiny nervous systems. A colony of ants, for example, often establishes a route to a food source. When that route is blocked, they will retreat in disorder, and then make a few more attempts to use the route again. But soon they will abandon the route and establish a new one. Their few specific defeats lead them to the generalization that the old route will always bring defeat. This is not human reasoning, but it *is* induction.

Among higher animals, induction is prevalent. For example, some insects protect themselves against birds by having an acrid taste. A bird is not born with an instinct to avoid such an insect. Yet often just one attempt to eat such an insect will "teach" an individual bird the permanent inductive generalization that such an insect is not good food. Experiments show that when a bird has learned its lesson, it can be surrounded by such insects and will not touch them even if deprived of all other food. In a sense the bird is using logic, though not complex logic.

But many mammals use logic in a complex way. For example, suppose a cat watches a dog through sliding glass doors. If, when the dog walks out of its view, the cat rushes to a window to get a continued view, it has put to use rather complex inductions that it has made a part of its central nervous system. And it is a confirmed fact that chimpanzees can learn rather complex symbolic languages, the learning of which demands induction of a high order.

In the general public mind there are a great many inductive generalizations not arrived at scientifically that are profoundly influential in our daily lives. Many of these inductions are soundly based on good evidence; many are false and cause harm. Many are of major importance, many only minor. First, let's see the general process by which public inductions enter our culture (though we must emphasize that not everyone believes any one particular public induction; controversial generalizations are plentiful).

One widely believed public induction is that most politicians are crooked. Why should many people believe this when no statistical study has been made to show that the generalization is valid and when the large majority of politicians are never even alleged to have acted illegally? The reason is simple. From long before the estabishment of our republic, various politicians have been "caught with their hands in the till." Most instances of bribery and graft are soon forgotten, but some linger long in the public memory. Scandals from President Grant's administration enliven every textbook of United States history. Almost everyone knows that a cabinet member of President Harding's administration went to jail for accepting bribes; and President Truman's and Eisenhower's administrations were troubled by scandals. The 1972 conviction of an Illinois judge and former governor is still discussed. And in 1973 the majority of the populace became convinced that President Nixon himself sanctioned illegal political activity and that Vice President Agnew accepted bribes. Even a few such specifics, working on human nature, have led many to believe the inductive generalization "They're all crooked." Thus many honest politicians suffer because of a public induction that grew out of a few specifics. The next chapter will show how inductions of this sort, which usually have some but not complete validity, should be qualified, or not taken as 100% true.

Many public inductions, of course, are not nearly so colorful and attention-getting as those just mentioned. For example, consider the quiet and automatic installation of bright street lights in new residential subdivisions. Why are such lights just automatically installed? Because over the years people have observed that burglary rates go down when street illumination goes up. When enough specifics showed this generalization to be true, the public accepted the induction (without realizing the logical process involved) and began to act on it. The inductive generalization comes into public consciousness only when some governmental agency fails to install sufficient street lights. Countless such public inductions — both valid and partially or wholly false — flow through the public consciousness. The most harmful, probably, are the false ones ascribing bad characteristics to entire races or nationalities of human beings.

Each individual, too, has a set of private inductions that he shares with few, if any, other individuals. For example, a new wife may soon discover that each time she is late in preparing dinner, her husband gets angry. After a very few specfic instances, she develops the inductive generalization that any time she is late with dinner, her husband gets angry. How she acts on the generalization depends on her own personality. She may conscientiously avoid being late with dinner, or she may at times deliberately be late for the express purpose of making her husband angry, out of spite. Or she might just adjust to his anger. Innumerable private inductions of this sort are in the minds of all normal people and greatly affect the way an individual conducts his life.

Individual inductions of personal taste are perhaps the most common. As one grows up, an incredible complex of specifics overwhelms him. He forms countless inductive generalizations about such things as the food, clothing, entertainment, women or men, literature, and so on that he likes or dislikes. For example, on one hand, the youngster (or adult for that matter) who simply will not drink buttermilk has formed an inductive generalization about it, probably on the basis of a very few specifics. On the other hand, simply growing up with something will by no means insure that a person will develop a taste (inductive generalization) for it. A child may grow up hearing his parents play classical records innumerable times, for example, but he still may have a private induction that he does not like such music.

The pervasive influence of public and private inductions in our lives is such that it is very interesting to investigate one's own beliefs and to judge whether they were arrived at on the basis of sound logic. The following exercises will give you some practice in understanding inductive generalizations.

A LESSON IN THINKING

Consider that you have got a temporary job (your great job, of course, is coming soon) as a bill collector for a finance company. During the first few days on the job, your approach to delinquents is always the same, but they react in widely varying ways, some being very belligerent and some cooperative. How would you go about determining whether to use different approaches to make most of the delinquents cooperative? How would your modification of your approaches be based on inductive logic?

EXERCISES

1. Cite a public induction about blacks (or any other minority) that you think is held by large numbers of whites. What specifics do you think led to the induction? Is the induction warranted?

2. Cite a public induction held by blacks (or any other minority) about the white majority. What specifics may have led to the generalization? Do you think the generalization is true?

3. The Chinese medical practice of acupuncture seems often to work well as an anesthetic and also as a cure for some diseases. Suppose you wanted to find out whether its success is due to psychological conditioning of the patient (that is, due to something like hypnotism). How would you use induction to see whether acupuncture works on infants not yet able to talk or on chimpanzees (which have physiology and anatomy almost identical to those of human beings)?

4. Think of a business concern, such as an auto repair shop, that you refuse to do business with. What specifics led to your generalization that it is a bad place of business? Do you think that you accumulated enough specifics to warrant your inductive generalization?

5. What specifics led to your inductive generalization that your most newly acquired friend is a really fine fellow or girl? How might new specifics alter your inductive generalization?

USAGE
LESSON
4

THE
APOSTROPHE
IN
POSSESSIVE
CONSTRUCTIONS

Nouns — but *not* pronouns — in the so-called **possessive construction** require apostrophes. Where the apostrophe is placed depends not on whether the noun is singular or plural but on whether or not it ends in *s*. In this chapter we will consider only nouns that do NOT end in *s*, some of them being singular and some plural.

To use the apostrophe correctly, you must first be able to identify the possessive construction that calls for the apostrophe. Some people can just feel a possessive construction, such as *the Witchers' Siamese cats*. Others need to learn that any possessive construction can be **transformed** (or changed) into an *of* or *belonging to* phrase which has exactly the same meaning as the original construction. Examples:

Terry's book = book belonging to *Terry*
the King's pride = pride of the *King*
Bruce's sister = sister of (or belonging to) *Bruce*

Anytime a construction can be transformed into such an *of* or *belonging to* phrase with identical meaning, that is 100 percent proof that the original construction is possessive and requires an apostrophe (unless a pronoun does the owning). If a construction cannot be transformed in this manner, that is 100 percent proof that the original construction is *not* possessive and must not have an apostrophe. For example, if you try to transform

The Smiths live on Oak Drive

into

live on Oak Drive of the Smiths,

you will see that an identical meaning does not result (in fact, no clear meaning results) and that therefore in the original sentence, *Smiths* is not possessive and must not take an apostrophe.

The transformation also tells **where** to put the apostrophe in the possessive construction. At the end of the *of* or *belonging to* phrase is the **base noun** you will make possessive. For example, in

the teacher's temper = the temper of the *teacher*,

the base noun (italicized) is *teacher*. If that base noun does not end in *s*, in the possessive construction an *'s* is added to make the base noun possessive. Whether the base noun is singular or plural has no bearing on the use of the apostrophe. For example,

the chldrens mother = mother of the *children.*

The base noun *children* does not end in *s;* therefore the correct possessive spelling is

the children's mother,

with an *'s* added to the base noun, which does not end in *s.* The fact that *children* is plural has no bearing on where the apostrophe is placed. Similarly,

five deers antlers = antlers of five *deer.*

The base noun *deer* (though plural) does not end in *s,* and therefore the correct spelling of the possessive construction is

five deer's antlers,

since an *'s* is added to the base noun to make it possessive. Remember, when the base noun does not end in *s*, in the possessive construction the apostrophe comes **before** the *s.*

Here are other examples of transformations that have base nouns that do not end in *s:*

one counselors office = office of one *counselor,*

making

one counselor's office

the correct spelling. Also

Mr. Tates wife = wife of Mr. *Tate,*

making

Mr. Tate's wife

the correct possessive spelling. Similarly,

my youngest cats sleeping pad = sleeping pad belonging to my youngest *cat,*

making

my youngest cat's sleeping pad

the correct possessive spelling. You must learn to make the *of* or *belonging to* transformation if you are to recognize possessive constructions and place the apostrophe correctly.

A rather common construction is a possessive noun at the end of a sentence with the thing it owns just understood. Example:

Mary's books are different from Bettys.

Books is understood at the end of the sentence, so that we really have

Bettys (books) = (books) belonging to *Betty.*

Thus the original sentence should read

Mary's books are different from Betty's,

since *Betty* does not end in *s* and is in a possessive construction. In English it is common to have a possessive noun at the end of a sentence with the thing owned just understood. An apostrophe is still required in the possessive noun.

EXERCISE 4A. Some of the following constructions can be transformed into *of* or *belonging to* phrases with identical meanings. Some cannot be transformed in that way. In the blanks provided, write out the transformations that can be made or state that no transformation is possible. In the constructions that are possessive (and can thus be transformed), the apostrophes are **omitted.** Enter apostrophes where needed.

1. my fathers second wife = _____

2. the fathers who came = _____

3. the Green Knights mission = _____

4. Mr. Bradys high-paying job = _____

5. the Bradys of Norwell = _____

6. televisions inferior programs = _____

7. a monkeys uncle = _____

8. the monkeys called "Uncle" = _____

9. Jerrys best girl friend = _____

10. Americas allies = _____

11. the wars tragedy = _____

12. the wars fought over trivialities = _____

13. a parents duties = _____

14. the parents at home = _____

15. for my consciences sake = _____

16. the audiences reaction = _____

17. the relatives of everybody = _____

18. my relatives relatives = _____

19. the cars at the race = _____

20. several cars performances = _____

EXERCISE 4B. In the blanks provided rewrite any words from the preceding sentence that need apostrophes, entering the apostrophes in their proper places. Remember that an apostrophe never goes directly above an *s*.

1. We saw that Bettys intentions were to deny Rosemarys accusations.

_____

2. No professors ever agree that another professors ideas are as sound as theirs.

_____

3. The presidents office is located next to Dean Witters.

_____

4. This peaches taste reminds me of an apples.

_____

5. For his consciences sake, Jeffrey refrained from stealing any childrens toys.

_____

6. The three sweetgum trees pruned branches made a bundle no bigger than one pomegranate trees branches.

_____

7. My counselors advice seemed to be sounder than Janices.

_____

8. Two sophomores grades made Jerrys look like the alphabets last letters.

_____

9. The Kennedys ordered the Mellons dog out of their estates boundaries.

_____

10. The Mobleys sons girl friend made Mr. Mobleys blood pressure rise.

_____

CHAPTER 5
QUALIFICATION IN INDUCTIONS

Some inductive generalizations are 100 percent valid. This means that for such generalizations, every specific ever observed has been the same; thus people believe that every such specific that will occur in the future will be the same. As we live our daily lives we unconsciously put into operation many completely true inductions that we have come to trust. For example, we just know that if we drive on a completely flat tire very far, the tire will surely be ruined; that if water is poured over cotton cloth, the cloth will become wet; that if wet cotton cloth is hung in bright, hot sunshine, it will soon become dry; that if a kernel of corn is allowed to sprout and grow, a stalk of corn and no other plant will result; and so on and on. Completely valid inductions of these sorts have arisen, naturally, because innumerable specifics have been observed and are known not to have varied. Of course, one can argue that you cannot be absolutely *sure* about the next specific — that, for example, the next time a kernel of corn is planted a pea vine of some sort may grow from it. But in spite of such logical quibbles, we go on putting our full faith in countless inductive generalizations that have never failed us.

However, all normal adult human beings also rely on countless inductive generalizations[1] that are not completely valid. These generalizations vary from being almost completely false to being almost completely true. For example, there are many drivers who have had their car engines knock or

---

[1] We are talking here only about inductive generalizations — those developed because of observations of specifics. Chapter 8 will show that human beings also believe generalizations that have no inductive basis at all.

ping on the first tank of gas they have bought at an independent, unaligned gas station. Some of these drivers therefore believe and will always believe that independent stations always sell inferior gas. That generalization is mostly false, for studies show that independent stations for the most part sell gas equal in quality to that sold by major oil companies. But even one or two specifics will put a permanent inductive generalization into the minds of some people, when further specifics would show the generalization to have only partial validity. At the other end of the scale, we have people who believe that *all* teenage boys at times drive cars faster than is safe. These people have observed many specific instances of teenagers driving too fast for safety and thus accept the generalization as completely true. Observation does bear out the generalization that a very large percentage of teenagers do at times drive too fast, but certainly there are a few who always drive at safe speeds, and thus the generalization, though mostly valid, cannot be accepted as 100 percent true.

Inductive generalizations not completely valid make up a large part of our mental storehouse. How should we handle such inductions? The answer is that people who use logic intelligently will **qualify** such inductions. To qualify anything is to restrict it or to put limits on it. To qualify a generalization, then, is to phrase it or use it in such a way that it does not apply to all specifics that it could cover. For example, suppose some teacher should say that "all football players are poor students academically." Without **qualification,** that generalization must apply to every individual football player, making it a manifest lie. But the qualified generalization that *"many football players are poor students academically"* has validity, for observation has certainly showed that many football players are poor students (as are some bookworms, for that matter). Or, for another example, a person may have had a couple of bad experiences in having his car repaired in a certain repair shop. Being human, he is likely to form the private inductive generalization that "that shop always does bad work." But is the *always* warranted? Probably not. Instead, the generalization should be qualified, perhaps in this way: "'that shop *often* does bad work." Thus an inductive generalization is qualified when it includes a word or phrase such as *many, often, sometimes, under certain circumstances, rarely, nearly always, some, most, a few, at times, mostly,* and so on.

Now you may argue that if a generalization must be qualified, it cannot be depended upon and thus is useless. Not so. A qualified induction[1] is useful as a guide, though not as an article of faith. For example, we must put our faith in the inductive generalization that in ordinary circumstances on earth the law of gravity always holds true. If every time we set a solid object on a flat surface we had to wonder whether it would fly into the air, we would live very unsettling lives. We must believe in the generalization that the law of gravity always works. However, if a person gets a "lemon"

---

[1] In Chapters 6 and 7 we will learn how inductions are actually put to use.

the first time he buys a new car of a certain make, he uses logic badly if he forms the unqualified generalization that all cars of that make are lemons. Instead, he should qualify the generalization and use it as a guide to make him be more wary and careful the next time he considers buying one of the cars. It might be that cars of that make are *usually* more reliable than most others; thus, to form a sweeping, unqualified generalization about their being lemons might actually prevent a person from making a good buy later. But the qualified generalization can be useful in making him careful about buying another new car of that make.

The use of sweeping, unqualified generalizations is a common weakness in student writing. Most English teachers would rather see an error in grammar in a paper than a generalization that is false because it is unqualified. And yet human nature is such that most people indulge too frequently in glittering, unsupported generalizations. For example, here is a paragraph from a student paper:

> Governor X is the only governor in over a generation who has given this state completely honest government. He has weeded out of governmental posts all incompetents and replaced them with people who will do the job right. He has cleaned up the welfare mess and stopped cheating in welfare. He has stopped unfairness in levying property taxes. He has made our school system the best in the nation, when it was on the verge of falling into the hands of soft-headed so-called intellectuals. He's the best governor we've ever had.

Such extravagant, unqualified claims (all are generalizations which the student thinks have inductive bases) can only make an intelligent user of logic suspicious of everything the writer says, for clearly such statements are not entirely valid.

Now note in this revision how qualification of generalizations can make the student's paragraph more believable:

> Governor X has been the originator of one of the most honest state administrations that we have had in over a generation. He has strengthened state government by firing a number of incompetent officials and replacing them with people more able to perform the jobs properly. He has organized the welfare system for more efficiency and has reduced the amount of welfare cheating. He has established more equity in levying of property taxes. He has improved the organization of the public school system and has removed some incompetents from it. Overall, I think he is one of the better governors our state has had.

Of course a great many people in this student's state might still disagree with these opinions[1], but at least the generalizations are qualified and are

---

[1] In Chapter 31, which may be assigned early in the course, and elsewhere in this text you will learn how to support generalizations of this sort with specific details that make them more believable.

not expressed so as to enrage opponents of the governor.

In all of your school work, and especially in such courses as sociology and psychology, learn to be aware of inductive generalizations and to inspect them for proper qualification. And by all means learn to qualify your own generalizations properly.

A LESSON IN THINKING

Many people have observed that some policemen and highway patrolmen seem always to be suspicious of everybody and never seem to believe any explanation a suspect gives. Discuss the aspects of logic and human beings' use of logic that might lead some police officers to behave in that way.

EXERCISES

1. You have been told that large dosages of vitamin C will prevent colds. When some members of your family come down with colds, you immediately take large dosages of vitamin C. You do not catch cold. What are you to think?
2. Two of your acquaintances whom you have known to be smokers of marijuana turn up one day in jail as heroin addicts. What, if anything, happens to your attitude towards the use of marijuana?
3. Some psychologists have maintained that it is good for a young teenager to try shoplifting and to be caught. Why should they think this?
4. Evaluate these statements:

   a. Blacks make superb athletes.
   b. People in the lower classes are lazy.
   c. Israelis work harder than Arabs.
   d. Slums cause teenagers to turn to crime.
   e. Students who cheat will not be as successful in life as students who don't cheat.
   f. Everybody has been dishonest at one time or another.
   g. Doctors care more about making money than about their patients.
   h. If an adult is poor, it's his own fault.
   i. Uncivilized people are just naturally cruel.
   j. Hard work will compensate for low intelligence.

5. Write a paragraph of *properly qualified* generalizations about the effects of sports on participants or on spectators or on both.

USAGE
LESSON
5

THE
APOSTROPHE
WITH
NOUNS
ENDING
IN
S

Remember that a noun in the so-called possessive construction requires an apostrophe. A possessive construction may *always* be transformed into an *of* or *belonging to* phrase. Example:

a freshmans worries = worries of (*or* belonging to) a freshman.

Since the transformation produces a phrase of identical meaning, the original is possessive and must be written as

a freshman's worries,

since the base noun *freshman* does not end in s. If a construction, such as

the boys in the band,

cannot be transformed into an *of* or *belonging to* phrase with identical meaning, the construction is not possessive and must not take an apostrophe.

When the base noun of a possessive construction ends in s, the placement of the apostrophe may be (though in certain cases need not be) different from its placement when the base noun does not end in s. The same transformation, however, tells both whether a construction is possessive and also where to place the apostrophe. The simple rule is that when the base noun ends in s, in the possessive construction a correct spelling is just to place an apostrophe after the s, regardless of the pronunciation. Example:

Mr. Davis (es) wife = wife of Mr. *Davis*.

The base noun *Davis* ends in s; therefore a correct spelling of the possessive construction is

Mr. Davis' wife,

even though in speech we pronounce an additional *es*. (It is also acceptable, and sometimes preferred, to use an *s* after the apostrophe [Mr. Davis's wife]). In the first transformation here, the *es* is put in parentheses to show that it is pronounced but is not a part of the possessive spelling. In English we *never* add *es* to a noun to make it possessive, but only to make it plural.

Here are three other examples of possessive constructions with the base nouns ending in *s*:

James (es) car = car belonging to *James.*

Since the base noun *James* ends in *s*,

James' car

is a correct possessive spelling, regardless of the pronunciation.

my boss (es) temper = temper of my *boss.*

Since the base noun *boss* ends in *s*,

my boss' temper

is a correct possessive spelling, regardless of the pronunciation.

Lois (es) boy friend = boy friend of *Lois.*

Since the base noun ends in *s*,

Lois' boy friend

is a correct possessive spelling.

When the base noun ends in *s* and also is singular, as in all the cases above, an alternate correct possessive spelling is to place another *s* after the apostrophe. Example:

Mr. Thomas (es) dog = dog belonging to Mr. *Thomas.*

Since the base noun *Thomas* ends in *s*, and also is singular, a correct possessive spelling is

Mr. Thomas's dog.

Another example:

one lioness (es) cubs = cubs of one *lioness.*

Since the base noun *lioness* ends in s and also is singular, a correct possessive spelling is

one lioness's cubs.

Many people prefer this variant spelling with the additional s because then the pronunciation is proper if one thinks of the apostrophe as replacing an e.

When the base noun of a possessive construction ends in s and is plural, the *only* correct possessive spelling is to place an apostrophe after the s. Examples:

the Millers son = son of the *Millers*.

Since the base noun *Millers* ends in s, the correct possessive spelling is

the Millers' son.

the Davises house = house belonging to the *Davises*.

Since the base noun *Davises* ends in s, the correct possessive spelling is

the Davises' house.

six bosses salaries = salaries of six *bosses*

Since the base noun *bosses* ends in s, the correct possessive spelling is

six bosses' salaries.

The above three base nouns have first been made plural by the addition of s or *es;* then they have been made possessive by the addition of an apostrophe after the final s. Since the nouns are plural and end in s, the only correct possessive spelling is to place an apostrophe after the s.

Never use an apostrophe with a last name that is only plural and NOT possessive. Examples:

correct: The Harrises are our neighbors.
correct: We visited the Crosses.
correct: The Smiths arrived late.

These last names are plural only and not possessive. The transformation will not work with them.

EXERCISE 5A. Some of the following constructions can be transformed into *of* or *belonging to* phrases of identical meaning, showing that they are possessive. Some cannot be transformed, showing that they are not possessive. In the blanks provided write the transformation of those which can be transformed and also in the original possessive constructions enter apostrophes in the proper places. In some cases an *es*, which causes a **misspelling**, is added for the sake of pronunciation. When you enter an apostrophe, strike out any erroneously used *e*; you may also strike out an unnecessary *s* if you wish or you may leave it in if you prefer the alternate spelling. When a construction cannot be transformed, write "No transformation possible" after it.

1. Thomases new car: _____

2. Mr. Thomases wife: _____

3. the Thomases children: _____

4. the Thomases on 10th Street: _____

5. an actresses role: _____

6. two actresses husbands: _____

7. two actresses in Hollywood: _____

8. Euripideses plays: _____

9. three dogs in the pound: _____

10. three dogs collars: _____

11. Mr. Wilkses job: _____

12. two boys mothers: _____

13. no boys allowed: _____

14. any boys around: _____

15. Phyllises college degree: _____

16. Mrs. Burnses liquor: _____

17. the Burnses milk: _____

18. all cops badges: _____

19. all cops on the beat: _____

20. Mrs. Wallises housework: _____

EXERCISE 5B. In the blanks below the following sentences, rewrite any words from the preceding sentences that need apostrophes, being sure to place the apostrophes properly. In the sentences some words are **misspelled** (other than lacking apostrophes) simply to indicate the proper pronunciation.

1. The Willises were visiting the McCalls friends.

   _____

2. The Grasses son entertained Loises parents.

   _____

3. There are three Henrys in my psychology class.

   _____

4. Mavises job requires the Johnsons approval.

   _____

5. A crocuses odor attracts many lionesses.

   _____

6. No others entries will be accepted after the Kennedys entry.

   _____

7. Mr. Luises class is larger than Mr. Joneses.

   _____

8. No companies spies have been arrested by Mr. Sheetses private detectives.

   _____

9. Mr. Dabbses salary is higher than Alexises.

   _____

10. Louises temper is more explosive than his bosses.

   _____

CHAPTER
6

DEDUCTION,
OR
REACHING
A
SPECIFIC
CONCLUSION

Induction — the forming of a generalization on the basis of observed specifics — is one of the two major kinds of logic. The other is **deduction,** the logical process by which we reach a *specific* conclusion rather than a general one.[1] Thus, while induction is reasoning from the specific to the general, deduction is reasoning from the general to the specific. We *make use of* our generalizations through the process of deduction. With that kind of logic, we start (usually unconsciously) with a generalization and end up with a specific conclusion.

For example, suppose you hear your mother, speaking on the phone, give evidence that her mother is coming to visit. When this information is divulged, you see your father turn red, slam down his paper, and stalk angrily out of the room. What logical process has been enacted? First, it is clear that your father has at some time in the past formed, on the basis of specifics, the private inductive generalization that a visit from his mother-in-law causes him pain of some sort. When he hears that she is to make a visit, he puts his inductive generalization to use and reaches the specific conclusion — a deduction — that this visit will cause him pain. His behavior is a reaction to the deduction he has made. Your father has reasoned from the general (any visit by his mother-in-law causes him pain) to the specific (this particular visit will cause him pain). Even though all of this involves emotions and thus might be thought by many not to be related to logic, a logical process has gone on in your father's mind.

---

[1] Some deductions may from certain points of view be generalizations, as Chapter 9 will show.

Though most of us live our daily lives without any thought of logic and with little understanding of logical processes, each of us daily reaches and acts on hundreds or thousands of specific conclusions — deductions — which have their origins in the generalizations stored in our minds. The validity and proper qualification of the generalizations in one's mind largely determines the soundness of his deductions and thus greatly affects the quality of his life.

For example, suppose a student decides a dozen times during a school term to cut a class in U.S. history. Each time he cuts he has reached a specific conclusion or deduction that cutting a class period of U.S. history will harm him very little if any. Thus at some time in the past he must have (perhaps unconsciously) put into his mind the generalization that frequently cutting U.S. history will not hurt him. His generalization may or may not be sound, but still he uses it in the process of deduction. Another student might, to go drag racing, cut a class in psychology that he knows will be helpful to him. His cutting the class is the product of a deduction, but the generalization he started with is that a session of drag racing will do more to provide him with what he wants than will a class period of psychology, valuable as it may be. Still another student may have perfect attendance in a course in African anthropology. He has, in effect, deduced the conclusion that he should not miss class, and the generalization he started with is that missing any class period of African anthropology will be detrimental to him.

These examples may not seem to involve logical processes, but they do. Some people think that logic is concerned only with such things as deciding whether P is true when Q is the same as P and Q is always true. But actually, our daily lives are very much affected by induction and deduction, and it is much more interesting to discuss the logic of our daily lives than it is to discuss abstractions with such symbols as P and Q.

A great many of our deductions help us safely through the day. For example, you may have learned that Niles Street is constantly prowled by traffic cops, and thus when you drive there you act on the deduction that you need to drive more slowly than usual not to get a ticket. Or you may have learned that you are allergic to chocolate and thus deduce on many occasions that you must decline the offer of a piece of chocolate candy. Or you may have learned the inductive generalization that eating lunch before a one o'clock class makes you inattentive in class and thus act on daily deductions that you should postpone lunch until 2:00. The more successful a person's daily life is, the more his deductions are made on the basis of sound generalizations.

Sometimes, of course, one's deductions can be harmful. For example, a person may form the generalization that he knows better than his boss how to perform a job and thus may deduce that he should ignore his boss's orders and do the job his own way. If he does, he may be fired as a result. Another person may have, because of luck, formed the generalization that he can hold his liquor well and drive safely while drunk; he may deduce at the end of a particular party that it is perfectly safe for him to drive home, and he may have a serious accident because of his drunk driving. Few of us are immune from occasionally making faulty deductions that hurt us.

Also some of our faulty deductions may be harmful to others. A personnel officer, for example, may hold the false generalization that all blacks are undependable and thus may deduce that he should not hire a particular qualified black applicant. The black person has thus suffered because of faulty logic on the part of the personnel officer. A composition teacher may have formed the false generalization that all football players are incapable of writing acceptable compositions, and thus he may use an unwarranted deduction to give a football player's paper a low grade when it really deserves a higher one. In other words, the many specific instances of prejudice that all of us display at one time or another, often harming others, are deductions based on false or improperly qualified generalizations which are general prejudices.

But what about an unpredictable decision that a person seems to make on impulse, such as a dieter's suddenly changing his mind and ordering a banana split after all? Is such a decision, which could go either way, a deduction based on a generalization? Yes, it is. Almost every decision is a deduction, and *every* deduction is deduced from a generalization. The answer to the above questions is that a person can carry contradictory generalizations buried in his mind; he may sometimes act on one and sometimes on the other. For example, an alcoholic may form the generalization that any drinking is bad for him and then act on repeated deductions in order to refuse drinks. But all the time there is buried in his mind the generalization that he will be able to control his drinking or that giving in to drinking will provide him more pleasure than staying away from it. Thus at any time such a person might suddenly act (make a decision) on the basis of the latter, long unused, generalization and begin a binge. In effect, when we are faced with temptation we have two contradictory generalizations, each vying to be the one we will use to make a deduction.

Sometimes it may seem that one is faced with the need to make a decision when he has *no* generalization in his mind to base a deduction on. For example, early in a course in political science you might feel the need to disagree openly with your professor. You have no generalization about him to guide you. So you just guess whether you can disagree with him with impunity. You decide to disagree, apparently with no generalization to base your decision on. Thus you accumulate one specific which will help lead you to generalizations about that professor. But have you really made a deduction not based on a generalization? Probably not. It is quite likely that you based your decision on generalizations formed in the past about other professors and the penalties or rewards of openly disagreeing with them. On the basis of your experience, from which you have formed generalizations, you wager in your mind that it is safe and maybe profitable to disagree with this professor. You have, in effect, made a deduction based on a generalization. It is probably rare for one to make a deduction without some kind of generalization in his mind being back of it.

A LESSON IN THINKING

Suppose that someone reads a newspaper article about some child being beaten to death. As he reads he sympathizes and thinks about how horrible the beating and death are. But then at the end of the article he learns that the child was black and says to himself, "Oh, well, that doesn't matter much." Discuss the logic this person has unconsciously used.

EXERCISES

1. What generalizations must have been in the minds of those who either said or did the following?
   a. "No thanks. I've got to drive."
   b. "Professor Stern is sure to give me a low grade."
   c. "Amos will never conquer his alcoholism."
   d. "Lorraine won' be able to finish out the school year."
   e. "Charlotte's new baby was born on August 12. He'll have a life full of good luck and fortune."
   f. A quarterback for the Rams called an audible.
   g. A diner in a cafe picked up a pinch of salt he had spilled and threw it over his left shoulder.
   h. A student who had received a low mid-term grade told his professor how much he was enjoying the course.
   i. A basketball player crossed himself just before shooting a free throw.
   j. A housewife saw that the directions on a bottle of pills called for taking one pill every four hours and promptly took two of the pills.

2. Specify some harmful deductions that might be made by a teacher who believes the generalization that Nordic people in general and Anglo-Saxons in particular are mentally superior to all other kinds of people.

USAGE
LESSON
6

OTHER
POSSESSIVE
CONSTRUCTIONS

Indefinite Pronouns

A fairly large number of words in English are called indefinite pronouns because they have indefinite, rather than specific, reference. The ones that can be used in possessive constructions are *one, no one, someone, anyone, everyone, nobody, somebody, anybody, everybody, other, others, another, one another,* and *each other*. These words function just as nouns do and thus take an apostrophe in the possessive construction. The *of* or *belonging to* transformation works with them. Examples:

someones car = car belonging to *someone*.

Since the base word *someone* does not end in *s*, the correct possessive spelling is

someone's car.

nobodys business = business of nobody.

Since the base word *nobody* does not end in *s*, the correct possessive spelling is

nobody's business.

all others tickets = tickets belonging to all *others*.

Since the base word *others* ends in *s*, the correct possessive spelling is

all others' tickets.

one anothers respect = respect of *one another*.

Since the base phrase *one another* does not end in *s*, the correct possessive spelling is

one another's respect.

Also the constructions *no one else, somebody else,* and so on may be used in possessive constructions. Example:

everyone elses dog = dog belonging to *everyone else.*

Since the base phrase *everyone else* does not end in *s*, the correct possessive spelling is

everyone else's dog.

You can be sure that anytime you hear the *s* on one of the *one* (except for *one*) or *body* words or on *else*, the correct spelling will be *'s*.

Words Naming Periods of Time

Words naming periods of time, such as *month, day, today, Wednesday, February,* and so on, are frequently used in the possessive construction and, when they are, require an apostrophe just like other nouns. The *of* transformation works with them. Examples:

one months vacation = vacation of one *month.*

Since the base noun *month* does not end in *s*, the correct possessive spelling is

one month's vacation.

two months vacation = vacation of two *months.*

Since the base noun *months* ends in *s*, the correct possessive spelling is

two months' vacation.

tomorrows newspaper = newspaper of *tomorrow.*

Since the base noun *tomorrow* does not end in *s*, the correct possessive spelling is

tomorrow's newspaper.

Tuesdays lesson = lesson of *Tuesday.*

Since the base noun Tuesday does not end in *s*, the correct possessive spelling is

Tuesday's lesson.

Words Naming Sums of Money

Words naming sums of money are often used in possessive constructions and, when they are, require apostrophes. The *of* transformation works with them. Examples:

one dollars worth = worth of one *dollar.*

Since the base noun *dollar* does not end in *s*, the correct possessive spelling is

one dollar's worth.

two dollars worth = worth of two *dollars.*

Since the base noun *dollars* ends in *s*, the correct possessive spelling is

two dollars' worth.

one nickels difference = difference of one *nickel.*

Since the base noun *nickel* does not end in *s*, the correct possessive spelling is

one nickel's difference.

a dimes value = value of a *dime.*

Since the base noun *dime* does not end in *s*, the correct possessive spelling is

a dime's value.

Remember, you must be able to use the *of* or *belonging to* transformation if you are to know when an apostrophe is needed in a possessive spelling and where to place the apostrophe.

EXERCISE 6. In the blanks below each of the following sentences rewrite any words from the preceding sentence that need apostrophes, being sure to place the apostrophe properly. *Some words are* **misspelled** *in a way other than having an apostrophe omitted; correct the spelling of those words.*

1. If ones dollars are not in Tuesdays collection, a months vacation may be denied him.

   _____

2. Nobodies desire to own a thousand dollars worth is different from anybody elses.

   _____

3. Februarys weather didn't cause a dollars difference in anyones electric bill.

   _____

4. Yesterdays assignment caused some others reactions to surprise everybodies parents.

   _____

5. Your two cents worth caused us all to doubt each others capacity to work next weeks problems.

   _____

6. An hours delay cost us two hours pay, as well as putting everyones temper on edge.

   _____

7. There wasn't a quarters difference at the years end.

   _____

8. Fridays lesson on Januaries eclipses was more interesting than Mondays on stellar parallax.

   _____

9. Let's respect one anothers feelings so that tomorrows party will be everybodies delight.

   _____

10. Ten dollars value in todays marketplace is about the same as one dollars value in the nineteenth centurys.

_____

11. Will nobody elses teacher explain the semesters work as clearly as Joans?

_____

12. The dollars value dropped even more after Fridays news reached everybodys TV.

_____

13. The days end saw nobodies work completed as well as the Turners.

_____

14. Six fives but no ones were in somebodys wallet at the weekends end.

_____

15. Ninety-eight cents worth of nails in California really costs more than a dollars worth in Maine because of Californias sales tax.

_____

16. Yours is just like everybody elses.

_____

17. As the centurys end neared, so did the Republics.

_____

18. After forty-four weeks work, nobodies project was in better shape than Thomases.

_____

19. A nickels purchasing power in 1975 was equal to a pennies in 1925.

_____

20. Yesterdays newspaper announced the end of Marches drought, to everyones delight.

_____

CHAPTER
7

THE
SYLLOGISM,
OR
THE
STRUCTURE
OF
A
DEDUCTION

We saw in the last chapter that we use **generalizations** to reach specific conclusions, or deductions. For example, you may have in your mind the generalization that the Republican (or Democratic) Party, when in power, gives the country poor government. On the basis of that generalization you might deduce the specific conclusion that you should not vote for the Republican (or Democratic) candidate for the presidency. You might assume, that is, that deduction is always a two-part logical process: the generalization and the specific conclusion. Actually, however, deduction is a *three*-part logical process, and it is now time to introduce you to this three-part process, which is known as a **syllogism.**

To explain the syllogism, we must reintroduce the term **premise,** which we defined in Chapter 1. To refresh your memory, a premise is a statement phrased so that it affirms or denies that something is true or false. It may be a *fact,* such as "Kentucky Beau whiskey costs $4.99 a quart in California" or "alcohol is an intoxicating beverage." It might be a *specific,* as in the first illustrative statement in the preceding sentence, or it might be a *generalization,* as is the second illustrative statement. Also a premise might be just an assumption rather than a fact, such as "the eclipse of the moon on June 19 caused my radish plants to die" or "the conjunctions of the stars and planets at the time of one's birth determine the course of his life." As you can see, the inductive generalizations we have been talking about are premises.

It is on the basis of premises that we draw specific conclusions, or deductions, but we use two premises rather than one. The first, called the **major**

premise, is a generalization that covers all or some members of a category, and the second, called the **minor premise,** is the identification of an object, idea, or the like as a member of the category covered by the major premise. The **conclusion** is the deduction that resutls from the application of the generalization of the major premise to the specific of the minor premise. If *both* premises are true, the conclusion *must* be true. Here is an example of a simple syllogism:

> *major premise:* All large cars are expensive to operate.
> *minor premise:* This car is large.
> *conclusion:* This car is expensive to operate.

As you can see, if the generalization of the major premise applies to the minor premise, the conclusion follows.

Though you may not realize it, this logical process of the syllogism is enacted in your mind hundreds or thousands of times a day. Almost every decision you make or conclusion you come to is the result of your unconscious use of a syllogism. For example, if at a party you say, "Boy, Marvin will have a dilly of a hangover tomorrow," you have unconsciously used this syllogism:

> *major premise:* Anyone of Marvin's constitution who drinks heavily at a party will have a severe hangover the next day.
> *minor premise:* Marvin is drinking heavily at this party.
> *conclusion:* Marvin will have a severe hangover tomorrow.

Or you might make the observation that you suspect your term paper will receive an F. Your unconscious syllogism might be this:

> *major premise:* Professor Stern fails any term paper he knows is plagiarized.
> *minor premise:* He will know my term paper is plagiarized.
> *conclusion:* He will fail my term paper.

Thus the process of deduction that we saw in Chapter 6 is embodied in the three-part syllogism.

Of course you should realize by now that the soundness of much of your thinking depends on using true premises in the syllogisms that you unconsciously enact. If either of the premises is false, the conclusion may very well be false. For example, you may hear a student say, "Professor Stern is mean to his students." His syllogism might be this:

> *major premise:* Any professor who assigns X amount of work and gives X percentage of grades below B is mean to his students.
> *minor premise:* Professor Stern assigns X amount of work and gives X percentage of grades below B.
> *conclusion:* Professor Stern is mean to his students.

The trouble here is that the major premise is open to serious doubt. It may be that Professor Stern cares so much for his students that he tries very hard to prepare them for further college work and for life after college. The student simply used a false major premise and therefore arrived at a false conclusion.

Or another student might declare that Professor Bedlam should be fired. His syllogism might be this:

major premise: Any professor who actively tries to convert his students to Communism should be fired.

minor premise: Professor Bedlam actively tries to convert his students to Communism.

conclusion: Professor Bedlam should be fired.

For the sake of argument, let's accept the major premise. But the minor premise may be false because the student misinterpreted evidence. Thus the conclusion is false. With a flaw in either the major or minor premise, the conclusion is likely to be false. For this reason, in our thinking we should do all we can to use only sound premises.

As we saw in Chapter 5, many inductive generalizations must be qualified if they are to be useful. When a qualified generalization is the major premise of a syllogism, the conclusion will also have to be qualified. Here is an example:

major premise: *Some* students who cheat never get caught.

minor premise: Sanchek is a student who cheats.

conclusion: Sanchek *may* never get caught cheating.

The qualifying word *some* in the major premise demands the qualifying word *may* in the conclusion. Thus one would just have to wait to see whether the conclusion will be true.

You may at this point feel frustrated because your sound use of logic does not always lead to a proven fact. You may ask, "If the conclusion must be qualified, of what use is it?" The answer is that in our daily lives we must constantly use qualified conclusions that come from qualified major premises simply because a very great deal of the information on which we base our behavior cannot be proved. But the qualified conclusion is often useful as a *guide*. For example, suppose you are a football quarterback and have noticed a weakness in pass defense in a team you are playing against. You might unconsciously act out this syllogism:

major premise: A pass play often succeeds against a team with weak pass defense.

minor premise: This team has weak pass defense.

conclusion: Many of my pass plays may succeed against this team.

You cannot be sure that any one of your pass plays will succeed; you may even suffer an interception. But the qualified conclusion, which grows out of the qualified major premise, is a very good guide for you. It's simply a fact that we constantly play the probabilities in almost all aspects of our behavior, and qualified conclusions let us play the probabilities more successfully than we would if we merely guessed. Deductive logic is very important to us even though it often does not lead to a proven fact.

A LESSON IN THINKING

A French woman who frequently eats snails and frog legs became sick when she learned that some delicious meat she had just eaten had come from a lizard. Discuss the logical processes that went on in her mind.

EXERCISES

1. Discuss any weaknesses you see in the following syllogisms.

a. *major premise:* Students who are put on the honor system will cheat.
   minor premise: Students at Wahoo State are on the honor system.
   conclusion: Students at Wahoo State cheat.

b. *major premise:* A Republican administration always causes a recession or depression.
   minor premise: We now have a Republican administration.
   conclusion: We will soon have a recession or depression.

c. *major premise:* A Democratic administration always gets us into a war.
   minor premise: We now have a Democratic administration.
   conclusion: We will soon be in a war.

d. *major premise:* College administrative committees with student members make more bad administrative decisions than the committees without student members.
   minor premise: We now have students on our college's administrative committee.
   conclusion: We will have more bad administrative decisions in the future than in the past.

e. *major premise:* The higher one's intelligence, the better grades he will make in college.
   minor premise: Susan's intelligence is higher than mine.
   conclusion: Susan will make higher grades in college than I will.

2. Starting with the following conclusions, invent proper major and minor premises to create syllogisms. If you wish, you may use generalized statements, such as "under such and such conditions." Following is a sample:

a. conclusion: Mary will break her engagement to Harry.

major premise: Any fiancée who is beaten severely by her fiancé will break the engagement.
minor premise: Harry beat Mary severely.
conclusion: Mary will break her engagement to Harry.

b. Jerry will probably be expelled from school.
c. War will soon break out in the Middle East again.
d. Dean Levinson will be the next president of our college.
e. Zero Condell is going to get hooked on drugs.
f. Charlotte's baby will probably be put up for adoption.
g. Freeman will lose his case before the Fairness Committee.
h. There will be a brawl at the dance tonight.
i. Professor Lax's class in human courtship will be full again next semester.
j. I hate Professor Montebank.
k. Our school paper will be suspended for six months when Friday's issue comes out.

3. Prepare a full syllogism for the deduction in the first paragraph of this chapter.

USAGE
LESSON
7

OTHER
USES
OF
THE
APOSTROPHE

Contractions

Apostrophes are used in the spelling of contractions, with the apostrophe indicating the omission of one or more letters. Examples:

I'm (I am)	doesn't (does not)	o'clock (of the clock)
I'd (I would)	can't (cannot)	don't (do not)

The contractions most involved in misspellings are the following:

it's (it is *or* it has)	you're (you are)
who's (who is *or* who has)	they're (they are)

Do not confuse these four contractions with the following four possessive pronouns:

its (belonging to it)	your (belonging to you)
whose (belonging to whom)	their (belonging to them)

And *never* use apostrophes in these possessive pronouns:

yours	ours
hers	theirs

These are never contractions but are possessive noun substitutes.

Plural Last Names

Never use an apostrophe in spelling the plural of a last name which is *not* also possessive. Examples:

64   *Logic, Language, and Composition*

correct:	The Davises visited the Harrises.
correct:	The Millers live near the Smiths.

When the pronoun you would substitute for a last name is *they* or *them,* an apostrophe must *not* be used.

The Apostrophe in Plural Spellings

An apostrophe may be used in spelling the plurals of capital and lower-case letters, numerals, and abbreviations. Examples:

correct:	There are four *s*'s and four *i*'s in *Mississippi.*
correct:	I made two C's and two B's.
correct:	There are three 7's and two 0's in that row of figures.
correct:	We hired two MA's and three PhD's.

Though some writers omit apostrophes in such plural spellings when there is no chance of their being misunderstood, careful writers insure complete clarity by using apostrophes. Try writing the first example sentence without apostrophes.

Apostrophes may also be used in spelling the plurals of words used *as words* and not for their meaning. Such words are also italicized in pirnt and underlined in typewriting or longhand. Examples:

correct:	Don't use so many *if*'s in your proposals.
correct:	But me no *but*'s.
correct:	There are three *therefore*'s in that sentence.

Some writers do not use apostrophes in such plural spellings, but when apostrophes aid clarity, they should be used. For example, how would you write the following sentence without an apostrophe?

There are six *is*'s in the first sentence of that book.

EXERCISE 7. Write meaningful sentences using the following pairs (that is, one sentence for each member of each pair):

1. a. its

   _____

   _____

   _____

   b. it's

   _____

   _____

   _____

2. a. you're

   _____

   _____

   _____

   b. your

   _____

   _____

   _____

3. a. the plural of a numeral

   _____

   _____

   _____

   b. the plural of a lower-case (small) letter

   _____

   _____

   _____

4. a. the plural of your last name

   _____

   _____

   _____

b. the plural possessive of your last name

_____

_____

_____

5. a. the plural of any favorite slang word of yours

_____

_____

_____

b. the pural of the preposition *on*

_____

_____

_____

CHAPTER
8

THE
DIFFERENT
KINDS
OF
MAJOR
PREMISES

Our minds cannot make a deduction — that is, cannot reach a specific (as opposed to a general) conclusion — without a major premise or generalization as an unconscious starting point. For example, if, on a picnic, you say, "We're going to be caught in the rain," you begin your logical process of deduction with a major premise or generalization something like this: Any time the sky has this kind of cloudy appearance, it will rain very soon. Your minor premise, of course, is that the sky has this kind of cloudy appearance. And so your conclusion follows. Our minds, then, need to be stocked with vast numbers of generalizations, or major premises, to serve as the starting points of the countless deductions we make.

In Chapters 2 through 5 we saw one broad kind of generalization or major premise — the *inductive generalization* based on observed specifics. After observing a sufficient number of specifics, a person (or a group of people) reaches a general conclusion. Many inductive generalizations, however, are false because of misinterpretation of evidence — either by one person or by a large body of people. For example, someone may get sick on one or two occasions when he drinks a cheap brand of liquor and not get sick the first time he switches to a more expensive brand. On the basis of so few specifics thousands of people have formed private inductions to the effect that not only a specific cheap brand of liquor but *any* cheap brand will make them sick. Even later pleasant experiences with cheap brands will often not erase the inductive generalization so quickly established on the basis of so few observed specifics. In general, human beings are reluctant to give up their inductive generalizations, even when new evidence shows them to be wrong.

Large groups of human beings also often misinterpret evidence and thus form false inductive generalizations. For example, some centuries ago Italians observed so many people becoming sick with malaria (literal meaning: bad air) after being out in the night air that they formed the inductive generalization that night air is foul and causes malaria. As a result, they kept their houses closed at night. Actually, the situation was that the mosquito that carries malaria comes out at night to bite people. The Italians just misinterpreted evidence. Similarly, in the seventeenth century large numbers of Europeans observed farm animals dying or individual human beings becoming insane after lonely old women had passed by. They then came to the general conclusion that the old women were witches and could cause animals to die or people to become possessed by evil spirits. On the basis of this generalization they drew many specific deductions which led to huge numbers of individual "witches" being burned at the stake. Again, faulty observation, or misinterpretation of evidence, led to a false inductive generalization.

Sometimes, however, people do not misinterpret observed specifics but actually accept as evidence incidents that by no stretch of the imagination should be considered evidence. This kind of behavior leads to **pseudoinductive generalizations,** that is, generalizations that people think are based on observed specifics but which are not. The following is a representative example: A woman in her late twenties, single but eager to meet men and in the habit of going places men frequent, goes to a palmist to get her fortune told. The palmist reads the creases in her palm and predicts that she will soon meet a dark, handsome man who will be attracted to her. Several days later, after increasing her visits to places men frequent, she meets a man who roughly fulfills the palmist's prediction. Presto! The woman promptly puts into her mind the pseudoinductive generalization that creases in the palm of one's hand foretell one's fortune, though naturally a palmist is needed to interpret the creases. Of course the palmist was simply predicting something that could be expected to occur sooner or later in some degree. Many superstitions, particularly those abounding in astrology, are nothing but pseudoinductive generalizations.

Everybody believes many generalizations, however, that are *not* inductive because they are not based on any observed specifics. These **noninductive generalizations** may generally be said to derive from ones **cultural value system** — that is, from the assumptions about religion, politics, economics, social behavior, and so on that a person absorbs from the society he grows up in. For example, do we Americans believe a fixed presidential term is better governmental policy than Britain's indefinite term for prime ministers because we have observed specifics that cause us to believe the generalization? Almost certainly not. We simply have grown up with that system and thus most of us think it best. Do Buddhists believe that their religion provides better psychological health than Christianity because they have observed specifics and have come to an inductive generalization? Again, certainly not. Most are Buddhists because they simply grew up being Buddhists. Or, for another example, does a young girl retain her virtue until marriage because observed specifics have led her to believe that such behavior produces a happier life in the long run? Or is she just acting on social or religious principles that her particular background has instilled in her? Almost surely the latter. Such *non*inductive generalizations grow out of everything from religion to superstition to what one considers his personal insight or an intelligent way of looking at things.

In making deductions, we use noninductive generalizations as major premises exactly as we use inductive generalizations. For example, when a person declines an alcoholic drink, he has made a deduction (in this case, a decision). For many, the syllogism would be this:

major premise: Drinking alcohol incites God's displeasure.
minor premise: I don't want to incite God's displeasure.
conclusion: I will not accept an alcoholic drink.

No observed specifics led to this person's major premise. It is simply part of his religious beliefs.

For another example, a personnel officer might say to himself, "I will hire this black even though he is not as highly qualified as one of the white applicants." He has made a deduction, and his syllogism might be this:

major premise: Blacks should be compensated for past oppression.
minor premise: Giving a job to a black less qualified than a white will help compensate for past oppression.
conclusion: I will hire this black even though he is not the most highly qualified applicant.

No observed specifics but only value judgments or social theory can account for the personnel officer's major premise.

For a final example, someone might say, "I'm certainly not going to vote for Gus Loosenoodle for president." He has made a deduction, and his syllogism might be this:

major premise: Creeping socialism in our national government is bad.
minor premise: Gus Loosenoodle, if president, would promote creeping socialism.
conclusion: Voting for Gus would be voting for bad government.

Now our voter almost certainly has no observed specifics on which to base his major premise. He just believes this political generalization because of the political environment he grew up in. Many people would, in such cases, insist that they have observed specifics which led them to their generalization, but in actuality everyone believes many noninductive generalizations that have grown out of his cultural value system.

Inductive generalizations are the only kind that can actually be proved true — through observation and experimentation. Noninductive generalizations are not subject to proof. For this reason, some people have maintained that we should not believe any deduction, or specific conclusion, that grows out of a noninductive generalization, since the noninductive generalization (major premise) cannot be proved and since no deduction can be known for sure to be true unless the premises are known to be true. For example, probably a great many men, if the truth were known, have tried to seduce women by showing them that their noninductive generalization that "premarital sex is wrong" cannot be proved and that thus no specific deduction based on it can be shown to be true. But such reasoning is foolish. Every normal member of every society — from Hottentots to Englishmen — must have a cultural value system containing many generalizations that can't be proved. We must make decisions and deductions on the basis of these noninductive generalizations, and it is not wrong for us to do so, so long as we do not harm other people.

A LESSON IN THINKING

If you contribute money or goods to a charitable organization to help birds and stray animals, you can deduct the amount of your contribution on your income tax forms. But if you help stray animals or birds directly — such as, for example, providing them with veterinary care — you cannot deduct the cost on your income tax forms. Examine and discuss the logic of this apparently contradictory situation.

EXERCISES

1. Separate the following generalizations into two categories: (1) those you think are inductive (based on observed specifics) and (2) those you think are noninductive.

   a. Being born under the zodiacal sign of Cancer increases a person's chances of being highly intelligent.
   b. Some diseases can be communicated by bodily contact.
   c. Murderers are punished by God.
   d. Advertising helps companies sell more goods than if they did not advertise.
   e. Nonbelievers are more dishonest than true Christians.
   f. Democracy is the best form of government.
   g. Wealth does not necessarily bring happiness.
   h. Redheaded people are more likely to have bad tempers than those not redheaded.

i. The Bible is the revealed word of God.

j. Violence on TV shows causes some people to commit violent crimes.

2. Using any of the major premises in Exercise 1, create one or more syllogisms.

_____

_____

_____

_____

_____

_____

_____

_____

_____

_____

THE
HYPHEN

The hyphen is a mark used in spelling, not a mark of punctuation. It should not be confused with the dash (—), which is a mark of punctuation (see Chapter 30) and which is twice as long as a hyphen (-).

1. When dividing a word at the end of a line of typewriting or script, use a hyphen, but place it *only* between syllables in the word. Examples:

correct: di-version; prac-tice; diction-ary; shift-ing; indi-vidual
wrong: div-ersion; pra-ctice; dictio-nary; shif-ting; indiv-idual

Never divide a one-syllable word at the end of a line. Examples:

wrong: flub-bed; stren-gth; tw-elve; prov-ed

2. Hyphenate all compound whole numbers; the hyphen, in a sense, acts as a + mark (i.e., twenty-one = twenty + one). Examples:

correct: twenty-three; forty-four; ninety-two; fifty-fifth; sixty-second
wrong: twenty three; forty four; fifty fifth

Do *not* hyphenate whole numbers that are not compound. Examples:

correct: one hundred; six thousand; two hundred and ninety-six
wrong: one-hundred; six-thousand

Hyphenate fractions that consist of two spelled-out numbers. Examples:

correct: two-thirds; three-fourths; eighty-two and nine-tenths
wrong: two thirds; eighty two and nine tenths

Do *not* hyphenate a fraction when *a* or *an* is used instead of *one*. Examples:

```
correct:   a half; an eighth
wrong:     a-half; an-eighth
```

3. No rule can be given for hyphenation of compound words. Practice among professional writers varies, and the spelling of compound words in English is now in a state of flux. For example, the spelling of *weekend* proceeded in a few decades from *week end* to *week-end* to *weekend*. You may, of course, follow the spelling given in any standard dictionary. Otherwise let clarity be your guide. Here are some examples of hyphens providing clarity:

```
preferred:   close-up; tie-up; well-being; cross-country; passer-by;
             Europe-firster; self-serving
```

4. More and more, the hyphen is being omitted with the use of such combining prefixes as *pseudo*. Examples:

```
acceptable:   pseudoclassic; noninductive; antimonarchical;
              semitrailer; postwar; antebellum; ultramodern
```

However, when the last letter of the prefix is the same as the first letter of the base word, a hyphen provides clarity. Examples:

```
preferred:   pseudo-organic; anti-industrial; semi-independent;
             pre-exist; de-emphasize; re-entry; utlra-articulate
```

Also when the base word is capitalized, a hyphen should separate it and the prefix. Examples:

```
preferred:   mid-July; anti-Christian; pro-American; pre-Roman;
             post-Reconstruction
```

And a hyphen should always be used when the prefix provides a different meaning from another word spelled the same except for the hyphen. Examples:

```
correct:   re-serve and reserve; re-cover and recover; co-op and coop
```

5. Hyphenate two or more words that function as a single modifier (adjectival) in front of a noun. This important rule provides for clarity. Example:

```
correct:   a double-parked car; all-to-human gestures; high-pressure salesmen; a
           soft-spoken type; ten-year-old boys; sewing-machine operators; extra-
           soft soap; moon-eyed cows
wrong:     high pressure salesmen; ten year old boys; extra soft soap
           (unless the meaning is "soft soap which is extra")
```

Do not hyphenate two or more describing words that follow the noun they describe. Examples:

> *correct:*   a boy who is ten years old; cars that are double parked; soap that is extra soft; operators of sewing machines

However, if you think of such words as compounds, you should hyphenate them in such positions. Examples:

> *correct:*   a man who is soft-spoken; cows that are moon-eyed

Always in the use of hyphens make clarity your chief objective.

EXERCISE 8. In the blanks below each of the following sentences rewrite any words that should be hyphenated or that should have apostrophes. Also correct the misspelling of a few words that are misspelled in other ways.

1. It seems that one half of Shirleys attention is worth less than a third of Jameses.

   _____

2. A twenty five thousand dollar a year man sometimes wont spend seventy five cents for Cubas best cigar.

   _____

3. A tie up in the cross country railroads will cost hard pressed manufacturers more than two thirds of their hard earned profits.

   _____

4. Mr. Lewises son in law took a rather red than dead attitude when the Russians power plays became noticeable.

   _____

5. An anti-intellectuals position on Congresses new civil rights bill is the same as a dairymans position on piled up manure.

   _____

6. In the pre Rooseveltian era Hoovers let 'em eat cake attitude towards the poor brought on a high blood pressure syndrome in church going people.

   _____

7. Forty six and one half percent of Americas state supported segregated schools were in a last stage financial crisis in 1967.

   _____

8. Dont be so week kneed in your gudgingly granted support of Susies highly praised science project.

   _____

9. One hundred Congressmens wives voted for a long term outlay of money for three fourths of the extra patient applicants.

   _____

10. The reentry of the trouble plagued space craft caused the rapidly beating hearts of the astronauts wives to race at one hundred and thirty two beats a minute.

---

11. A fool proof lock didnt fool Jacks partner as he entered the money crammed safe.

---

12. As Jims sister tried to resort the cards, a hard blowing wind scattered them again.

---

13. Joes wife couldnt recover from recovering her sofa with prickly pear cloth.

---

14. One third of the ninety six hard pressed soldiers decided to surrender to their better equipped enemy.

---

15. Your coming to Joans imitation Founding Fathers party, aren't you?

---

16. Nobodies power hungry superior should deemphasize his affection for twelve year olds.

---

17. The Scraggses own the ninety first parcel of the Harrises new subdivision.

---

18. Cant you reserve muscle building beans to hungry athletes after the not so tasty beans are cold?

---

19. Is the dirty gray water in the thirty second reservoir as pure as the chalky white water in the twenty second?

---

20. Your well being is more important to me than Charleses.

CHAPTER
9

DEDUCTIONS
AS
PREMISES

So far we have, for the sake of simplicity, said that a deduction is a specific conclusion formed on the basis of a major premise, which is always a generalization, and a minor premise, which may be a specific or may be a generalization on a lesser level than the major premise. For example, you might say, "I adore Cheri Marshall." The syllogism for your deduction might be this:

major premise:	I adore all natural blondes.
minor premise:	Cheri Marshall is a natural blonde.
conclusion:	I adore Cheri Marshall.

This major premise is a private induction of personal taste; on the basis of specifics you have concluded that, for you, all natural blondes are adorable. But the minor premise is wholly specific with no suggestion of generality. For another instance, you might make the observation, "I think trial marriages are desirable." The syllogism for this deduction might be as follows:

major premise:	Any marriage arrangement that will increase the number of happy people is desirable.
minor premise:	Trial marriages would increase the number of happy people.
conclusion:	Trial marriages are desirable.

This major premise is a broad noninductive generalization; many people would agree with it, but many, on religious or other grounds, would disagree. But the minor premise, though not as broad, is also a generalization, since it applies to a great many individual trial marriages.

Now we must see that, though countless deductions are specifics in that each applies to just one individual situation, many deductions are themselves generalizations and thus may become major premises (and occasionally minor premises) in making other deductions. In fact, sometimes in a long reasoning process a person may use a deduction as the major premise for another deduction, and then that deduction as the major premise for another, and so on and on to the final idea he is seeking. Human thought is extremely complex, and one can begin to understand the nature of it only if he breaks it down into small bits as we are doing in these short chapters.

Here is the way a seemingly specific deduction can actually be a generalization to serve as a major premise for another deduction. A friend wishing to argue about your second deduction in the first paragraph of this chapter might say, "Contract marriages for a specified length of time are desirable." The syllogism for this deduction might be this:

major premise: Any marriage system that can lead to a desired dissolution of marriage without court proceedings is desirable.
minor premise: Contract marriages for specified lengths of time can allow dissolution of marriage without court proceedings.
conclusion: Contract marriages for specified lengths of time are desirable.

Now in one sense (considering the major premise) this conclusion is a specific, but in another sense it too is a generalization, though less broad than the major premise because it is concerned with one marriage system rather than with "any marriage system that . . . ."

Here is how that conclusion can be used as a major premise: Continuing his argument, your friend might say, "I'm going to seek a three-year contract marriage." His syllogism might be this:

major premise: A contract marriage for a specified length of time is desirable.
minor premise: I want a desirable marriage.
conclusion: I'm going to seek a three-year contract marriage.

His major premise in this syllogism is the conclusion of his previous deduction. Thus a conclusion of one syllogism often serves as a major premise in another. Though few of us realize the logical processes going on in our minds, all of us use deductions constantly in making other deductions.

Here is another example of the conclusion of one syllogism functioning as the major premise of another syllogism:

major premise: Any school calendar which requires students to study too much material in too short a time is inferior.
minor premise: The quarter system requires students to study too much material in too short a time.

conclusion: The quarter system represents an inferior school calendar.

The conclusion appears to be a specific but in fact is a generalization that can be used as a major premise, as in this syllogism:

major premise: The quarter system represents an inferior school calendar.
minor premise: Our college operates on the quarter system.
conclusion: Our present school calendar is inferior.

It is also possible for the conclusion of a syllogism to function as the minor premise in another syllogism. Here is an example using the above conclusion that "Our present school calendar is inferior."

major premise: Any inferior school calendar harms the educational process.
minor premise: Our present school calendar is inferior.
conclusion: Our present school calendar is harming the educational process.

Thus we see that conclusions that we reach through the logical process of deduction often themselves function as premises in other deductions. Also we see again that logical processes are concerned not only with provable facts but also with the many value judgments we make daily because of our participation in a pluralistic cultural value system. The logical process involving unprovable premises and conclusions is the same as the process involving provable premises and conclusions.

A LESSON IN THINKING

It seems that almost everybody who has witnessed a complex situation later written up in a news article has maintained that the news article was not accurate. What does this kind of situation indicate about our logical processes? What does it make you think about news articles concerning situations you are not familiar with? In considering this problem, you might ask a psychology teacher to give you a few facts about human perception.

EXERCISES

1. Following are five syllogisms. Following directions given by your teacher, use one or more of the conclusions as either a major or minor premise in another syllogism.

    a. *major premise:* Grades in college courses cause a harmful educational situation.
       minor premise: We do not want a harmful educational situation in college.
       conclusion: We should abolish grades in college courses.

b. *major premise:* Grades in college courses provide a competitive situation that promotes more learning on the part of students than a noncompetitive situation would provide.

minor premise: We want college students to learn more.

conclusion: We should retain grades in college courses.

c. *major premise:* Only students with high academic potential should be enrolled in college.

minor premise: Currently many students with low academic potential are enrolled in college.

conclusion: The number of college students in this country should be reduced.

d. *major premise:* Every normal American between the ages of 18 and 25 deserves an opportunity to achieve a college education.

minor premise: Many normal Americans between the ages of 18 and 25 are not now in and have never been to college.

conclusion: College enrollments in America should be increased.

e. *major premise:* Required courses in college cause more students to drop out than if there were no required courses.

minor premise: We do not want college students to drop out.

conclusion: We should eliminate required courses in college.

2. Discuss the logic of the syllogisms in Exercise 1, concentrating on what you think are flaws in the logic.

USAGE
LESSON
9

CAPITALIZATION

The use of capital letters varies enough among experts so that in some constructions you may let your personal preference dictate whether you capitalize a word or not. For example, all of the following illustrative sentences are acceptable because such capitalization or lack of it has been repeatedly used by professional writers:

correct: The president of the United States is elected quadrennially.
correct: The President of the United States is elected quadrennially.
correct: President Nixon claimed Executive privilege.
correct: President Nixon claimed executive privilege.
correct: There will be an English staff meeting tomorrow.
correct: There will be an English Staff meeting tomorrow.

Thus each writer must, in certain cases, just follow his own judgment in using capital letters.

However, below are listed a number of fixed rules of capitalization that all good writers adhere to. You, too, should observe these rules.

1. Everyone knows that the first word in a sentence, the pronoun *I*, and people's names are always capitalized. In quoting lines of poetry, one must follow the capitalization the poet used.

2. In titles and chapter headings, capitalize the first word and all other words except prepositions of four or fewer letters, the articles *the*, *a*, and *an*, and the coordinating conjunctions *and*, *but*, *yet*, *or*, *nor*, and *for*.

   Examples:

   title of a book: The Grevious Case of the Battle Between the Yahoos and the Houyhnhnms
   title of an article: *A Scramble for Power Among the Republicans, Democrats, and Whigs*
   chapter heading: Chapter 6. A Matter of Life or Death for the Condors

3. Capitalize the names of individual geographic regions or formations and of streets and avenues. These are known as place names and are proper nouns, which means that they are always capitalized. Examples:

the Western Hemisphere	Walden Pond
North America	the Red River of the North
the Mideast	Moscow Mountain
Mexico	the Friant Canal
Kern County	Tenth Street
Weedpatch, California	Wilshire Boulevard
the South	Gin Alley
Lake Louise	Broadmoor Court

Also capitalize all adjectives formed from proper nouns. Examples:

French	Midwestern
English	Scandinavian

Do *not* capitalize the names of directions. Example:

correct: The farther south we drove. the more convinced I was that we should be driving west.

4. Capitalize the names of relatives, officers, and officials when a particular individual is meant. Examples:

Aunt Grace	the Senator (meaning a particular one)
Secretary of State Malone	the Chairman (meaning a particular one)
Lieutenant Flibi	the General (meaning a particular one)

Do *not* capitalize *mother, grandfather,* and so on when used with a possessive pronoun but otherwise do capitalize them. Examples:

correct: My mother is a social worker.
correct: I think Mother was not happy with my decision.

5. Capitalize the names of organizations and buildings. Examples:

the Veterans Administration	the U.S. Army
the Masons	the Bijou Theater
the State Assembly	the Chrysler Building

6. Capitalize the days of the week and the months of the year, but do *not* capitalize the seasons. Examples:

Monday	February
January	spring

7. Capitalize specific course names, but do *not* capitalize subject-matter fields. Examples:

correct: I am taking History 17A and Introduction to Literature.
correct: I would like to take courses in history, art, and music.

8. Capitalize the names of all organized religions, all references to the Deity, and the titles of divine books. Examples:

the Church of Christ	Allah
the Baptists	Does God make His will known?
Buddhism	the Bible
the Holy Ghost	the Upanishads

9. Capitalize the names of historical documents and events and of specific eras. Examples:

the Declaration of Independence	World War II
the Diet of Worms	the Renaissance
the Battle of Midway	the Middle Ages

10. Capitalize brand names but not the name of the product. Examples:

a Dodge car	Dial soap
Boroteem pills	Chevron gasoline

11. Do *not* capitalize the names of foods, drinks, plants, animals, games, musical instruments, diseases, or occupations. Examples:

ravioli	bridge
whiskey	violoncello
pine trees	mumps
elk	engineer

But do capitalize a proper noun that is part of the name of one of the above. Examples:

Douglas fir trees	Thompson's gazelle

EXERCISE 9. In the blanks below the following sentences, rewrite words from the sentences above that should be capitalized but are not, that are capitalized but should not be, that need apostrophes, and that need hyphens.

1. I read *an escape from the drudgeries of work* while I was waiting in a Doctors office in the graham Building.

   _____

2. Our canary pine tree begins to grow in february and grows throughout Spring if mother waters its tap root.

   _____

3. In the midwest the farmers never ending problem is to eradicate carters blight from their Hybrid Corn.

   _____

4. I enrolled in a course in English Literature entitled Shakespeares history plays.

   _____

5. Nobodys french accent will be improved in any french course taken from professor Duex.

   _____

6. Bettys case of Measles subsided on wednesday, when she was visited by some do-gooders from the lions club.

   _____

7. The east coast is not as far east as greenlands Capital City.

   _____

8. My Mothers job at the Southland Oceanarium makes her entertainment—minded even in Winter.

   _____

9. The Palace theater has been turned into a Burlesque House because everyones interest in good Movies declined.

   _____

10. The Members of the church of god have christ-centered beliefs like those of the Holy rollers.

    _____

11. An anaconda snake may reach thirty-two feet in length, making ordinary-looking rattlesnakes appear harmless.

_____

12. The Gillises like to take summer vacations in the lake moraine country, which has canada's best awe-inspiring scenery.

_____

13. I joined the swiss navy after I read about its war-winning exploits in the mid-century war.

_____

14. The atlantic charter, signed on a ship in the atlantic ocean, affirmed the freedoms of all peoples of the western hemisphere.

_____

15. The childrens maternal grandmother bought their father a copy of the koran, the holy book of the mohammedans.

_____

16. A methodist is more likely than a catholic to consider going to church a god-inspired social event.

_____

17. I like january's weather better than july's because the oak trees branches look beautiful when snow-laden.

_____

18. My doctor prescribed combid pills when my father's doctor thought any common anticholinergic would be satisfactory.

_____

19. Though Billys mother had introduced me to him before, the general didn't remember my name.

_____

20. The troops thought captain Floogie was a spit-and-polish officer.

_____

CHAPTER
10

THREE
LOGICAL
FALLACIES

A **fallacy** is an erroneous, misleading, or unsound idea, belief, or argument, and the error is the result of some misuse of the reasoning processes. We do not normally use the word *fallacy* to apply to a simple error in fact — such as that George Washington died in 1900 — but to apply to some sort of conclusion that has been reached on the basis of unsound logic — such as that all Mexicans should want Mexico to become part of the United States because Americans have a higher standard of living than Mexicans. Even well-informed, highly intelligent human beings are often guilty of fallacious reasoning, though the more one knows how the mind uses logic, the less likely he is to be illogical. In the following four chapters we will examine thirteen common **logical fallacies.**

The Sweeping Generalization

In the first five chapters of this text we have alluded to the fallacy known as a **sweeping generalization.** Such a fallacy is, in fact, just a faulty induction based on insufficient sampling of specifics or lack of qualification of the generalization. For example, some people — and probably a great many — have said, "The columnist Jack Anderson never tells the truth." Since Anderson writes a daily column and often has several news stories in a single column, he is likely to slip into some faulty reporting. Seeing two or three such slips, a person who strongly opposes what he thinks are Anderson's political beliefs may jump to the sweeping generalization that Anderson **never** tells the truth. A sufficient sampling of Anderson's news stories, however, would result in the qualified generalization that "Anderson occasionally reports as truth news stories that are untrue."

Many aspects of racial prejudice represent sweeping generalizations. For example, a well-to-do family might have had two chicano maids who stole a few household objects. The family might then leap to the sweeping generalization that "they all will steal." Such faulty induction is very unfair to other individuals of the minority race, for most of them will refrain from stealing. Also the family in question should realize that some members of any race or nationality will steal. Minority groups in this country have suffered much real harm because of sweeping generalizations.

In their themes and term papers students often misuse sweeping generalizations. Here are some examples:

1. Students are eager to be a part of the college's decision-making committees.
2. Students resent the attempt of older people to guide their lives.
3. Teachers are unaware of the students' most pressing problems.
4. Union organizers use deceptive tactics to trick people into joining.
5. Policemen work off their aggressions by bullying citizens.

Teachers may justly criticize student compositions that contain such sweeping, unqualified generalizations. The little word *some* can change all of these sweeping generalizations into acceptable statements.

In sampling for the purpose of drawing inductive conclusions, the representativeness of the samples is often as important as the number. For example, if the Gallup pollsters in making a prediction of the outcome of a presidential election should interview only residents of rich suburbs, their prediction could not be depended upon because of the poll's faulty or unrepresentative sampling. Similarly, if one wanted to draw a conclusion as to how great a percentage of a college's student body uses hard drugs and if he did his sampling only at rather wildly swinging parties, he no doubt would come to a false conclusion. If in sampling one allows himself to be completely arbitrary in choosing those to be sampled, he can come to almost any conclusion he wants to, such as that no college students cheat or that all college students cheat. So beware of the sweeping generalization that does not have a sound inductive basis.

Use of Faulty Premises

The use of faulty premises may be called **faulty deduction** and has been explained somewhat in Chapters 6 through 9. When one uses a faulty premise in drawing a deductive conclusion, the conclusion is very likely to be false. For example, no doubt countless students have said that such-and-such a teacher is unfair. It is likely that such a false conclusion has usually been based on comments that his tests are too hard, he assigns too much material, or, simply, he gave me a low grade. The first two sample premises represent value judgments that the student is probably not capable of assessing properly. The third sample premise may be true, but the major premise it derives from — that any teacher who gives me a low grade is unfair — is very probably false.

Or, for another example, one might hear the comment, "Mr. Dupple is really a good citizen." The major premise from which the comment derives may be that "any person who votes regularly is a good citizen" — a premise that most certainly cannot be depended upon. Similarly, someone might say, "Shirley is certainly a good Christian." The major premise for this conclusion might be, "Anyone who attends church regularly is a good Christian." But that premise cannot be depended upon because many who attend church regularly do not behave as good Christians outside of church.

The use of faulty premises is very common in human thought — so common that in any serious argument or discussion it is often useful to pause and ask just what premises one is using when he makes some sort of declaration. For example, if in the course of an argument about the place of varsity football in colleges and universities someone says, "Well, we certainly should keep football because it helps build character in the players," it might be enlightening to ask what major premise that conclusion is derived from. Pause a moment and answer that question.

Here are some other examples of the use of faulty premises:

1. It's perfectly safe for me to drive. I haven't drunk a great deal.
2. The used car I bought had only 15,000 miles on it. It's bound to be an excellent car.
3. Lois's baby is growing up without a father. He'll be a problem child in school.
4. Mr. Lovee is a devout Catholic. You can depend on him to treat you right in business dealings.
5. Rory started on alcohol and is now on marijuana. He'll be on addictive drugs soon.

The conclusions in these statements cannot be trusted because the premises are faulty. For practice state each major premise in clear terms.

Non Sequiturs

The Latin phrase *non sequitur* means "it does not follow," and it represents a fallacy related to the misuse of premises. A *non sequitur* derives from a sort of wild jump from a premise to a conclusion that has little if anything to do with the premise. Of course there almost always *seems* to be a relationship between the premise and the conclusion; otherwise one would probably not indulge in the *non sequitur*. But a real relationship is lacking. Here are some examples of *non sequiturs*:

1. Rufus is always cheating on his wife. He probaby treats her very badly at home.
2. Alan Cranman drinks. How could he be a good senator?
3. Merry Jane has perfect attendance in all her classes. She'll do well on the final exams and will make all high grades.
4. Senator Snort comes from a rich family. He'll be against allowing farm laborers to unionize.
5. Cheri teases the boys a lot. She's probably a hot date.

The *non sequitur* differs from a faulty deduction only in that there is less of a relationship between it and its premise than there is between the faulty deduction and its premise. None of the above conclusions follows from the premise given, though at first glance there is a reasonableness about the statements. In our daily lives most of us are at times disappointed with an outcome because we let our reasoning go astray because of a *non sequitur*. For example, the person who will buy only a General Motors car because he assumes the world's biggest car maker will also make the best cars may be in for a bitter disappointment.

A LESSON IN THINKING

Ponder the following question, give an answer, and then examine the logical basis of your answer: Should a drunk person who causes a serious accident be punished the same as, more than, or less than a sober person who causes exactly the same kind of accident?

EXERCISES

Decide whether or not there is a fallacy in each of the following statements and, if there is, specify which logical fallacy is involved. Remember that there is much similarity between faulty deductions (use of faulty premises) and *non sequiturs*. Therefore members of your class may argue about which fallacy is involved.

1. Alfred has finally decided to go to a doctor. He'll be well soon now.
2. You just can't depend on anyone who has been on welfare to work hard when he has a job.
3. Luis argued in class with Professor Turrett. You can bet he will get a low grade.
4. Look at that pine tree's needles. It will be dead in a few weeks.
5. William Bradford can trace his ancestry in this country back to 1630. Boy, he must be devoted to American political principles.
6. Ruby kissed Brad right out in public. What a promiscuous floozy she must be.

7. Those umpires in the National League are the most incompetent officials in the sports world.
8. Louise was born under the sign of Aries. She'll suffer tragedy late in life.
9. Give me a sip of that vodka. I've got to do well on a test next period.
10. American Indians don't want to be self-supporting.
11. Governor Retread raised taxes again. He can't be a real Republican.
12. Billy Horsetoe has an IQ of 140. He'll make the best grade in class.
13. You just can't depend on blacks to hold down jobs that require high responsibility.
14. There's a church. There must be a saloon somewhere nearby.
15. The more brilliant a person is, the more he contributes to society.

USAGE
LESSON
10

SENTENCE
FRAGMENTS

A sentence is most simply defined as a group of words with a subject and predicate which can stand alone. A sentence begins with a capital letter and ends with a period, question mark, or exclamation point. Many people very early develop "sentence sense," which means having the intuitive ability to recognize whether a group of words is a sentence or not. For example, people with sentence sense recognize that such a construction as

She thought they would

is a sentence even though the meaning of *she, they,* and *would* must come from previous sentences. Similarly, they recognize that such a construction as

Because the game ended in a tie

is not a sentence even though it contains a complete thought ("The game ended in a tie."), since the word *because* prevents the construction from standing alone.

Some people, however, lack sentence sense, though the reason *why* they lack it is not known. For example, some students have a hard time understanding why the italicized constituents in the following examples are not sentences:

I expect college to make me a better person. *To give me a better understanding of life.*

I decided not to enroll in college that semester. *Since I wanted some work experience first.*

Since the two constructions in each example do make sense, some people erroneously assume that the second construction is a sentence. But, in fact, both of the second constructions are unacceptable **sentence fragments.**

Though certain kinds of sentence fragments are acceptable in certain kinds of writing, almost all fragments in student papers are unacceptable and are usually considered to be serious errors. Occasionally sentence fragments in student papers are due to simple carelessness. Example:

> Although the patrolman seemed sympathetic. He wouldn't accept my excuse and gave me a ticket.

Very few students would out of ignorance let such an introductory clause stand as a fragment. Careful proofreading will prevent almost everyone from committing such an error.

The most common kind of unacceptable fragment written out of ignorance is the **detached phrase** or **clause** that should be attached to the preceding sentence. Here are typical examples:

> *wrong:* The law should allow eighteen-year-olds to buy alcoholic beverages. In order to give them full status as adults.
>
> *correct:* The law should allow eighteen-years-olds to buy alcoholic beverages in order to give them full status as adults.
>
> *wrong:* People often forget that they are the ones who make the laws. Not the police officers on the street.
>
> *correct:* People often forget that they, not the police officers on the street, are the ones who make the laws.
>
> *wrong:* I will make law enforcement my career. Because I think I can serve people well in that capacity.
>
> *correct:* I will make law enforcement my career because I think I can serve people well in that capacity.

Students who habitually leave phrases and clauses as detached fragments need to study sentence structure carefully to develop sentence sense.

You should know, however, that sentences beginning with coordinating connectives are *not* fragments. The most common coordinating connectives used to introduce sentences are *and, but, yet, for, so, therefore, however, nevertheless, furthermore, thus,* and words like these. Examples:

> *correct:* But I was still unable to convince my parents of my sincerity.
>
> *correct:* However, love alone will not cause a child to grow up to be a good Christian.

Many students report that they have been taught not to begin a sentence with *and* or *but,* but any such rule is completely in error. In fact, good writing demands that some sentences be started with *and* and *but,* which express a coordinate relationship between the sentences they start and the preceding sentences. You will find examples of such sentences on pages 52, 61, 62, 72, and elsewhere in this text.

EXERCISE 10. In the blank *before* each of the following constructions write an S if the construction following and ending with a period is a complete sentence and an F if it is a sentence fragment.

Example: __S__ One mark of a good policeman is unfailing courtesy. __F__ To all citizens of whatever status. __F__ Even those who have committed crimes.

1. _____ If a car is not properly tuned. _____ It will consume more gas than a well-tuned car. _____ And will often stall. _____ Making its owner angry and disgusted.

2. _____ My intentions were honorable and I had sufficient money to carry them out. _____ But my associate was suspicious and did not give me sufficient support. _____ Causing me to lose favor with Alice.

3. _____ I was not able to enroll at Pitzer College. _____ Not having high enough high school grades. _____ Which are given careful consideration by the Dean of Admissions. _____ And so here I am at Saddleback College.

4. _____ I want to be free. _____ To soar like a bird. _____ To live fully. _____ And by all means to use my mind to the fullest.

5. _____ The overhead-cam engine is highly efficient. _____ Because it can operate at high RPM's. _____ A feature that produces more horsepower per cubic-inch displacement. _____ Thus such an engine gets good gas mileage.

6. _____ When the leaves of the deciduous trees turn color. _____ Especially in Western Massachusetts. _____ The quality of the air also changes. _____ Announcing the arrival of fall. _____ Which is my favorite season of the year. _____ And my wife's too.

7. _____ Most businesses are eager to hire people who can write clearly. _____ For the ability to express oneself clearly is usually accompanied by many other desirable mental traits. _____ Such as the ability to make decisions quickly. _____ And make good ones.

8. _____ We can't know the future for sure. _____ But we can know the past. _____ And knowledge of the past can help us make good plans for the future. _____ Which will increase our chances of having a desirable future.

9. _____ My decision to attend college was a sudden one. _____ Not a carefully thought-out plan. _____ Nevertheless, I am succeeding well in my studies. _____ Which are giving me more pleasure than I anticipated.

10. _____Never will I understand women. _____Who are more unpredictable than New England weather. _____But I expect always to love them. _____For even their unpredictability is a delight. _____Especially in affairs of the heart.

11. _____He can. _____I know it. _____Because I have seen others with similar capacities perform the task. _____Which really doesn't require great talent.

12. _____I refused to donate. _____Because I knew that little of the money would reach the poor. _____Many charities spend as overhead 90% of the money they collect. _____That knowledge reduces my desire to contribute.

13. _____The solution to the problem is easy. _____To increase the per-acre yield by using more fertilizer. _____Which has been shown to be feasible.

14. _____A notorious case of putting the cart before the horse and thus getting priorities all confused. _____Which should be avoided at all costs. _____For success depends on proper timing.

15. _____Diversionary tactics won the day. _____Giving us victory when defeat was expected. _____Thus we were triumphant. _____An unusual occasion for us.

CHAPTER
11
THREE MORE LOGICAL FALLACIES

Polarized, or Simplistic, Thinking

It is common for speakers of English to say that two ideas are *poles apart* — meaning that they are completely opposed to each other. For example, one politician might advocate a wholly communistic government and another advocate that we have no governmental interference at all in a free economy, not even social security or welfare. Their ideas may truthfully be said to be poles apart.

But probably neither of their positions is sound, for in areas of complex human behavior, ideas (or things, if you prefer) are seldom either good or bad, right or wrong, black or white, and so on. Instead, mixtures of good and bad, black and white, and so on are the rule. But some people, when dealing with complex ideas, illogically indulge in **polarized thinking,** maintaining that you must be either for or against an idea, either on this side or on that side — either, that is, at the north pole or at the south pole, and not somewhere in-between. For example, there are some people who will not see government control of the entire transportation system as a very complex matter; instead they want either complete control or none at all. Others will get an idea fixed in their minds and then say that any other seemingly contrary idea is wrong, even though there may be no real connection between the two ideas. Some people, for instance, maintain that if a person does not believe in God (or, more narrowly, is not a Christian) he must be an immoral, untrustworthy person.

Trying to reduce a very complex issue to black or white or trying to oppose two ideas that need not be related to each other is **simplistic,** since doing so oversimplifies matters. This sort of thinking is also sometimes called **either-or thinking,** since its practitioners are continually saying, "Either you're for me or you're against me." People who are more logical see the complexities involved in an issue and try to break the issue down into smaller component parts so that they can take a rational stand on less complex parts of the whole issue. Or they simply refuse to establish a complete connection between two ideas when such a connection does not exist.

Here is an example of polarized thinking on a complex issue: One educator takes the position that high school seniors and college freshmen should not be allowed to do any independent study for credit, citing as his reason that such students are not mature enough for such study. Another educator takes the position that a complete program of nothing but independent study should be available to all high school seniors and college freshmen. But the issue is too complex for such either-or thinking. A person who reasons well would try to determine what kinds of independent study might be feasible for such students and what kinds might not, perhaps depending on the subject matter. Such a logical person might, for example, conclude that some students would be able profitably to study independently in some aspects of music but that few if any students should be turned loose to learn laboratory chemistry without supervision. In essence, instead of indulging in polarized or simplistic thinking, he divides a complex issue into manageable parts so that he can think soundly about each part.

And here are some examples of either-or thinking involving ideas not necessarily related.

1. Either you boycott California table grapes or you are against justice for the farm laborer.
2. You either vote in every election or you're a poor citizen.
3. You either abstain from drinking alcohol altogether or you have no will power and are morally bankrupt.
4. Either every student in a teacher's class earns an A grade or the teacher has failed in his job.
5. No one can use profane language and be a good, right-thinking person.

When one sees either-or ideas phrased so starkly, he is likely to say that nobody *really* thinks like that. But listen carefully to fifteen or thirty minutes of spirited discussion or argument and you will hear many people indulge in such polarized thinking.

Begging the Question

Begging the question is a logical fallacy in which a reasoner puts his conclusion into his premise and then tries to use that premise to prove his conclusion. For example, a person may argue that we are sure to have eternal life because the immortality of the soul guarantees that we will. The conclusion maintains that we will have eternal life, but the premise from which the conclusion derives contains the assumption that the soul is immortal. Thus the reasoner has begged the question. One major aspect of logic, as we made clear in earlier chapters, is the process of demonstrating that because one idea is true, another must be true as a consequence. But the above reasoner simply said that eternal life is certain because immortality is certain. His conclusion and premise are the same.

Begging the question is also sometimes called **circular reasoning,** because the reasoner simply argues in a circle. Here are further examples:

1. The Republican Party is the best political party; therefore Republicans provide the best government. Or, Republicans provide the best government; therefore the Republican Party is the best political party.
2. Your conscience forbids you to commit a certain act because it is wrong. Or, a certain act is wrong because your conscience forbids it.
3. Education is desirable because educated people are desirable. Or, educated people are desirable because education is desirable.

When you engage in discussions or arguments, watch to see whether any of those speaking assume in their premises the conclusions they are trying to convince you to accept.

False Analogy

An **analogy** is a comparison used to try to make an idea believable or to make a difficult concept clear. For example, if a person has a hard time understanding why a common stock that pays a high dividend sells for less than a seemingly identical stock that pays little or no dividends, he might be enlighted by an anology. Someone might explain to him that if the interest on a savings account were allowed to stay in the account, the account would become more and more valuable. But if the interest were regularly withdrawn, the account's value would stay the same. Similarly, if dividends are not taken out of a company's treasury, the worth of the company continues to grow, but if dividends are taken out regularly, the company's worth remains the same and the price of its stock will not go up. Such an analogy is fairly sound and useful.

However, many people use *false analogies* in their arguments, a false analogy being one that tries to make one idea seem true by comparing it with another idea that really has no relationship to the first. For example, if a person compares the federal government to a family in trying to show that a huge national debt means financial disaster, he has used a false analogy, for the federal government is not like an individual family. Or suppose a politician uses George Washington's phrase "no entangling alliances" to urge that present-day America should not make treaties with foreign countries. He would, in effect, be using a false analogy because he would be comparing a small, agrarian country of the late eighteenth century to a giant industrial country of the twentieth century.

Analogies and comparisons of all kinds can be very useful in making essays clear and interesting, but they seldom *prove* anything. False analogies, of course, mislead. They should be avoided by sound thinkers and exposed in the arguments of unsound thinkers.

A LESSON IN THINKING

Many intellectuals of the eighteenth century, including most of our Founding Fathers, were *Deists* — that is, proponents of a religion based on reason rather than on faith. Their reasoning began something like this: "We see the world around us; therefore we know there was a creation. If there was a creation, there must have been a creator. Thus we demonstrate by reason that an omniscient, omnipotent God exists." Discuss their logic. Also examine the logic of the person who replied in approximately these terms: "If the world could not exist without being created, then God could not exist without being created. What created God?"

EXERCISES

Decide which of the following statements contain logical fallacies and identify each fallacy by name. The six fallacies discussed in Chapters 10 and 11 are represented, but remember that faulty deduction (use of false premises) and *non sequiturs* are very similar.

1. General Eisenhower was a poor president because all military men make poor presidents.
2. I wouldn't read Flak Miserene's novels. He divorced his wife.
3. A teacher is like a Marine drill sergeant. If he is to be successful, he must be relentless with his students.
4. You just can't go in debt and be a good manager of money.
5. All drinkers eventually come to grief.
6. The Dean of Instruction recommended this teaching technique. It must be good.
7. Diplomats must be like quarterbacks. They must always try to deceive the diplomats of other countries.
8. Taking any drugs is harmful to the body. Therefore one's body suffers when one ingests drugs.
9. Every educational system that eliminates competition among students is bad.
10. Entering college is just like taking a job. You've just got to please your "employer."

11. I failed two courses last semester. My parents are going to be angry.
12. The administration of this college cannot make any intelligent decisions.
13. You shouldn't have said the car is running well. Now we're sure to have a breakdown.
14. Keeping a wife happy is just like keeping a pet dog happy. Pat her on the head often and give her plenty of good food.
15. All college courses should be electives. There should be no specific course requirements for graduation, only a certain number of units.

USAGE
LESSON
11

COMMA
SPLICES
AND
RUN-TOGETHER
SENTENCES

In Chapter 10 we defined the term *sentence sense*, which means having the ability to distinguish between a construction which is a complete sentence and one which is not a sentence. We showed that lack of sentence sense leads some people into writing unacceptable sentence fragments. Lack of sentence sense also leads some into committing the serious errors known as **comma splices** and **run-together sentences.**

Sentences are opened with capital letters and closed with periods, question marks, or exclamation points. Or, in certain cases, two constructions (independent clauses) that are in effect two sentences are separated with a semicolon, with the second sentence *not* beginning with a capital letter. Also in certain cases two constructions (independent clauses) that are in effect two sentences are joined by one of the coordinating conjunctions: *and, but, yet, or, nor, for,* and *so.* Usually a comma precedes the coordinating conjunction (see Chapter 25). When two sentences do not have a mark of end punctuation or a semicolon between them or are not joined by a coordinating conjunction, they form run-together sentences if there is nothing between them and comma splices if there is only a comma between them. Either error is very serious and is usually an indication that the writer does *not* have sentence sense and should therefore study sentence structure.

Run-together sentences are sometimes just the result of carelessness, but when the second sentence begins with a lower-case letter the writer is usually committing an error out of ignorance. Here are examples of run-together sentences:

wrong: Money is what makes the world go round it is needed by everybody.

wrong: Caring for other people is an important quality to develop in children too many parents spoil their children.

wrong: Blacks are striving to better themselves this is shown by greater numbers of blacks going to college.

Either periods or semicolons are needed after *round, too,* and *themselves.* Such errors are not especially common, but they are inexcusable in any writing. Most often, run-together sentences occur when the second sentence begins with *it* or *this.*

The above sentences would represent the much more common, but almost as serious, error called the **comma splice** if a comma were placed after *round, too,* and *themselves.* The writer of a comma splice recognizes that the distinct pause between the sentences calls for a mark of punctuation, but he uses a comma, showing that either he does not recognize that the second construction is a sentence or that he does not know that a sentence is to be followed by a mark of end punctuation, a semicolon, or a coordinating conjunction (usually accompanied by a comma). Though it is true that in certain kinds of writing, comma splices are acceptable in certain cases, almost all comma splices written by students are serious errors. Here are examples of comma splices used with no connective word at all between the sentences:

wrong: I didn't ask to come into this world, it was my mom's idea.
correct: I didn't ask to come into this world; it was my mom's idea.

wrong: A child should not eat sweets just before a meal, they will ruin his appetite for the meal.

correct: A child should not eat sweets just before a meal, for they will ruin his appetite for the coming meal.

wrong: People without money tend to complain that they are beaten down, they don't want to admit their own failure.

correct: Moneyless people tend to complain that they are victims of society. They don't want to admit their own failure.

The wrong pairs of sentences are spliced together with commas. Instead, they should either be separated by a semicolon or period or joined by a coordinating conjunction. The writer must choose which method of separating (or joining) sentences he prefers in avoiding comma splices.

When a coordinating connective other than a coordinating conjunction joins two sentences, either a semicolon or period must separate the sentences to prevent the comma splice. The most common such coordinating connectives are *however, therefore, consequently, otherwise, nevertheless, then, furthermore, moreover, thus, for example, also, second, next* and other words like these. Examples:

wrong: The rich continue to suppress the poor, however, poverty is declining.
correct: The rich continue to suppress the poor; however, poverty is declining.

wrong: Children just naturally get all the exercise they need, therefore parents should be more concerned with their children's diets.

correct: Children just naturally get all the exercise they need; parents, therefore, should be more concerned with their children's diets.

wrong: Parents must of course first provide their children with the essentials of life, then they should be concerned about bringing them up to behave morally.

correct: Parents must of course first provide their children with the essentials of life. Then they should be concerned about bringing them up to behave morally.

Even though coordinating connectives (they are *not* coordinating conjunctions) are used between these sentences, comma splices still exist in the examples labeled *wrong*. One good tip to remember is that if the connective can be shifted to the interior of the second sentence, a period or semicolon (*not* a comma) must be used to separate the sentences, regardless of where the connective is placed. Example:

wrong: The blacks are making progress, however I do believe some communistic leaders are trying to use the blacks.

correct: The blacks are making progress. I do believe, however, that some communistic leaders are trying to exploit them.

Most coordinating connectives that require periods or semicolons can be shifted in this way.

EXERCISE 11. In the blanks provided rewrite any of the following sentences that run together or have comma splices. A few of the sentences are correct; do not rewrite them.

1. Nowhere could a police officer be found, not even a meter maid.

2. The American jury should be replaced by panels of trained judges, this would assure a greater degree of justice.

3. Coed dormitories have been called highly successful, however, the rate of illegitimate births among college coeds has been rising.

4. First we must do our homework then we can take in a movie.

5. Some of the townspeople complained that several of our cheers at the football game were obscene, therefore, to maintain good attendance, we discontinued the offensive ones.

6. A student who does not occasionally read good books on his own will probably never be well educated, he will at most be well trained.

7. This is a pomegranate, its juice makes both good jelly and good wine.

_____

_____

8. We should be more God-fearing, for we know that God destroys the Sodoms and Gomorrahs.

_____

_____

9. It was not Belgium it was, of all places, Bulgaria.

_____

10. First I removed the engine from the car, next I removed the L-head and oil pan from the engine.

_____

_____

11. Emerson's essays were highly recommended to me, nevertheless I remained much more attached to Thoreau's writings.

_____

_____

_____

12. That did it, I refused to write another term paper for that course.

_____

_____

13. The storm abated the streets, however, remained river-like for hours.

_____

_____

14. Sugar is a simple carbohydrate honey, however, is a complete food.

_____

_____

15. We sent our ads by third-class mail, this left us money to pay a telephone receptionist.

_____

_____

CHAPTER 12

THREE MORE LOGICAL FALLACIES

Misinterpretation of Causation

In human life and in the world in general there occur simple events, events of moderate complexity, and events of great complexity — and they all have causes. The cause of a simple event may be very easy to determine. For example, if you have a flat tire, examine it, and find a nail sticking into the air chamber, you can be fairly certain that running over the nail caused the flat tire. The cause of a slightly more complex event, however, may not be so easy to determine. For example, if on a routine date your steady girl friend treats you coldly rather than with her usual sweetness, you may find it hard or even impossible to discover the cause of her behavior. And for highly complex events, such as World War II or a raging urban riot, experts may argue for years and never come to an agreement as to what the real causes of the events were.

Since our logical thinking deals with events as well as ideas, we often need to know the cause or causes of one or more events to pursue an argument or to come to a sound and beneficial conclusion. And unfortunately, we often **misinterpret causation** and thus engage in unsound thinking. One of the most common types of misinterpretation of causation is known as *post hoc, ergo propter hoc,* which means "after this, therefore because of this." For example, suppose that shortly after a Democratic president and Congress have been elected, the country experiences a sudden and sharp burst of inflation. Millions of citizens would assume that the cause of the inflation was the election of a Democratic administration because the inflation came after the election. But the real causes of the inflation might lie in events that occurred before the election. The economy is so complex that it may be directly influenced by events perhaps far in the past.

In another example, students at a university might note that an unusually large number of professors left for other positions shortly after the university acquired a new president. The *post hoc* fallacy might cause the students to assume that the professors left because of the new president, since they left shortly after he was appointed, whereas the true causes might be completely unrelated to the new president. The *post hoc* fallacy is common, especially in matters that have to do with people's health. For example, countless people have thought that taking a certain medicine brought relief because relief came directly after taking the medicine. Under these circumstances, many have continued to take the medicine, thinking that it wards off the undesirable symptoms. But in many cases the relief was coming anyway (most minor ailments cure themselves), and the symptoms were not going to appear again with any regularity. The *post hoc* fallacy has made many fortunes in patent medicines.

Similar to the *post hoc* fallacy is the fallacy of misinterpretation of causation because of coincidence. When two events occur at the same time, some people will assume that one is the cause of the other even though there may be no real connection between the events. Many people, for example, have maintained, because of the fallacy of coincidence, that telepathy is real and that some dreams come true. For instance, a person might get a sudden impulse to telephone a friend and have the friend say, "Why, I was just wishing you would call." While it is quite possible that telepathy can occur, most such cases as the example just given are surely coincidences.

In reasoning yourself and in evaluating the reasoning of others, keep causation in mind. Beware of such statements as these:

> The legislature cut our college's appropriations again because we had a losing football season.
> The president won't appear before the congressional committee because he's got something to hide.
> The prisoners rioted because the guards treat them like animals.

Close investigation will usually divulge complex causes of complex events.

Diversionary Arguments

It is difficult for most people to stick to the point in an argument. Most of us tend to drift off to a side issue or to ignore the issue altogether. For example, in the famous Watergate case of 1973 many people tried to justify the illegal activities of some Republican campaign officials on the grounds that the Democrats probably acted illegally too. But if the Democrats did act illegally, they too should have been prosecuted. Their wrong, if they committed one, did not justify the Republicans' wrong, and citing it in an argument was simply resorting to a side issue. And while the Watergate scandal was wracking the country, the obscure Democratic presidential candidate Shirley Chisholm was shown to have handled her campaign contributions illegally. Then many Democrats resorted to a side issue and dismissed that charge lightly just by saying, "Look at what the Republicans did." Few of us can resist using side issues to try to clinch our arguments. But we should try to resist them and should expose them in the arguments of others.

The fallacy of ignoring the issue has the Latin name *ignoratio elenchi.* This means straying from the point completely. For example, when President Nixon was in the midst of his most serious troubles, some people, instead of citing Nixon's considerable talent as a statesman, tried to justify his competence to remain president on the grounds that he was a very good family man, devoted to his wife and daughters. That devotion, of course, did not make him competent to serve as president. If it did, then there are millions of uneducated American who would make good presidents. Or, for another example, some people considered President Lyndon Johnson to be an unfit president because he swore mightily, drank whisky, and played poker. Of course none of those habits had any bearing on his presidential capacities. Another interesting example of ignoring the issue was the attempt of some to prevent Grover Cleveland from becoming president because he was the father of an illegitimate child. Cleveland's proponents merely replied that if he could just get the votes of all the men in a similar position he would be elected easily. He did get elected and made a good president, for the charge against him had no bearing on his capabilities to govern the nation. People who reason well will not ignore the issue and will not let their opponents in an argument ignore it.

Ignoring Differences in Degree

Philosophically, people can argue till doomsday as to whether stealing ten cents is just as much a sin as stealing a million dollars. But the law says it is not nearly so serious a *crime.* And certainly differences in degree are important when events are cited in support of an argument. People who ignore differences in degree in their reasoning are guilty of a logical fallacy. For example, some political leftists of the 1930's tried to dismiss Stalin's monstrous purges and his starvation of 10,000,000 peasants by calling our attention to the oppression and occasional lynching of blacks in the South. Certainly the oppressive treatment of the blacks could by no means be justified, but there was a huge difference in degree between their oppression and the Communist terror. Similarly, when Hitler later began his systematic murder of 6,000,000 Jews, a few fanatic political rightists again pointed to the treatment of blacks in America in an effort to justify Hitler. In the argument, of course, the question of degree was most important.

We see the fallacy of ignoring degree almost everywhere. For example, a youngster once tried to justify his setting a cat on fire by pointing out that his sister had pulled the cat's tail. Embezzlers of huge sums have been known to try to minimize their crimes by accusing neighbors of cheating lightly on their income taxes. Many a student has tried to justify turning in a wholly plagiarized term paper on the grounds that some other student copied one passage. And who knows? — perhaps some giant food corporation has justified adulterating or short-weighting large quantities of foods on the grounds that some people shoplift in their stores. Differences in degree should be taken into consideration in the use of examples in arguments.

A LESSON IN THINKING

Many Christians have accepted the theological concept of **predestination** — the idea that all occurrences are predestined, or absolutely bound to occur. A simplification of the reasoning that leads to predestination is this: "God is omniscient, or all-knowing. Therefore He knows every single happening that will occur from the beginning to the end of time and knows what occurrences will not happen. Thus, since what is going to happen is known in the mind of God, what is to happen must happen, and nothing else. Therefore everything is predestined." Discuss the logic of this concept.

EXERCISES

Most of the following statements contain logical fallacies. Identify each fallacy by name, but remember that some fallacies can correctly fit more than one category. Fallacies from the nine discussed in Chapters 10, 11, and 12 are represented.

1. TV programs should not be interrupted by commercials. Movies in theaters aren't.
2. I'll just not report this $10,000 fee on my income tax. President Nixon paid almost no taxes in 1970 and 1971.
3. If a teacher can't put up with students chatting to each other in class, he can't teach well.
4. Arabs are too lazy to accomplish what individual Israelis accomplish.
5. Learning is just like medicine. It must be unpleasant to do you any good.
6. After learning that Craig Reamer owns part of an "adult" theater, I refused to vote for him for mayor.
7. It's easy to see that his ulcers caused Napoleon to lose the battles he lost.

8. Hilda's illness is all in her mind. A placebo will cure it.
9. Doubleday publishes the best mystery stories because they are the most interesting.
10. Professor Johnson doesn't like to have girls in his chemistry classes. Joy Ann is sure to get a low grade in his chemistry course.
11. Professor Tuggard said, "Steele is on drugs, and I'm not going to pass him."
12. Everybody deserves damnation.
13. That wine I had at dinner really made me sleep well. I'll have wine for dinner every evening now.
14. Don't take English lit from Professor Dabbs. He reads detective stories every night.
15. You can't ignore the Bible and be a good Christian.

USAGE
LESSON
12

SUBJECT-VERB
AGREEMENT,
PART
ONE

Most verb forms in English are the same for both singular and plural subjects, thus preventing the possibility of errors in agreement in number between subject and verb. However, the verb *to be* has different forms for the singular and plural in both the present *(is, are)* and past *(was, were)* tenses. Also all verbs have a singular form for the third person singular, present tense *(I talk, he talks; you hear, she hears; many eat, one eats)*. Since **verbs are supposed to agree in number with their subjects, you should take care to use the proper form of *to be* and of other verbs in the simple present tense. Following are discussions of the chief trouble spots in subject-verb agreement.

Intervening Prepositional Phrases

A preposition usually has a noun as an object, and when a prepositional phrase intervenes between the simple subject of a sentence and its verb, the object of the preposition has no effect on the verb. In the following examples, the intervening prepositional phrases are italicized and the simple subjects and verbs are in boldface.

wrong: Several **students** *on the dean's list* **was selected** to receive scholarships.

correct: Several **students** *on the dean's list* **were selected** to receive scholarships. (The noun *list* has no effect on the verb.)

wrong: **One** *of the teachers* **have resigned.**

correct: **One** *of the teachers* **has resigned.** (The noun *teachers* has no effect on the verb.)

wrong: **Professor Maynard** *as well as several students* **were** to go on a field trip.

correct: **Professor Maynard** *as well as several students* **was** to go on a field **trip.** (The noun *students* has no effect on the verb.)

wrong:	**Mr. Beal** *together with his children* **were** hospitalized.
correct:	**Mr. Beal** *together with his children* **was** hospitalized.
	(The noun *children* has no effect on the verb.)

Omitting the prepositional phrase will usually show you which verb form is correct. Note especially that *as well as* and *together with* are prepositions.

Indefinite Pronouns as Subjects

Of the many indefinite pronouns in English only *either, neither,* and *each* give much trouble in subject-verb agreement. All three are always singular and always take singular verbs. Examples:

wrong:	**Neither** of you **walk** as rapidly as I want to.
correct:	**Neither** of you **walks** as rapidly as I want to.
wrong:	**Either** of these books **are** enjoyable to read.
correct:	**Either** of these books **is** enjoyable to read.
wrong:	**Each were** responsible for their own equipment.
correct:	**Each was** responsible for his own equipment.

The indefinite pronouns *any* and *none* are correctly used with either singular or plural verbs and thus give no trouble.

Compound Subjects and Correlative Constructions

A compound subject is by definition plural and requires a plural verb. Examples:

correct:	The **candor** and **earnestness** of the student **were** reassuring.
	(*Was* would be wrong.)
correct:	**Returning to the house** and **entering through the cellar were** not easy.
	(*Was* would be wrong.)

When parts of the subject are joined by *and,* the subject is compound and requires a plural verb.

The verbs that go with the subjects that include the correlatives (two-part conjunctions) *not only . . . but also, either (neither) . . . or (nor), not . . . but,* and *whether . . . or* agree with the part of the subject closest to the verb. Examples:

correct:	Not only Joy but also the **twins are** coming.
correct:	Not only the twins but also **Joy is** coming.
correct:	Either the judge or the **lawyers are** crazy.
correct:	Either the lawyers or the **judge is** crazy.

correct: Not two potatoes but one **squash is** preferable.

correct: Not one squash but two **potatoes are** preferable.

Collective Nouns

Collective nouns are those singular in form but plural in meaning, such as *number, crowd, jury, family, team, crew,* and so on. In formal writing a singular verb should be used with such nouns, but in informal or semiformal writing either a singular or plural verb is satisfactory. Examples:

formal: A **number** of bills **was placed** before the Ways and Means Committee.

semiformal: A **number** of students **were** present. (*Was* would not be wrong.)

EXERCISE 12. Complete the following sentences with either a form of *to be (is, are, was, were)* as the verb or with the present tense of some other verb *(run, runs; smile, smiles;* and so on). If your teacher approves, you need only supply a verb and not a complete sentence.

1. Every one of the students _____ *is* _____

2. Not only Bob but also Alice and Ted ____ *are* _____

3. Growling and frowning _____ *are* _____

4. A crowd of spectators ____ *was or were* _____

5. Everybody but the Joneses ____ *is* _____
   prepo.

6. Each of you ____ *is* _____

7. Neither rain nor sleet nor snowflakes ____ *are* _____

8. Neither snowflakes nor sleet _____ *is* _____

9. My sister together with my brothers ____ *is* _____

10. As I looked over the books, I said that either ____ *is* _____

11. Doris as well as her parents _____ *is* _____

12. The jury ___are___ staying in different hotels.

_____

13. Walking in the rain and exploring caves ___are___

_____

14. Either a dog or two cats ___are___

_____

15. Either two cats or a dog ___is___

_____

16. I think that either ___is___

_____

17. Whether the jury or the judges ___are___

_____

18. Neither of you ___is___

_____

19. Whether the judges or the jury ___are~~ is___

_____

20. A list of honor students ___is___

_____

21. Kindness and sweetness in a girl ___are (is)___

_____

22. I wonder whether each ___is___

_____

23. Not only my aunts but also my Uncle Bernard ___is___

_____

24. The Kennedys as well as Mr. Mann ___are___

_____

25. One of those dogs ___is___

_____

118   *Logic, Language, and Composition*

CHAPTER 13

TWO MORE LOGICAL FALLACIES

Appeal to False Authority

In trying to make a point in a discussion or argument, we all occasionally cite an authority to lend weight to our reasoning. For example, in discussing whether human beings have free will or not, a person arguing for free will might cite the world-famous physicist Werner Heisenberg and his Principle of Uncertainty, which seems to show scientifically that events are not determined. On the other hand, someone arguing against free will and in favor of determinism might cite the great scientist Albert Einstein, who rejected Heisenberg's theory and claimed that the universe is deterministic. Both of these men were important experts in their fields and worth citing in an argument involving their fields. That they disagreed is not relevant, for in matters of great complexity we find most disagreement among the greatest experts.

Thus citing an expert in making a point is quite justifiable and worthwhile. The fallacy lies in making an **appeal to false authority.** For example, Albert Einstein was not an expert on nutrition. Therefore someone trying to make out a case for some nutritional theory could cite as an authority any of millions of educated people with as much justification as citing Albert Einstein. And yet there is a tendency on the part of most of us to cite any famous person as though he were an authority in the field we are discussing as well as in his own field. Some political leftists, for example, eagerly cited

119

Einstein's socialistic views to support their own position. But Einstein had no special credentials as a political thinker.

Many people's willingness to be taken in by an appeal to false authority perhaps shows up most noticeably in the field of advertising. That is, many people will buy a particular brand of merchandise solely because some celebrity endorses it. A famous athlete or entertainer, for example, can increase sales of a particular make of car simply by appearing in an ad for the car. Some people are willing to accept him as an expert on cars when he undoubtedly is not. Similarly, in an argument some people will resort to statements such as this: "Well, Elliott Gould is going to vote for so-and-so, and so am I." You could probably walk into any faculty meeting and find many better authorities on politics than Elliott Gould. Fame in one field of endeavor does not prepare a person to be especially expert in another field. Thus when you cite an authority, be sure he is an expert in the field you are discussing and refuse to accept the arguments of others who make an appeal to false authority.

Argument *ad hominem* and *ad populum*

Ad hominem means "against the man" and *ad populum* means "against the people." When, in a discussion or argument, one ignores the real issues and attacks the man or the people instead, he is indulging in a logical fallacy, one similar to ignoring the issue. For example, suppose that in trying to show that a professor you don't like is a poor teacher you attack his mode of dress, his social life, and his political views. You would be engaging in **argument ad hominem.** You would be attacking the man instead of the issue, since his mode of dress and so on need not have any bearing on the quality of his teaching. Or suppose you are in an argument in which you take a stand against abortion on demand and suppose your opponent cites a woman sociologist who is an authority on abortion laws. If you attack the sociologist because she has had an illegitimate baby and ignore her well-reasoned views, you again would be engaging in argument *ad hominem*. You should instead attack the sociologist's views on abortion and should try logically to show that they are not sound.

Argument *ad hominem* appears most frequently in politics. It probably can be safely said that no serious contender for the presidency has ever escaped argument *ad hominem*, probably not even George Washington. Thomas Jefferson's opponents attacked the man savagely, citing among other things his illegitimate children. Lincoln's personal life was attacked with a viciousness that makes modern political invective look mild. John F. Kennedy was not only attacked as a Catholic but also had it hinted that there were scandals in his personal life. Politicians are, of course, used to such treatment and they even more or less expect it. But the person who wants to be sound in his reasoning will try to stick to the issues and not attack individuals personally.

Argument ad populum involves the same kind of name-calling argument as *ad hominem*, except that the attack is on a population group rather than an individual. The Women's Lib movement uncovered not only much prejudice against women but also many unfair attacks on them as a group. When Colonel Kaddafy, ruler of Libya, visited Cairo in 1973, he attacked the feminist movement on the grounds that women are "unclean" and "physiologically inferior." Or, for another example, just suppose a well-qualified black should run for the presidency of the United States. Can you imagine the amount of abuse that would be heaped on the black race as a whole? Countless people would ignore the issues and engage in argument *ad populum*. Such argument is, of course, a fallacy.

A LESSON IN THINKING

Suppose you overhear an argument in which one person maintains that all pornography, no matter how hard-core, should be legally available to all people and his opponent maintains that all people should be protected, even against their will, from any kind of sexual exhibition. Examine the logic of each.

EXERCISES

By now you are aware of considerable overlapping in the logical fallacies, though you should see that each term we have used has its own validity. Most of the following statements contain logical fallacies. This time see how many different, but suitable, labels you can give to each of the fallacies. Here is an example of what you are to do:

A. I'm against a volunteer army. Who wants drifters defending his country?

Any of the following logical fallacies fit this statement: (1) use of faulty premise, (2) *non sequitur*, (3) polarized thinking, and possibly (4) argument *ad populum*.

1. I see that the great pianist Van Cliburn uses a Steinway piano. I think I'll have my father buy me that make.
2. Mabel Maykluck, star of "Forty Joints," endorsed Candlelight brand marijuana. It must be the best.
3. Senator Mugwump isn't fit to be dogcatcher. He divorced his wife of twenty-five years and married a young girl.
4. I knew there would be a national catastrophe. The comet Kohoutek came close to the earth.
5. Governor McCall should either run for president or get out of politics altogether.
6. I didn't know the Israelis were such religious fanatics.

7. I'll just slip this hundred-dollar bill from Dad's wallet. He made me wash the car when I was late for a date.
8. Marriage is just like riding a merry-go-round. You have to go up and down and stop and pay again every once in a while.
9. Abortion is murder because it is a sin against God.
10. Abortion is murder. I'm going to give up sex.
11. The Indians shouldn't be given any more food until they change their religious habits.
12. Those farm laborers are ignorant and uncouth. Why should we pass laws to help them?
13. The Jews are known to be dishonest. Therefore Sid Greenberg should not be elected president.
14. How can you be in favor of so few required courses? On the job we're going to have to meet many requirements.
15. The Arabs don't even keep clean. They shouldn't even be in the United Nations.
16. Athletes sure are dumb off the playing fields.
17. College professors don't need a raise in pay. They have an average standard of living now.
18. Doris is a constant church-goer. She probably isn't much fun on a date.
19. A lot of people can't hold their liquor. Therefore all liquor should be prohibited.
20. Organized labor has committed abuses. The unions ought to be outlawed.

USAGE
LESSON
13

SUBJECT-VERB
AGREEMENT,
PART
TWO

There is and There are Constructions

Errors in subject-verb agreement occur frequently in sentences that begin with *there is* or *there are*. This is a common type of sentence and not one to be avoided. However, when you use such a sentence, be sure that you know what subject follows the verb so that you can correctly use *is* or *are* (or *was* or *were*). The tendency for many people is to use *is* or *was* every time, since the subject has not yet been uttered and *there* sounds singular. But in this kind of sentence the subject follows the verb, and the verb must still agree in number with the subject. Examples, with the verb and subject in boldface:

correct: There **is** only one pound's **difference** in our weights.
correct: There **were** many **disagreements** among the members.
correct: There **was** very little **disagreement** between us.
correct: There **were** ten **errors** in Mildred's paper.
correct: There **was** hardly an **error** in my paper.
correct: There **are** two **holes** in the seat of Brad's pants.
correct: There **is** a gaping **hole** in my tent.
correct: There **are** two **differences** to be considered.

The *there* in these sentences has no meaning but serves only as a filler to stand in the normal subject position.

Inverted Sentence Order

Though you may not often write sentences with inverted order — with the verb preceding the subject — you should understand this structure and know that the verb agrees with the subject even though it precedes the subject. Examples, with the verbs and subjects in boldface:

correct:	To the right of me **were** several additional **cops.**
correct:	Out of the cave often **come** weird, banshee-like **noises.**
correct:	Out of the other cave often **comes** a demon-like **wail.**

This kind of inverted sentence order is occasionally used by good writers to give variety to their styles.

Relative Pronouns as Subjects

The relative pronouns that can function as subjects are *who, which,* and *that.* These pronouns are both singular and plural, and thus the verb one takes agrees in number with the antecedent of the pronoun, or the noun it refers to. Here are example sentences with the relative pronoun, its antecedent, and its verb in boldface:

correct:	The **wine which wins** the grand prize will be auctioned off.
correct:	The **wines which win** blue ribbons will not be sold.
correct:	The **professors** of English at UCLA, **who have** unanimously protested the ruling, are prepared to resign.
correct:	The **professor** of computer science at tiny Piedmont College, **who has** published forty articles, is world-famous.
correct:	The first six **chapters** of *Modern Linguistics,* **which are** required reading, are especially difficult.
correct:	The first six chapters of *Modern Linguistics,* **which is** required reading, are especially difficult.

Note how proper agreement in the last two sentences is essential for proper meaning.

Another agreement problem with relative pronouns occurs in sentences like this one:

Jerry is one of those alcoholics who (get *or* gets) busted every week.

Many people think the relative pronoun refers to *one* and thus requires a singular verb (*gets*). But *who* refers to the plural noun *alcoholics* and thus the verb should be the plural *get.* Here are two other examples:

| *correct:* | I am one of those **people who** always **lose** at poker. |
| *correct:* | Earl is one of those **potheads who know** how to elude cops. |

A simple way to test such a sentence is to rearrange its structure so that the antecedent of the relative pronoun is absolutely clear. Examples:

| *correct:* | Of those **people who** always **lose** at poker, I am one. |
| *correct:* | Of those **potheads who know** how to elude cops, Earl is one. |

Of course when *one* is the antecedent of the relative pronoun, the verb is singular. Example:

correct: I am **one** of the club members **who detests** Scotch.

The sentence means that some of the members do not detest Scotch.

Sums of Money, Periods of Time, and Measurements

When a sum of money, a period of time, or a measurement is used as a subject, the verb should usually be singular, for the sum of money, period of time, or measurement is thought of as a single unit. Examples:

correct: I think **thirty-five dollars is** enough to cover the damages.
correct: **Four years is** a long time to wait for a husband to return.
correct: **Three miles is** a long way to walk.

Of course when pieces of money and so on are thought of as individual units, the verb should be plural. Examples:

correct: Three silver **dollars were** on the table.
correct: Twelve individual **inches were** marked off on the blackboard.

These usages are rare.

EXERCISE 13. In the blanks in the following sentences write the correct **present-tense** form of the verb in parentheses below the blank. Past tense forms may be used for the verb *to be*.

1. At the end of the last row _____ *sit* _____ some noisy sophomores.
   (to sit)

2. There _____ *are* _____ many medical technicians who _____ *wish* _____
   (to be)   (to wish)
   they had gone to med school.

3. Jerry is one of those who _____ *are* _____ good in all sports.
   (to be)

4. But Terry is one who _____ *has* _____ trouble even with tiddlywinks.
   (to have)

5. Running counter to Heisenberg's theory _____ *are* _____ the discoveries
   (to be)
   of Einstein.

6. Professor Turnipseed is one of those scholars who _____ *want* _____ to
   (to want)
   make everything scientific.

7. There _____ *are* _____ unknown causes of some flu-like diseases.
   (to be)

8. Tommy's first six tries to enlist in the Navy, which _____ *were* _____
   (to be)
   even less than unsuccessful, only spurred him to try again.

9. Promptly at midnight every night, out of the clockworks _____ *comes* _____
   (to come)
   a voice like an angel singing.

10. The early theories of the structure of the atom, which now _____ *seem* _____
    (to seem)
    naive, did help researchers come closer to the truth.

11. On the back of the truck _____ *sit* _____ six disgruntled farm laborers.
    (to sit)

12. Sally is one who _____ *puts* _____ dates ahead of homework.
    (to put)

13. But Betty is one of those students who _____ *stay* _____ ahead in their
    (to stay)
    homework.

14. Keeping Jackie out of the running _____ *are* _____ some outside ex-
    (to be)
    perts the ATO brought in.

15. Frank is certainly one of those players who _____ *try* _____ to show
    (to try)
    that sports build character.

16. There _____ *are* _____ a half-dozen or more rules frequently broken.
    (to be)

17. Peter is one of those students who _____ *have* _____ a ready answer for
    (to have)
    any question — ready but usually wrong.

18. The Carroll sisters of the hamlet Horton Bay, who _____ *date* _____ any
    (to date)
    boys that come along, are being spied on by the police.

Two More Logical Fallacies 127

19. There _is/was_ two dollars' difference at the day's end.
    (to be)
20. On the floor _is_ the shifting shadow of the two intruders.
    (to be)
21. Professor Rolfe handed out a reading list of novels that _was/is_
    (to be)
    not clearly typed.
22. Professor Longueil handed out his reading list of poems, which
    are (is?) sure to be entertaining.
    (to be)
23. There, behind the rose bushes, _kneel_ the runaways.
    (to kneel)
24. Sara is one of those people who _keep_ up with the Joneses at
    (to keep)
    all costs.
25. There _are_ , according to the findings of Skinner, several
    (to be)
    ways to train pigeons to dance.
26. It seems to me that forty-seven dollars _is_ a lot to pay for
    (to be)
    that jacket.
27. Did the coach say that twelve miles _is_ the normal dis-
    (to be)
    tance we have to run each day?
28. There _seem_ to be several ways to solve this problem.
    (to seem)
29. A hundred meters _is_ a somewhat greater distance than a
    (to be)
    hundred yards.
30. I hardly see that thirty cents _makes_ up for the crime you com-
    (to make)
    mitted.

PART TWO

LANGUAGE

CHAPTER
14

THE
USES
OF
LANGUAGE

Many scientists like to differentiate man from other advanced mammals by calling him "the talking animal," and indeed it is language more than anything else that sets man apart from the higher primates, which physiologically are almost identical to man. Though language is with us all the time, it may justly be called a miracle, for it works wonders. It not only allows very complex human cultures to exist, but it is also the necessary medium for transmission of cultures from generation to generation. Most people take language for granted, since it is so natural, but it is actually so complex that many long books would be required to describe its many aspects in detail. The study of language is a science called **linguistics,** to which many research scholars devote their professional lives. But some of the important aspects of language can be discussed simply and briefly, as the following chapters will show.

Our culture is one of the most advanced in the world; some others are very primitive. By studying cultures in varying degrees of development, we learn that the more advanced a culture is, the more important language skills are to its members. In the United States most of our citizens — particularly those holding jobs requiring a college education — need extensive verbal (language) skills. The need to speak and write effectively and correctly is of course basic; but many other verbal skills, such as the ability to evaluate propaganda, are also important. A general study of some of the basic characteristics of language can help you improve your various verbal skills and thus can greatly enhance your education. The chapters in this part provide you with materials for such study.

Perhaps the very first question to ask about languages is how did it originate? — a question no one can answer. Many theories about the origin of language have been proposed, but none has been generally accepted by linguists. In fact, in the late nineteenth century the French Academy became so disgusted with wild speculation about the origin of language that it forbade any further papers on the subject to be presented to the academy. But there is always the urge to speculate. The Biblical story in Genesis says that the original language God gave to Adam became diverse at the Tower of Babel. The ancient Greeks believed that originally every word corresponded to an object in nature but that "corruption" caused, say, a horse to be called different names in different languages. Some theories say that language originated as an imitation of sounds in nature. Two of these speculations have been called the "ding-dong" and "bow-wow" theories. The "ouch-ouch" theory says that instinctive yelps of pain started language on its evolution. The "yo-de-ho" theory claims that language began with the singing sounds men make at hard labor. And so the speculation goes, with no final answer.

But whatever its origin, we do have language and perhaps the second question to be asked about it is what are the uses of language? In spite of its enormous complexity, language has only three basic uses. The first of these is to convey information, and language with this use is called **informative language.** Here are simple examples:

"I got in a traffic jam on my way over. That's why I'm late for our date."

"We're all out of Smokies brand, and when we get a new stock the price will be higher."

The heliocentric theory of the solar system was first presented by Copernicus, a Polish monk who lived from 1473 to 1543.

Of course informative language may not be true. The fellow above who was late for his date might just be lying to cover his having stopped off to see another girl. Or the birth and death dates for Copernicus could be in error. Nevertheless, such language is still classified as informative, even if it is language which *mis*informs. All knowledge (and incorrect knowledge) is transmitted through informative language; thus this use of language is the most important one for transmitting a culture from generation to generation and for the expansion of a culture.

The second use of language is to produce an emotional reaction in the hearer or reader. Such language is called **expressive.** Expressive language is more widely used than you may think; aside from its use between lovers, loved ones, and friends it abounds (often in disguise) in political, social, and religious propaganda. For example, if in a speech on welfare a politician emphasizes how many able-bodied men and illegitimate children are on welfare, he is doubtless playing on the emotions of his listeners. But perhaps the purest expressive language appears in poetry. Consider this little poem by Emily Dickinson:

> The bustle in a house
> The morning after death
> Is solemnest of industries
> Enacted upon earth, —
>
> The sweeping up of heart,
> And putting love away
> We shall not want to use again
> Until eternity.

This poem is intended solely to arouse emotion.

Third, we use **directive language,** the purpose of which is to cause (or prevent) action or belief. All request or command sentences are directive. Examples:

> Stay away from those porno shows.
> Get that cat out of here!
> Believe in Him and you will be saved.

Directive language may also appear in nonrequest sentences. For example, if in a sermon a preacher says, "The way of the transgressor is hard," he is using directive as well as informative language, for he is urging the congregation not to transgress God's will.

As you have already perceived, the three uses of language may be mixed to produce complex layers of meaning. For example, informative and expressive language may be mixed to produce **narration,** or story-telling. The story-teller both informs his reader (or listener) and affects his emotions. For example, here is the ending of a story about how the relationship between two teen-agers was misunderstood:

> They're going to send Helen to a convent — I found out that. Maybe they'll let me see her before she goes. But, if we do, it will be all wrong and in front of people and everybody pretending. I sort of wish they don't — though I want to, terribly. When her mother took her upstairs that night — she wasn't the same Helen. She looked at me as if she was afraid of me. And no matter what they do for us now, they can't fix that.

The informative and emotional aspects of the passage can be identified but they cannot really be separated.

Also **description** makes use of a mixture of informative and expressive language. For example, here is a short portion of Jack London's description of the great San Francisco earthquake and fire:

> By Wednesday afternoon, inside of twelve hours, half the heart of the city was gone. At that time I watched the vast conflagration from out on the bay. It was dead calm. Not a flicker of wind stirred. Yet from every side wind was pouring in upon the city. East, west, north, and south, strong winds were blowing upon the doomed city. The heated air rising made an enormous suck. Thus did the fire of itself build its own collossal chimney through the atmosphere. Day and night this dead calm continued, and yet, near to the flames, the wind was often half a gale, so mighty was the suck.

The passage conveys much information but also stirs the reader's emotions.

Persuasion is usually a mixture of informative and expressive language, often with some directive language included. For example, here is the opening of an argument against "welfarism" in the United States:

> In the first half of the 1960's, important people proposed that the United States make a social revolution, but without the inconvenience of changing any basic institutions.
> The president declared "unconditional war" on poverty, and the Congress obligingly proclaimed that it was the public policy "to eliminate the paradox of poverty in the midst of plenty." President Johnson declared that this goal, and the abolition of racial injustice as well, were "just the beginning." He looked toward nothing less than a Great Society, "a place where men are more concerned with the quality of their goals than the quantity of their goods," where leisure would mean "a welcome chance to build and reflect, not a feared cause of boredom and restlessness," where the city would serve "the desire for beauty and the hunger for community."
> An excellent case can be made for dismissing all this talk as windy futurism.

The author is using informative language but he is also playing on the emotions of the reader with such phrases as "windy futurism."

Thus, though the three distinctive uses of language may be identified and isolated, they can exist in mixtures of varying proportions, and all these various mixtures let language serve us in all the ways that we desire.

EXERCISES

1. Speculate as to how language might have originated and explain your own theory.
2. Explain how informative, expressive, and directive language are mixed in this portion of a *dirge* (death song) by Shakespeare.

Fear no more the heat o' the sun,
  Nor the furious winter's rages;
Thou thy worldly task hast done,
  Home art gone, and ta'en thy wages:
Golden lads and girls all must,
As chimney-sweepers, come to dust.

3. Explain how informative and expressive language are mixed in this passage from Hitler's *Mein Kampf*. Remember that, technically, informative
language need not be true.

   Since nationality or rather race does not happen to lie in language but in
the blood, we would only be justified in speaking of a Germanization if by
such a process we succeeded in transforming the blood of the subjected
people. But this is impossible, unless a blood mixture brings about a change,
which, however, means the lowering of the level of the higher race. The final
result of such a process would consequently be the destruction of precisely
those qualities which had formerly made the conquering people capable of
victory. Especially the cultural force would vanish through a mating with the
lesser race, even if the resulting mongrels spoke the language of the earlier,
higher race a thousand times over. For a time, a certain struggle will take place
between the different mentalities, and it may be that the steadily sinking
people, in a last quiver of life, so to speak, will bring to light surprising
cultural values. But these are only individual elements belonging to the higher
race, or perhaps bastards in whom, after the first crossing, the better blood still
predominates and tries to struggle through; but never final products of a
mixture. In them a culturally backward movement will always manifest itself.

4. Find out approximately how many live languages are now in existence.

USAGE
LESSON
14

PRONOUN
CASE
FORMS

Some of our pronouns occur in one form when they are subjects and another form when they are objects of verbs or prepositions. They are the following:

Subjects	Objects
I	me
we	us
he	him
she	her
they	them
who	whom

Other pronouns have the same form as both subjects and objects.

Pronoun Forms in Compound Structures

Many people wrongly use an object pronoun form in a compound subject when they do not use a wrong form singly. For example, some people will **wrongly say**

   Jess and me got busted,

but never

   Me got busted.

Similarly, many people wrongly use a subject form in a compound structure which is an object when they do not use a wrong form singly. For example, some people will wrongly say

The gift was for Herbert and I,

but never

The gift was for I.

So be careful in using pronouns in compound structures and test when you need to by omitting one part of the compound structure. You can avoid most mistakes in this aspect of pronoun usage if you will remember that constructions similar to the following are the correct ones:

between **you** and **me**   (*I* is wrong.)
between **her** and **him**   (*She* and *he* are wrong.)
for **him** and **me**   (*He* and *I* are wrong.)
to **her** and **me**   (*She* and *I* are wrong.)

Who and *Whom*

In colloquial (informal, casual) English *who* is now acceptable whenever it sounds natural, but in semiformal English *who* should be used only as a subject and *whom* as an object. In conversation you usually don't have time to determine which is the right form, but for writing you can test a construction to see whether *who* or *whom* is needed. The test is to substitute *he* (or *she* or *they*) or *him* (or *her* or *them*) for *who* or *whom*; if *he* sounds natural, then use *who*, and if *him* sounds natural, use *whom*. Usually a sentence must be rearranged for the test to work. Examples:

Terry is the one _____ we think will supply the feed.
                          (who *or* whom?)

We think **he** will supply the feed. (Therefore use *who*.)

Joe was the student _____ Dean Slater accused.
                            (who *or* whom?)

Dean Slater accused **him**. (Therefore use *whom*.)

_____ did old Cueball admonish?
(Who *or* Whom?)

Old Cueball admonished **him**. (Therefore use *whom*.)

With a little practice you can learn to choose the proper form.

Pronoun Forms after *to be*

In colloquial English it is acceptable to say *it's me, it's them, that was her,* and so on. In semiformal English it is best to say *it's I, that was she,* and so on.

The *we students–us students* Construction

In the *we Americans–us Americans* construction use whichever pronoun sounds right when the noun *(students, Americans,* and so on) is omitted. Examples:

> **We** (girls) will help you study. (*Us* would be wrong.)
> The coach really gave **us** (players) a dressing down. (*We* would be wrong.)

The nouns in parentheses are omitted for testing purposes. They would be included in the actual sentences spoken or written.

Pronoun Forms in Comparative Constructions

The common comparative constructions *more than, less than,* and *as . . . as* are frequently followed by pronouns. The way to choose the proper pronoun form is to complete the understood part of the sentence to see which pronoun form sounds right. Examples, with the understood part of the sentence in parentheses:

> Jo Ann is as well prepared as **I** (am prepared). (*Me* would be wrong.)
> Carrie gave Luis more attention than (she gave) **me.** (*I* would be wrong.)
> Carrie gave Luis more attention than **I** (gave Luis) (*Me* would be wrong.)

The test is easy to apply. And, as you can see, in some comparative constructions the form of the pronoun determines the meaning.

EXERCISE 14.   In the following sentences write in the blanks provided the correct form of the pronouns in parentheses below the blanks. When necessary, use the pronoun tests discussed in the previous section.

1. Just between you and _____, Frank is the one _____
        (I or me?)   (who or whom?)
    I expect to be expelled.

2. It was _____ who claimed that the joints were intended for
        (she or her?)

    Janice and _____ .
        (I or me?)

3. Do you know _____ it was who supplied more snow than
        (who or whom?)

    _____ ?
        (I or me?)

4. The cop told _____ fellows that he would arrest _____
        (we or us?)   (whoever or whomever?)
    he needed to.

5. The accident was reported to Jack and _____ after we discov-
        (he or him?)

    ered _____ the real culprit was.
        (who or whom?)

6. No one knows less than _____ about that stupid lesson on
        (I or me?)
    pronoun reference.

7. When _____ investigators found that it was _____
        (we or us?)   (they or them?)

    _____ the cops thought were responsible, we called in the
        (who or whom?)
    sheriff.

8. That affair is just between _____ and their consciences.
        (they or them?)

9. Jeannie gave Don a bigger hug than _____ .
        (I or me?)

10. When the stranger spoke to Rufus and _____ , we suspected
    (I or me?)

    that he was the one _____ the narks believed was pushing.
    (who or whom?)

11. Nobody else in the class is as well-informed as _____ .
    (I or me?)

12. While Josie was talking to Greg and _____ , we learned that it
    (I or me?)

    was George and _____ the mob was tracking.
    (she or her?)   (who or whom?)

13. Can David and _____ discover whether Malcolm is better
    (she or her?)

    liked than _____ ?
    (they or them?)

14. Where will all of _____ sinners end up?
    (we or us?)

15. Neither you nor _____ can spike the cabbage as well as
    (he or him?)

    _____ .
    (I or me?)

16. Just between you and _____ , there's no one _____
    (I or me?)   (who or whom?)

    Professor Turner likes better than _____ .
    (I or me?)

17. Where are _____ the angels prefer to Jackie
    (they or them?)   (who or whom?)

    and _____ ?
    (I or me?)

18. _____ did you say was narcoed?
    (Who or Whom?)

19. It was _____ the Royals stonkered.
    (they or them?)   (who or whom?)

20. No one has popped more dogtails than _____ .
    (she or her?)

CHAPTER
15

LEXICOGRAPHY
AND
THE
USE
OF
THE
DICTIONARY

Lexicography is the art and science of dictionary-making and has been brought to a high point of development in our language-conscious culture. The first significant English dictionary — Nathaniel Bailey's *Universal Etymological Dictionary* — was published in 1721, to be followed in 1755 by Dr. Samuel Johnson's great *Dictionary of the English Language*. Noah Webster's important *American Dictionary of the English Language* came in 1828. The greatest of all English dictionaries, the *Oxford English Dictionary*, which consists of twelve very large volumes, was begun in 1888 and published in 1933. It is so inclusive that it devotes eighteen long columns (enough to fill at least twenty-five normal book pages) to the single word *by*. Supplements to the twelve volumes have been published. Most people nowadays, however, depend either on the two important so-called unabridged dictionaries—*Webster's New International*, Third Edition, and *The Random House Dictionary of the English Language* — or on one of the five excellent collegiate dictionaries — (1) *Webster's New Collegiate Dictionary* (based on the *New International*), (2) *Webster's New World Dictionary*, (3) *Standard College Dictionary* (also known as *Funk and Wagnalls*), (4) *The Random House Dictionary of the English Language, College Edition*, and (5) *The American Heritage Dictionary*. These dictionaries will be referred to below.

Lexicographers do their work by collecting short citations (quotations) from writing and speeches of all sorts, with one particular word in a citation being marked as the one to be entered into the dictionary under preparation.

After collecting and alphabetizing millions of citations, scholars are ready to prepare an entry for each word, with all the information which is discussed in the following pages. Years of work by dozens or hundreds of scholars have gone into the preparation of each of the excellent dictionaries mentioned in the preceding paragraph.

The purpose of a dictionary is a matter of dispute among scholars. Nowadays the large majority of linguists maintain that the purpose of a dictionary is simply to record what current language usage *is*, not to prescribe what it *should be*. The publisher (Merriam-Webster, Inc.) of *Webster's New International* and *Webster's New Collegiate* dictionaries follows this philosophy fully. For example, those dictionaries do not label as slang a great many words that other dictionaries do label as slang. *Punk* (meaning "of poor quality") is an example. Those dictionaries also refuse to label any word informal (or colloquial), though all other good dictionaries do use one or the other of those labels.

Another example of those two dictionaries' liberal philosophy is their refusal to warn users of "incorrect" definitions, pronunciations, or spellings that have come into public use through ignorance. By contrast, most other dictionaries do give such warnings. For example, most warn that *disinterested* should not be used to mean "not interested" or "indifferent" but should instead be used to mean "impartial" or "having no personal motive." But the two dictionaries cited above do not give any such warning, on the grounds that the general public actually uses the word to mean "not interested."

Or, for another example, those two dictionaries list the spelling *alright* (for *all right*) as fully acceptable, whereas all of the other dictionaries warn in some way that this spelling is not in good usage. The other dictionaries mentioned in the first paragraph do purport to record language as it is rather than as it should be, but they do also in fact guide the user to a considerable extent. A few scholars still maintain that a dictionary should be authoritative and prescribe what is right and what is wrong, and the general public takes this view of a dictionary's purpose. Otherwise, they reason, anything goes, and that would lead to chaos. So in actual fact, contemporary dictionaries are in a sense just a record of our vocabulary as it is but are also authoritative guides for the public.

Dictionaries vary in the methods in which they list the definitions of any one word. *Webster's New Collegiate Dictionary* uses an historical method, which lists definitions of a word in the order in which they entered the language. Students often find this method inconvenient, for the first definitions listed may be out of date and may mislead the student when he looks a word up. *The American Heritage Dictionary* and *Webster's New World Dictionary* use a method in which the first-listed definition is a central sense of the word, with other definitions flowing from that one. *The Random House Dictionary* and the *Standard College Dictionary* use a statistical method, with the most common meaning listed first and so on. Here are examples of the methods of *Webster's New Collegiate* and *The Random House Dictionary*, with the dates of the definitions taken from the *Oxford English Dictionary*. (*N.e.* means that the OED does not list the definition.)

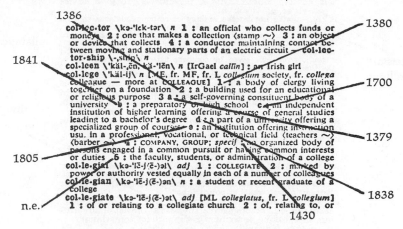

WEBSTER'S NEW COLLEGIATE DICTIONARY

Historical Method

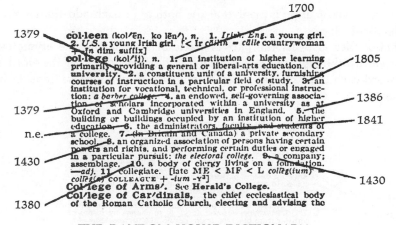

THE RANDOM HOUSE DICTIONARY

Statistical Method

Many students prefer the *Random House* method of listing definitions because they can usually depend on the first definition of a word being the one they want.

Dictionaries are most often used for looking up **definitions, spellings,** and **pronunciations.** Here is a segment from *Webster's New World Dictionary* showing how these items of information are entered:

definitions

alternate spellings

syllabification

alternate pronunciations

recommended; being good advice —ad·vis′a·bil′i·ty, ad·vis′a·ble·ness *n.* —ad·vis′a·bly *adv.*

ad·vise (əd vīz′) *vt.* -vised′, -vis′ing [ME. *avisen*, orig., to consider < OFr. *aviser* < ML. *advisare* < *advisum*: see ADVICE] 1. to give advice or an opinion to; counsel 2. to offer as advice; recommend 3. to notify; inform [he was *advised* of the facts] —*vi.* 1. to discuss something and get advice; consult (*with* a person) 2. to give advice —ad·vis′er, ad·vi′sor *n.*

SYN.—advise implies the making of recommendations as to a course of action by someone with actual or supposed knowledge, experience, etc.; counsel implies the giving of advice after careful deliberation and suggests that weighty matters are involved; admonish suggests earnest, gently reproving advice concerning a fault, error, etc., given by someone fitted to do so by age or position; to caution is to give advice that puts one on guard against possible danger, failure, etc.; warn, often interchangeable with caution, is used when a serious danger or penalty is involved

ad·vised (əd vīzd′) *adj.* showing or resulting from thought or advice; considered: now chiefly in WELL-ADVISED, ILL-ADVISED

ad·vis·ed·ly (əd vī′zid lē) *adv.* with due consideration; deliberately

ad·vise·ment (əd vīz′mənt) *n.* [ME. & OFr. *avisement* < *aviser*, ADVISE] careful consideration —take under advisement to consider carefully

ad·vi·so·ry (əd vī′zər ē) *adj.* 1. advising or given the power to advise 2. relating to, or containing advice —*n.*, *pl.* -ries a report or warning, esp. one issued by the Weather Bureau about weather conditions

ad·vo·ca·cy (ad′və kə sē) *n.* [ME. & OFr. *advocacie* < ML. *advocatia* < L. *advocatus*: see ADVOCATE] the act of advocating, or speaking or writing in support (*of* something)

ad·vo·cate (ad′və kit, -kāt′; *for v.* -kāt′) *n.* [ME. & OFr. *avocat* < L. *advocatus*, a counselor < *advocare*, to summon (for aid) < *ad-*, to + *vocare*, to call] 1. a person who pleads another's cause; specif., a lawyer 2. a person who speaks

A key to pronunciation is printed at the bottom of each odd-numbered page of the dictionary.

Dictionaries also list the **part** or **parts of speech** and the **etymology** of most words, the etymology being the origin or derivation of the word. Here is a word from the *Random House Dictionary* showing these items of information:

parts of speech

etymology

transf., 1. transfer. 2. transferred.
trans·fer (*v.* trans fûr′, trans′fər; *n.* trans′fər), *v.*, -ferred, -fer·ring, *n.* —*v.t.* 1. to convey or remove from one place, person, etc. to another. 2. to cause to pass from one person to another, as thought, qualities, power, etc.; transmit. 3. *Law.* to make over the possession or control of: *to transfer a title to land.* 4. to imprint, impress, or otherwise convey (a drawing, design, pattern, etc.) from one surface to another. —*v.i.* 5. to remove oneself or be moved from one place to another. 6. to withdraw from one school, college, or the like, and enter another: *He transferred from Rutgers to Tulane.* 7. to be moved from one place to another: *The entire military unit will transfer to overseas duty.* 8. to change by means of a transfer from one bus, train, or the like, to another. —*n.* 9. the act of transferring. 10. the fact of being transferred. 11. means or system of transferring. 12. a point or place for transferring. 13. a ticket, issued with or without extra charge, entitling a passenger to continue his journey on another bus, train, or the like. 14. a drawing, design, pattern, or the like, that is or may be transferred to another surface, usually by direct contact. 15. a person who changes or is changed from one college, military unit, business department, etc., to another. 16. *Law.* a conveyance by sale, gift, or otherwise, of real or personal property, to another. 17. *Finance.* act of having the ownership of a stock or registered bond transferred on the books of the issuing corporation or its agent. [ME *transferre* < L — *trans-* TRANS- + *ferre* to bear, carry] —trans·fer′a·bil′i·ty, *n.* —trans·fer′a·ble, trans·fer′ra·ble, *adj.* —trans·fer′rer, *n.*
trans·fer·al (trans fûr′əl), *n.* transference; transfer. Also,

The dictionary has a guide to the abbreviations: *v.t.* means "transitive verb"; *v.i.* means "intransitive verb"; *n.* means "noun"; ME means "Middle English"; and L means "Latin." All other abbreviations and symbols used in any good dictionary are clearly explained in the preface of the dictionary.

Dictionaries also enter **usage labels** and **subject labels.** A usage label tells the standing in the language of a word or one definition of a word. The most common usage labels are *slang* (such as *cop-out*), *colloquial* or *informal* (such as *quitter*), *substandard* (such as *nowheres*), *nonstandard* (such as *irregardless*), *obsolete, archaic,* and *dialectal.* A subject label indicates that a particular definition is used only in one field of endeavor, such as law, medicine, physics, and so on. The prefatory material in each dictionary clearly explains all usage and subject labels. Here is a segment of *The American Heritage Dictionary* showing usage and subject labels:

subject label → usage labels →

> **horse** (hôrs) *n.* **1.** A large hoofed mammal, *Equus caballus,* having a short-haired coat, a long mane, and a long tail, and domesticated since ancient times for riding and to pull vehicles or carry loads. **2.** An adult male horse. **3.** Any of various other equine mammals, such as the wild Asian species, *E. przewalskii,* or certain extinct forms related ancestrally to the modern horse. **4.** Mounted soldiers; cavalry: *a squadron of horse.* **5.** A supportive frame or device, usually having four legs. **6.** A gymnastic device having four legs and an upholstered body used for vaulting and other exercises. **7.** *Slang.* Heroin. **8.** *Informal.* Something larger or cruder than the average. **9.** *Often plural.* Horsepower. **10.** *Geology.* **a.** A block of rock interrupting a vein and containing no minerals. **b.** A large block of displaced rock that is caught along a fault. —*a horse of another (or a different) color.* Another matter entirely; something else. —*be (or get) on one's high horse.* To be or become disdainful, superior, or conceited. —*hold one's horses.* To check or rein one's eagerness; restrain oneself. —*the horse's mouth.* Any source of information regarded as original or unimpeachable. —*to horse!* Used to express a command or the intention to mount one's horse. —*v.* **horsed, horsing, horses.** —*tr.* **1.** To provide with or place upon a horse. **2.** To haul or hoist energetically: *horse in a bluefish.* **3.** To subject to horseplay. —*intr.* **1.** To mount or ride upon a horse. **2.** *Informal.* To indulge in horseplay. Usually used with *around.* **3.** To be in heat. Said of mares. —*adj.* **•1.** Of or pertaining to a horse. **2.** Mounted on a horse or horses. **3.** Drawn or operated by a horse or horses. **4.** Larger and cruder than its fellows. [Middle English *hors,* Old English *hors,* from Germanic *hors-* (unattested).]

Webster's New Collegiate Dictionary refuses to use the label *informal* or *colloquial,* on the grounds that people mistakenly think that such a label means the word is tainted in some way, but all the other dictionaries do use one or the other of these labels (which have the same meaning). Colloquial words are not to be avoided in informal situations but usually should be avoided in semiformal or formal situations.

Most of the good dictionaries also give **citations** and **synonyms** for some words. A citation is a quotation, usually from a well-known person, of the word in actual use for a particular definition. Synonyms are words with meanings identical or similar to the word in question. Here is a segment of *Webster's New Collegiate Dictionary* showing the use of citations and the listing of synonyms:

synonyms ——

¹dirty \'dərt-ē\ *adj* **dirt·i·er; -est** **1 a** : not clean or pure <~ clothes> **b** : likely to befoul or defile with dirt <~ jobs> **c** : tedious, disagreeable, and unrecognized or thankless <undertook the ~ tasks that no one else wanted to bother with> **d** : contaminated with infecting organisms <~ wounds> **2 a** : BASE. SORDID <war is a ~ business> **b** : UNSPORTSMANLIKE <a ~ trick> <~ players> **c** : highly regrettable : GRIEVOUS <it's a ~ shame> **3** : INDECENT. SMUTTY <~ language> **4** : FOGGY. STORMY **5 a** *of color* : not clear and bright : DULLISH <drab *dirty*-pink walls> **b** : characterized by a husky, rasping, or raw tonal quality — used esp. of jazz **6** : conveying ill-natured resentment <gave him a ~ look> **7** : having considerable fallout <~ bombs> — **dirt·i·ly** \'dərt-ə-lē\ *adv* — **dirt·i·ness** \'dərt-ē-nəs\ *n*

syn DIRTY. FILTHY. FOUL. NASTY. SQUALID *shared meaning element* : conspicuously unclean or impure. DIRTY emphasizes the fact of the presence of dirt more than an emotional reaction to it <children *dirty* from play> <a *dirty* littered street> FILTHY carries a strong suggestion of offensiveness and typically of gradually accumulated dirt that begrimes and besmears <a stained greasy floor, utterly *filthy*> FOUL implies extreme offensiveness and an accumulation of what is rotten or stinking <the *foul* oil-and-garbage whiffs from the river —Herman Wouk> NASTY applies to what is actually foul or is repugnant to one used to or expecting freshness, cleanliness, or sweetness <it's a *nasty* job to clean up after a sick cat> In practice, *nasty* is often weakened to the point of being no more than a synonym of *unpleasant* or *disagreeable* <had a *nasty* fall> <his answer gave her a *nasty* shock> SQUALID adds to the idea of dirtiness and filth that of slovenly neglect <living in *squalid* poverty> <*squalid* slums> All these terms are applicable to moral uncleanness or baseness or obscenity. DIRTY then stresses meanness or despicableness <the creature's at his *dirty* work again —Alexander Pope> while FILTHY and FOUL describe disgusting obscenity or loathsome behavior <*filthy* language> <a *foul* story> and NASTY implies a peculiarly offensive unpleasantness <a cheap and *nasty* imitation of the real thing —Robert Wilkes> Distinctively, SQUALID implies sordidness as well as baseness and dirtiness <her life was a series of *squalid* affairs> **ant** clean

—— **citations**

antonym ——

Occasionally, dictionaries also list **antonyms,** or words of opposite meaning, as illustrated here with the word *clean.*

In addition to guides to the use of the dictionary, all of the good dictionaries also include much useful miscellaneous information. *Webster's New Collegiate* has separate sections listing very brief information about famous persons and geographic names; the others include this information with the main entries. Otherwise the dictionaries have separate sections for (1) tables of weights and measures; (2) a list of colleges and universities in the United States and Canada; (3) an essay on usage; (4) rules of capitalization and punctuation; (5) a chart or list of historical events; (6) a brief history of English; (7) an essay on dialects; (8) an essay on grammar; and (9) various other essays or lists, such as a list of home remedies. The person who learns to use his dictionary well has a world of reliable information at his fingertips.

EXERCISES

1. How many definitions of *beat* does your dictionary list? What method does it use to order the numerous definitions?
2. How should the words *exquisite, combatant,* and *harass* be pronounced if the first-listed pronunciation in a dictionary is the preferred one? Do you hear these words given a nonpreferred pronunciation? Do you find the pronunciation key in your dictionary easy to use?
3. Find three words in your dictionary that have alternate spellings.

4. How many parts of speech does the word *present* function as?
5. Write out the etymologies of *cynic, algebra, boycott,* and *moo.*
6. What usage label, if any, does your dictionary give for *snot?*
7. See how many slang words for *drunk* you can find in your dictionary. If *Webster's New Collegiate Dictionary* is available to you, see if any of these words are *not* labeled slang. Or if *Webster's New Collegiate* is your dictionary, see if words for *drunk* that it does not label slang are labeled slang in another collegiate dictionary.
8. How many subject labels does your dictionary list for *neuter?*
9. How many synonyms, if any, does your dictionary list for *new?*
10. Using your dictionary's tables of weights and measures, find out (1) how long a rod and a furlong are; (2) how many centimeters make an inch; and (3) how much liquid is contained in a liter.
11. What information about Michigan State University does your dictionary give?

PRONOUN
REFERENCE

In our speech and writing we constantly use pronouns to refer to (or take their meaning from) particular nouns or, in some cases, whole ideas previously expressed. We call the noun or idea the pronoun refers to the pronoun's **antecedent.** Thus when we construct a sentence so that the reference, or antecedent, of a pronoun is unclear, we either confuse a reader or make **him** stumble in his reading.

When pronoun reference is **ambiguous,** the reader may be genuinely confused and not just momentarily stopped because of poor style. Ambiguity in language occurs when a statement has two or more possible meanings, often without the reader's being sure which meaning is intended. Here is an **example:**

> *ambiguous reference:* Just as our uncle was ushering us into his living room, one of his cronies stopped by for a visit. We sat down around the fireplace to thaw out. Then **he** began to tell a strange story.

Now it is probable that the writer meant *he* to refer to *uncle,* but it can also refer to *one of his cronies.* Thus the pronoun reference is ambiguous. Even if the pronoun's antecedent is made clear later in the paragraph, the damage has already been done, for the reader has momentarily lost his way. The alert writer would repeat the word *uncle* in order to avoid the ambiguity.

Here is another example:

> *ambiguous reference:* The small conference room at the south end of the gym, **which** incidentally is poorly ventilated, is often the scene of underhanded financial dealings between the players and college officials.

Is the whole gym or just the conference room poorly ventilated? The ambiguity of *which* keeps the reader from knowing. The careful writer is alert to such ambiguity and would recast the above sentence for clarity, perhaps like this:

> The small, poorly ventilated conference room at the south end of the gym is often the scene of underhanded financial dealings between the players and college officials.

The best of writers will occasionally use pronouns ambiguously, but they proofread their work carefully and revise unclear sentences.

Vague or **indefinite pronoun reference** may not completely confuse a reader, but it will annoy him and perhaps cause him to waste time as he ponders the writer's meaning. The pronoun *this* is frequently involved in vague or imprecise reference. Examples:

vague reference: Professor Turner was an Army officer for twenty years. There are many example of **this.**

vague reference: The McCalls' apartment was raided by the police in a mix-up of addresses. Many people have been subjected to **this.** And the police don't even apologize.

Though the reader can pause and work out the meaning of the pronoun *this* in these sentences, the reference, nevertheless, is indefinite or vague, and thus the writing is poor. The good writer will think more carefully about the structure of his sentences and will compose or revise for clarity. Examples:

clear style: Many Army officers have become teachers after retirement. Professor Turner, for example, was an Army officer for twenty years.

clear style: Because of a mix-up of addresses, police have too often raided the wrong apartment or house. The apartment of my friends the McCalls, for example, was mistakenly raided, and the police did not even apologize.

The pronoun *this* may be correctly used to refer to whole ideas, but since it is so subject to misuse, as illustrated, you should pay particular attention to its use in your writing.

In general, pronouns should not be used to refer to nouns not stated but only understood, for such reference is vague and distracting to the reader. Examples:

vague reference:	"The Second Choice" is about a young girl who fell in love and then lost **him.**
vague reference:	When I took an air flight to England I was surprised at how many passengers **they** can carry.

Neither *him* nor *they* has a specific noun as an antecedent. True, the reader knows that *him* refers to the young girl's loved one and *they* to some kind of passenger airplane, but the writing is nevertheless poor because the reader's attention is distracted by the lack of specific pronoun reference. The sentences should be cast to make the pronoun reference definite and clear.

Also pronouns should not be used to refer to adjectives. Example:

vague reference:	Cheri is lovely, but **it** doesn't make her conceited.

Again, the reader understands the meaning, but the experienced reader is irritated by the poor style caused by *it* referring to the adjecive *lovely*. The sentence can be recast like this:

clear reference:	Cheri's loveliness is admired by everybody, but **it** doesn't make her conceited.

Now *it* has the noun *loveliness* as a clear antecedent.

EXERCISE 15. In the spaces provided, rewrite the following sentences, eliminating ambiguous or vague pronoun reference. The first sentence is taken from a sign posted in the rooms of a hotel in Moscow, Russia. Do not rewrite it but just discuss why the specific pronoun reference in it is funny.

1. If this is your first visit to the USSR, you are welcome to it.

2. The penthouse on the Cabot Building, which my uncle owns, rents for $1500 a month.

   My uncle's penthouse on the _____

   _____

3. Though Baylor had the superior team, it lost its first game in twenty-six starts. ~~This often happens. Gamblers are aware of this.~~

   Gamblers are aware that the superior
   team may lose in any game.

4. You won't enjoy your visit to England because ~~they~~ _the British_ are so haughty.

   _____

   _____

5. Francis Macomber is hunting big game, but ~~misses him~~ _missed the lion before he had a clear shot at._ Robert Wilson talks to ~~him~~ _Francis_, but ~~his~~ _Francis's_ wife doesn't like that.

   _____

   _____

   _____

6. Harry said that the cop had complained about his making obscene phone calls. This wasn't true.

   Harry said that he had not made obscene phone calls,
   as the cop had asserted.

7. I objected to having to read the extra books, which turned out to be the thing to do. _____ _, but it turned out that_
   reading was profitable for me,

8. Ruth is too compliant, and it gets her into trouble.

Ruth is too compliant, and as a result she often gets into trouble.

9. The story is about a young man who learned to fly and then crashed *but* ~~it~~ *airplane* on his first solo.

_____

_____

10. My mother and older sister are always quarreling, ~~and~~ *mother* she always thinks she is right and knows best.

_____

11. We spent most of the semester just having rap sessions and then suddenly we had a lot of reading assigned. This was hard on me.

After spending most of the semester in rap sessions, we suddenly had a lot of reading assigned. It was hard for me to get accustomed to studying.

12. When you sit far back at a basketball game you don't realize how tall *the players* ~~they are.~~

_____

_____

It was interesting that

13. Some of the top administrators showed up at our supposedly secret meeting, ~~which was interesting.~~

_____

_____

14. Ronald had the best GPA, but he didn't get the scholarship. ~~This often happens.~~

Often the best student in a class doesn't get a scholarship.

CHAPTER 16

THE PHILOSOPHY OF USAGE

Many students feel that almost from their very first day in school they are hounded about their incorrect use of English, when they are just using the kind of language they hear everyday. Gradually they come to believe that correctness and incorrectness in language are real and that their teachers, English textbooks, and dictionaries can help them differentiate right usage from wrong usage. Many students do remain resentful, but most resign themselves to the need for having their language usage doctored. Though some teachers and textbooks are undoubtedly overzealous in promoting "correct" usage, it nevertheless is true that many if not most students do need to have some aspects of their language usage repaired or polished, because standard English usage is necessary for social acceptability among educated people and for success in many occupations that require a level of education above the average. For example, countless people have not received invitations to parties because the hosts have not liked their nonstandard language usage, and countless secretaries have been fired because of poor spelling.

Usage is the term applied to correctness and incorrectness in language (many people say "grammar" when they mean "usage"), but a distinction must be made between conventional usage and nonconventional errors. The word *convention* literally means "a coming together," and thus a convention is any aspect of behavior that a particular group of people tacitly agree is proper for them. By standard conventional usage we mean usage that the educated segment of our population agrees is proper for them. For example, standard usage calls for *haven't any* rather than *ain't got none* and *I saw it* rather than *I seen it*. Errors in conventional usage, then, are constructions that some people habitually use but that educated people avoid.

Nonconventional errors, however, are those not used habitually by any group. Such errors may be committed only once by one person and never again by anybody else. The most serious of these are **wrongly-used words, faulty idioms,** and **faulty sentence structure.** Even though a misspelling may be unique, spelling is nevertheless considered conventional, as is punctuation. Here is an example of a wrongly-used word:

I am **solicitous** for spring.

Solicitous does mean "anxious for" but not in the sense intended in the example sentence. It is likely that this particular error (this kind of error is known as a malapropism) has been made only once in the history of English, and therefore it is not an error in conventional usage. Strictly speaking, an idiom is a construction "peculiar" to a language and not literally translatable into another language. Most idioms in English involve prepositions or words that look like prepositions. Here is an example of a faulty idiom:

Poe won acclaim **of being** a truly great writer.

Of being as used in this sentence is not natural, native English for any English speaker. The proper idiom is

Poe won acclaim **as** a truly great writer.

Again, this particular error is not one in conventional usage, for it probably has been made only once in the history of English. However, errors in idioms, though often unique, are common in writing, though not in conversation. And here is an example of faulty sentence structure:

The soldier received some civilian clothes, which later he was arrested for wearing them.

Though some particular types of errors in sentence structure are so common that they may be called errors in conventional usage (see Chapters 34 and 35), the sentence just illustrated is jumbled in a unique way and thus does not represent an error in conventional usage. Since the three types of errors illustrated in this paragraph are mostly nonrecurring, they will play no part in our discussion of the philosophy of usage. Instead, we will consider only "errors" in conventional usage.

In the preceding sentence the word *errors* is in quotation marks because most errors in conventional usage are errors only in a relative sense; that is, they are errors for educated speakers of English but not for speakers of various dialects. Chapter 18 will be wholly devoted to dialects, but here we can say that the so-called "bad grammar" that people of small education use is not ungrammatical at all but simply belongs to a nonstandard dialect (and thus is sometimes scorned by users of the standard English dialect *if the user of the nonstandard constructions tries to pass himself off as educated*). For example, the grammar of

Them there potatoes ain't as full growed as the Sims's is

can be analyzed just as easily as that of

Those potatoes aren't nearly as large as the Sims's are.

Thus for the most part when schools teach "correctness" in language usage they are trying to remove from the students' speech and writing certain constructions that are socially unacceptable to speakers of the standard dialect but that are perfectly natural to people to whom the standard dialect is of small importance. However, many overlapping dialects exist, and thus it is not possible to specify with completeness just which words and constructions belong to the standard dialect and which do not, a problem to which we will return below.

Now we have arrived at the question, What makes for correctness in conventional usage in the standard dialect? In past centuries, particularly the eighteenth century, the answer to that question was that *a priori* rules of grammar dictated what was right and what was wrong. *A priori* means "independent of observation" or "existing in the mind prior to experience." Thus early experts in language, now called prescriptive grammarians because they prescribed what was correct and what incorrect, did not try to observe what the English language was really like, but, proceeding from Latin grammar, dictated what it *should* be. Of course they could not eradicate many long-established usages, but they did manage to codify a large body of standard usage, much of which educated people today adhere to.

Using the rules of the prescriptive grammarians, large numbers of schoolmarms (both women and men), hired in the eighteenth century by a newly rich middle class in England, worked tirelessly to polish their pupils' language usage so that they could circulate in cultivated society without being laughed at. The schoolmarm tradition flourished, and by the middle of the nineteenth century schoolmarmism was being applied to children of the lower classes as well as to those of newly rich middle-class families. Schoolmarmism was especially strong in America in the early twentieth century and to a degree it still lingers. It is fashionable today to laugh at school-marmism, but the tradition did a very great deal of good and can still do good, for nothing excludes a person from a well-paying job or from acceptance by educated society more quickly than language usage thought to be "incorrect."

Nowadays the answer to the question posed in the preceding paragraph is that correctness in conventional usage is established by custom only and not by *a priori* rules. That is, whatever usage is accepted by a majority of the educated segment of the population is perforce correct usage, regardless of any rules of grammar. For example, *Webster's New International Dictionary* now recognizes that *ain't* is used by educated people in some areas of the country, and it may be that in the distant future *ain't* will enter the standard dialect for everybody. There is no rule of grammar which excludes *ain't* from correct usage; only custom does that. All linguists nowadays take as their creed that rules of grammar must be derived from observation and analysis of language as it is, not that the rules come first with usage obeying the rules. You might think that under such a system all must be chaos, since human beings are notoriously diverse in their opinions. But on the whole there is surprising unanimity of opinion among experts and educated people alike as to the boundaries of the standard dialect. Textbooks, teachers, and dictionaries do a great deal to maintain uniformity in conventional usage.

Still, there are many differences of opinion among experts in English usage. Some of these differences exist because of the overlapping of dialects. Indeed, it is probably not valid to speak of *the* standard dialect; instead, there are probably many nearly identical standard dialects in our country. For example, the standard dialect of many requires that they say *yours is different* **from** *mine,* whereas many others who must be recognized as speakers of the standard dialect say *yours is different* **than** *mine.* Also linguists have recognized that every person has his own **idiolect;** that is, the totality of any person's language usage is not exactly the same as that of any other person. But idiolectal differences are mostly insignificant in any dialect.

But the chief reason experts (and ordinary educated people) differ in their opinions about a few aspects of conventional usage is that language — any language — is always in a process of slow change, and thus it is inevitable that some people will accept a recent change while others will not. *The American Heritage Dictionary* demonstrated this cleavage among experts by selecting a panel of 104 linguists and noted writers to pass judgment on various aspects of usage now in dispute. For example, 72 percent of the panel objected to the use, in writing, of *anxious* to mean "eager"; 75 percent objected to *I feel badly* and approved *I feel bad;* 92 percent objected to *infer* to mean "imply"; 92 percent objected to *most* to mean "almost"; 62 percent accepted *will* in constructions in which the old rules called for *shall;* 75 percent objected to the use of *like* as a conjunction to mean "as"; and, oddly enough, 70 percent objected to the use of *likely* by itself as an adverb, as in *she is likely to come*, even though that 70 percent maintained that *quite likely, very likely*, and so on are correct.

Most of these disputed points of usage represent recent changes in our language. For example, before about 1930 virtually no one ever used *badly* for *bad* or *most* for *almost*. But changes creep into any language, and differences of opinion among learned people do develop; but these differences usually disappear after a few decades. A most important point, however, is that the makers of *The American Heritage Dictionary* called for their usage panel to rule on only an infinitesimal percentage of the words in the dictionary, showing that there is almost unanimous agreement about usage in the standard dialect. Also, it should be noted, the usage panel approved of many expressions in casual conversation that they condemned in writing.

Changes in language have various causes. One of the most important is the rise to the level of respectability of slang words and expressions (see Chapter 17). For example, at one time *mob* (from *mobile vulgus*, meaning "the rabble") was a slang term vehemently opposed by such great writers as Jonathan Swift. Or, for another example, *hot dog* was once a slang term that drove *sausage sandwich* out of use. Clipping — the cutting off of a part of the front or the end, or both, of a word — also brings much change. For example, just recently high-quality magazines started using the word *perk* (a kind of fringe benefit that goes with high office), which is a back-clipping of *perquisite*. Even *sport* is a result of the fore-clipping of *disport*. Both fore- and back-clipping produced *flu* from *influenza*. Other changes come from an application of new meaning to old words or from the use of a word as a new part of speech, such as the now old but famous "Everything is *go*." Ignorance, too, contributes to language change. For example, the use of *would have* for *had* is a recent change due to ignorance, as in "If I **would have** run, I wouldn't have been busted." Most older people still say "If I **had** run . . . ." Another change due to ignorance that is now occurring is the use of the verb *lay* for *lie* (but no one ever uses *lie* for *lay*). In connection with language change due to ignorance we have the phenomenon of **overcorrection**, which means making one error because you think you are avoiding another error. For example, so many people have been taught so thoroughly to use *Tom and I* (and not *Tom and me*) as a subject that many (including some of high education) have begun to use the incorrect constructions *for Tom and I, between you and I*, and so on. They are victims of overcorrection.

What then is the proper attitude to take towards conventional usage? The sanest attitude is probably to take all reasonable measures to make your usage conform to the standard dialect, because language usage is undeniably important in social, and therefore also economic, matters, but to realize that there is no completely rigid and fixed standard dialect and that therefore there will always be some points of dispute even among experts.

EXERCISES

1. Is it correct or incorrect to begin a sentence with *and* or *but*? Why?
2. Is it correct or incorrect to end a sentence with a preposition? Why?
3. Make a list of three words – such as *phone* for *telephone* — that have undergone clipping.
4. How do you change your language usage according to the social situation you are in (for example, talking to your close friends and talking to your minister)?
5. Which of the following italicized words would you accept as standard and which would you reject?

    a. *Anymore*, I really like Ponski's.
    b. If you *would have* stayed, you would have had fun.
    c. He's guilty, *alright*.
    d. I feel *badly* about your accident.
    e. I feel *sadly* about your accident.
    f. *Lay* down for a while.
    g. *Aren't* I your friend?
    h. I *dove* into the empty pool.
    i. *Most* all of us escaped.
    j. Winstons taste good *like* a cigaret should.
    k. *Us* Tareyton smokers *ain't* bright.
    l. *Being as* it's raining, let's have a pot party.
    m. I *could of* made an A.
    n. Where's the quince juice *at*?
    o. How long has he *laid* there?

USAGE
LESSON
16

CONFUSED
WORDS

A number of pairs and triplets of standard words in English are occasionally confused because they are in some way similar — perhaps in spelling or pronunciation or meaning. Words mistaken for each other are not numerous, but some of them are commonly used and often confused. Following are the chief of these, with definitions and explanations.

accept *verb:*	to receive; to take; to agree to; to believe
except *prep.:*	excluding; not including

In normal speech the two words are pronounced alike.

right:	I **accept** your excuse. Will you **accept** my apologies?
right:	No one **except** members will be **accepted** as contestants.

affect *verb:*	to produce a change in; to influence
effect *noun:*	something that is produced by a cause; a result

In normal speech the two words are pronounced alike.

right:	His insult did not **affect** me.
right:	The **effect** of his insult was not what he intended.

anecdote *noun:*	a little story of an amusing event
antidote *noun:*	a counteractant to a poison; anything that counteracts

anyway *adv.:*	in any case
any way *noun phr.:*	whatever method is available
right:	I didn't want your invitation, **anyway.**
right:	We count not find **any way** to reach Norman.

censor *verb, noun:*	to suppress or restrict publication of supposedly objectionable material; one who does this
censure *verb, noun:*	to criticize or condemn supposedly bad behavior; the act of doing this
right:	I don't think *Playboy* should be **censored,** for it does no harm.
right:	Professor Toley **censured** me for cheating.

cite *verb:*	to quote; to mention; to refer to as an example (The noun form is *citation*.)
site *noun:*	a place where something is, was, or is to be
right:	That's a poor **site** for an apartment building.
right:	The judge **cited** a precedent for his ruling.
colloquialism *noun:*	a word or expression suitable for informal use in *any* locality (The adjective form is *colloquial*.)
localism *noun:*	a word or expression used only in one locality; a regionalism
right:	Some dictionaries consider *goofed* a **colloquialism** and others consider it slang.
right:	The word *spider*, meaning "a frying pan," is a **localism** used in parts of Pennsylvania.
conscience *noun:*	what gives a person a knowledge or feeling of right and wrong
conscious *adj.:*	aware; awake; alert
right:	Cheating makes my **conscience** hurt.
right:	I was not **conscious** of your mistake.
council *noun:*	an official group; a deliberative group
counsel *verb, noun:*	to give advice; advice or instruction; a legal adviser

The word *counselor*, such as a school counselor, means one who counsels. The word *councilor* means a member of a council, *not* one who gives advice.

right:	The Department Chairmen's **Council** will not meet this week.
right:	My **counselor** gave me good **counsel** when he recommended Professor Watts.
credible *adj.:*	believable; worthy of trust (*Incredible* means "beyond belief.")
creditable *adj.:*	worthy of praise
credulous *adj.:*	willing to believe readily; easily imposed upon (*Incredulous* means "skeptical" or "unbelieving.")
right:	José's excuse sounds **credible** to me.
right:	Your large donation is quite **creditable.**
right:	Mary is so **credulous** that she believes Jeff's lies.
delusion *noun:*	a false belief; a deception not based on visual appearances
illusion *noun:*	a deceptive appearance; something that deceives by a false visual impression
right:	Do not disturb his **delusion** that he is an important person.
right:	He had an **illusion** that the doorman was an Army officer.
wrong:	His **illusion** that he was a reincarnation of Patton amused everyone. (*Delusion* is proper.)
everyday *adj.:*	ordinary; commonplace; occurring daily
every day *noun phr.:*	each day; one of several days specified
right:	Bill's getting a traffic citation is almost an **everyday** occurrence.
right:	On **every day** from now until Christmas we will sing carols.

everyone *indef. pro.:* everybody; all of a particular group
every one *noun phr.:* each one; one of several people or objects specified
    right: **Everyone** will receive his wages.
    right: **Every one** of your answers was wrong.

imply *verb:* to hint; to suggest without actual expression
infer *verb:* to come to a conclusion by reasoning; to guess
    right: You **implied** by that remark that I am conceited.
    right: On the basis of his actions I **inferred** that he intended to take vengeance on Maurice.

its *poss. pro.:* belonging to it
it's *contraction:* it is; it has

lay *verb tr.:* to place an object somewhere (The principal parts of this verb are *lay, laying, laid, laid.* When this verb is properly used, someone always lays something somewhere or something is laid somewhere by someone.)
lie *verb intr.:* to be in or to take a reclining position (The principal parts of this verb are *lie, lying. lay, lain.* When this verb is used, nobody lays anything anywhere and nothing is laid anywhere by anyone.)
    right: I will now **lay** these cards down.
    right: I have **laid** these cards down.
    right: These cards have been **laid** down (by someone).
    right: The cards are **lying** on the table.
    right: Yesterday the cards **lay** on the floor.
    right: The cards have **lain** there many days.
    wrong: I think I'll **lay** down. (*Lie* is correct.)
    wrong: I **laid** down. (*Lay* is correct.)

liable *adj.:* likely; subject to occurrence; legally bound
libel *noun, verb:* slanderous statements; defamation; to slander or defame
    right: You're **liable** to get a punch in the nose if you **libel** me.
    right: A husband may be **liable** for his wife's debts.

loose *adj.:* not tight; unfastened
lose *verb:* to come to be without by accident; to mislay; to be deprived of
    right: I want any noose around my neck to be **loose.**
    right: Dont **lose** your **loose** change.

moral *adj.:* right; ethical; virtuous; adhering to principles (*Morals* is a noun usually used in the plural, except in the *moral* of a story or incident.)
morale *noun:* A mental condition as regards cheerfulness, depression, and so on
    right: **Moral** behavior is desirable among politicians.
    right: The **morale** of the class was low because of **low grades.**

principal *noun, adj.:* head of a school; chief; money used as capital
principle *noun:* a rule, law, or doctrine (often in the plural)

right:	The **principal** export of Turkey was once opium.
right:	Grammatical **principles** are very complex.
quiet *adj., noun:*	not noisy; calm; the state of silence
quite *adv.:*	entirely; actually; almost completely
wrong:	Do be **quite,** please.
set *verb tr.:*	to place something in a position (The principal parts of this verb are *set, setting, set, set.* When this verb is used properly, someone always sets something somewhere or something is set somewhere by someone.)
sit *verb intr.:*	to occupy a seat or be in a resting (sitting) position (The principal parts of this verb are *sit, sitting, sat, sat.* When this verb is used properly, nobody *sits* anything anywhere and nothing is *sat* anywhere by anyone; *sets* and *set* would be proper.)
right:	I wlll **set** the punch bowl on the table.
right:	Toby is **setting** the punch bowl on the table.
right:	The punch bowl is now **sitting** on the table.
right:	The punch bowl has **sat** there all day.
right:	Let's **sit** down.
wrong:	Don't just **set** there.
sometime *adv.:*	at some future time
sometimes *adv.:*	at times; occasionally
some time *noun phr.:*	a certain amount of time
right:	I'll get a job **sometime.**
right:	**Sometimes** it rains here for days.
right:	Please spend **some time** with me.
suppose *verb:*	*the stem of the verb, not to be confused with the past participle*
supposed *verb:*	*the past participle of the verb* Always use *supposed* when it is followed by *to* or preceded by a form of *to be* (*is, was, were, been,* and so on).
wrong:	Judd was **suppose** to bring the cattails.
than *conj.:*	*used in comparisons*
then *adv., conj.:*	at that time; as a consequence of
right:	Your bracelet is prettier **than** mine.
right:	We started to study; **then** we fell asleep.
right:	The proper move, **then,** is to escape to Mexico.
their *poss. pro.:*	belonging to them
there *adv., exp.:*	at a particular place; *expletive used to begin a sentence*
they're *contraction:*	they are
wrong:	**Their** are many ways to skin a cat.
wrong:	Have you seen **there** cappers?
wrong:	Are you sure **their** here?
to: *prep.:*	*Various meanings generally having to do with direction*
too *adv.:*	to an excessive extent or degree; more than should be
wrong:	Jerry's **to** credulous to see through your lies.

whose *poss. pro.:*	belonging to whom
who's *contraction:*	who is; who has
wrong:	**Who's** horse is that?
your *poss. pro.:*	belonging to you
you're *contraction:*	you are
yours *poss. pro.:*	belonging to you.
wrong:	**Your** the pull-out this time.
wrong:	Is that gray cat **your's?** (no apostrophe)

EXERCISE 16. In the following sentences cross out wrongly-used words and in the blanks provided write the correct word.

1. Its suppose to effect mine more than your's.

   _____

2. Did you mean to infer that Sally's councilor was too credible to believe Joan's antidote about her uncle?

   _____

3. Every one should lay down and be quite so that everyone of the children can go to sleep.

   _____

4. Don't loose the principals you're conscious excepts as right.

   _____

5. Mac labored under the illusion that his mind was a machine, any way.

   _____

6. What affect did the elected members of the city counsel have on the preachers' attempt to censure the pornography being published in the city?

   _____

7. Your libel to believe all sorts of things that are incredulous.

   _____

8. The colloquialisms of the Great Smoky Mountains are quainter then those of any other cite I've investigated.

   _____

9. Who's principle is going to set down with me and explain the school's morale code?

   _____

10. I want to spend sometime watching the bottle of whiskey just setting there.

_____

11. The professor's antics while he was censoring me for misbehaving gave me the delusion of the devil tormenting a saint.

_____

12. Everyday I infer that I'm leaving home because of every day tensions, but I never loose the high moral my homelife gives me.

_____

13. Their are to many children to quite; they must not be laying down or setting in their chairs.

_____

14. The lawyer hired as county council would not except more than $40,000 a year because of his conscious.

_____

15. I don't believe their suppose to loose by more than ten points.

_____

16. Children are not suppose to except rides from strangers.

_____

17. When I tell my dog to lay down, it's tail is libel to wag.

_____

18. Sometime we select our fishing cite by the affect of the wind on the clouds.

_____

19. My councilor inferred by his behavior that he expected me too loose my high GPA.

_____

CHAPTER
17

SLANG

Slang, though difficult to define, is perhaps the aspect of our vocabulary dearest to the hearts of young people. And it should be dear to their hearts, for it is expressive of their wonderful world of youth and in no way is disreputable or reprehensible *per se*. True, slang is chiefly oral and should be oral. It enlivens the casual conversation of speakers on all educational levels. For example, a college student emerging from a final exam and saying, "Boy, I really blew that one" has used more pungent and effective language than the student who says, "I think I failed that exam badly." But though slang is usually oral, a racy slang term can occasionally be used in college writing with admirable effect. For example, few teachers would object to such a sentence as this in a theme: "After devoting some weeks to the study of some of the modern composers, I began to get the old kick out of Bach again." Many teachers would be pleased with the slang term and would note the otherwise generally high level of word choice in the sentence. The main point, then, is that slang should be used in college writing only sparingly; it should be consciously chosen for its spicy effect and should not be limp. For example, such expressions as *peachy keen, outa sight, guys and gals, real cool,* and so on will impoverish rather than enrich your writing. Like ideas, some slang expressions are strong and some weak. The good writer will use slang only carefully and effectively.

Almost every youngster knows what slang is, but, as we said, it is hard to define. The origin of the word is unknown. One of the most original attempts to account for the word is that it is "language that is slung around"; *to sling language* became *slanguage,* which became *slang.* Undoubtedly that speculation is far-fetched. No modern dictionary lists an etymology for *slang,* and all speculation about its origin seems futile. But several terms in English once had the same meaning as slang and those and others are now occasionally mistaken for slang. The chief of these are *argot, cant, jargon, gibberish, idiom, lingo, shoptalk, vernacular,* and *vulgate.* As an exercise, you may want to look these words up. Though some dictionaries still list a few of these words as meaning slang, in our modern vocabulary none, with the possible exception of *argot,* should be equated with slang.

The American Heritage Dictionary's definition of slang is perhaps as definitive as that of any dictionary: "The nonstandard vocabulary of a given culture or subculture, consisting typically of arbitrary and often ephemeral coinages and figures of speech characterized by spontaneity and raciness." It should be added, however, that slang expressions are usually the result of linguistic inventiveness on the part of the young and that they usually just pop up with their origin uncertain — though most must have had a specific point of origin. That is, for example, some irreverent youth must have at one time referred to an attractive sorority girl as a "biscuit," with the word catching on with others — for a time at least.

One point, however, should be emphasized about every slang term: it must have some sort of equivalent in standard diction; else it is not true slang. For example, many people still regard *jazz* (the music) as a slang term, but since it has no equivalent standard term (unless one uses a long, circuitous definition), it is not slang. Or, for another example, *drag racing* is not slang, for it was not invented as a pungent substitute for some stodgy or pretentious or colorless standard term, but for a once-new activity. Such terms as *jazz* and *drag,* as defined above, are the equivalent of the invention of the term *Borodin* to name a new medicine. But when *jazz* was used in the phrase *and all that jazz* (meaning activity, nonsense, and such), it became slang for that meaning.

On one hand, slang should not be confused with **vulgate,** which means, not "vulgar," but the nonstandard vocabulary and grammar of the uneducated masses. For example, when quizzed, many students will say say they think such vulgate expressions as *ain't, nowheres, bust* (for *burst*), *hisself* and *theirselves, nohow,* and so on are slang, but they are not. They belong to nonstandard dialects and are not racy, pungent, irreverent substitutes for familiar activities and social situations. Also the familiar so-called four-letter words are not slang but are **vulgarisms,** though contemporary polite society is using them more and more in mixed company. For example, the word *snot,* which used to be the least offensive of this group of words, is now the one least likely to be used in polite, mixed social groups. These words existed in the standard dialect long before such euphemisms as *urinate* allowed society to reject them as vulgar.

On the other hand, distinguishing between slang and **colloquialisms** (see p. 160) or even standard words is not an exact science for lexicographers.

Though there is uniformity of opinion about the status of most words, experts and ordinary people alike often disagree about the status of a small percentage of our words; thus usage labels in our five good collegiate dictionaries do vary. For example, *rib* (to tease) is labeled slang in three of the dictionaries cited in Chapter 15 and standard (no label) in the other two; *get the goods on him* is labeled slang in three, colloquial (or informal) in one, and is not entered in one; *cop* (policeman) is labeled slang in one, colloquial in three, and standard in one; *gravy* (easy profit) is labeled slang in four and standard in one; *jive* (deceptive talk) is labeled slang in three, standard in one, and is not entered in one; and *phony* is labeled slang in one, colloquial in three, and standard in one. And so it goes: Like most things in human life, the status of a word is not always firmly ascertainable. However, there is near unanimity of opinion about most slang words, and certainly you need not hesitate to accept the labeling in your own good dictionary. We should say, though, that *Webster's New Collegiate Dictionary* is the one most likely to accept as standard various words and expressions that most of us consider slang.

General slang — that which is widespread and cross-cultural — seems mostly to center on just a few aspects of human behavior — chiefly sex, drink and drugs, and social situations in which approval or disapproval of an individual is expressed. The number of current slang terms for attractive or unattractive young women, for example, runs into the dozens. And hundreds of slang terms used over the centuries for *drunk* have been catalogued. But slang may also be specialized (in fact, originally the word and words like *argot* and *cant* meant the specialized vocabularies of underworld groups). Many, if not most, occupations have their own slang, often closely protected. Popular musicians, for example, are almost notorious for their specialized slang. Some examples are *apple* (New York City), *balling* (having a good time), *cat* (a musician), *juice* (liquor), *ofay* (a white person), *scroff* (food), *twister* (a key), and hundreds of other expressions. Taxi drivers use such slang as *riding the ghost* (driving an empty cab with the meter running), *on the arm* (driving a passenger without the meter running), *pork chops* (a girl-hustling cab driver), *working a single* (working overtime), and so on. Most games have their own vocabularies of slang. For example, in surfing there is *bomber* (a sea gull), *ding* (a dent in the surf board), *hodad* (a surfer with small ability), *gremmie* (worse than a hodad), *heavies* (the really big waves), and *kook* (a beginner). And of course a whole world of slang has grown up around drug addiction, as it did much earlier around prostitution.

Though both general and specialized slang exists, slang is to a large extent class structured and regional. For example, much of the slang of the lower classes of Manhattan is unknown to upper-class youths in Westchester County. But probably the least amount of slang is used by uneducated rural people and most by middle- and lower-middle-class city youth. Much of what outsiders take for slang in the vocabulary of the lowest classes of the big cities is really dialectal; its strangeness causes outsiders to consider it slang. Also, though modern communication and transportation help slang to sweep the country quickly, much slang also remains regional. For example, the slang of St. Louis and of Seattle overlap to a considerable extent, but each also has slang foreign to the other — for example, *bebe* (an unwanted illegitimate baby) in St. Louis and *siwash* (half-breed Indian) in Seattle.

There are two broad kinds of slang terms. One — by far the most common — gives some sort of new, nonstandard meaning to a standard word or a variation of a standard word. For example, *off* (somewhat mentally unbalanced), *burn artist* (a con man), *pass* (an amorous overture to a girl), *dirt* (slanderous gossip), *knock it off* (stop what you're doing), *heller* (a wild, noisy person), and so on are not completely new inventions, for there is a relationship between them and standard words. Many such slang terms are **figurative language,** for they are not meant literally. For example, dirt is soil, but when used as slang it refers to behavior which, figuratively, is soiled or dirty. Some slang terms, however (though not many in the total vocabulary of slang) are pure inventions. Some examples are *goop* (a sticky mess), *floozy* (a disreputable woman), *blurb* (an ad on a book jacket), *goof* (to make a mistake), *pooped* (exhausted), and *snozz* (a large nose). Thus in dictionaries usually only some definitions of a word will be labeled slang, though a few will be categorized wholly as slang.

Considering the nature of slang, an interesting question is, "What happens to it?" The answer is that almost anything may happen to a slang term. A very tiny number of slang terms may remain slang for generation after generation — even for centuries. For example, Chaucer (died 1400) used the slang word *gab* as we do. As early as the 1300's a woman was called a *piece* and the slang term *broad* for woman originated in the 1600's. *Cough up* (meaning "to give a donation or pay a debt") was used in the 1500's. *High* for *drunk* originated in the eighteenth century. (The great *Oxford English Dictionary* lists the date of origin of many such slang terms.) However, the great majority of slang expressions either rise on the scale of respectability to become colloquial or standard or else simply vanish from oral usage. The incorporation of slang into the standard vocabulary (even if colloquial) is one of the prime sources of language change. For example, some words once scorned by the pretentious as mere slang (and therefore to be despised) are *trip* (not the drug-induced kind, but a journey), *glib*, *swagger, nice* (meaning "desirable"), *freshman, bored, club* (an organization), *dwindle, foppish, mob, scoundrel, tidy* (meaning "neat"), and *tantrum*. But most slang expressions simply disappear from the oral language, often not long after their first use. Eric Partridge's *Dictionary of Slang and Unconventional English* (5th Edition, 1961), for example, contains 1362 pages and nearly 50,000 entries, the great majority of which are not currently in use. But even short-lived slang expressions, if they are expressive and racy, play an important role in our vocabulary.

EXERCISES

1. Find one word or expression which in different dictionaries is labeled slang, colloquial (or informal), and standard (if a word is not labeled, it is standard. Also only one meaning may be involved).

2. See whether you can find two of your favorite current slang terms which do not have their definitions listed in any dictionary.

3. List two slang terms that for your peer group are out of date.

4. Choose one of the following terms and see how many slang expressions you can think of for it: *drunk, food, gun, petting,* and *an attractive* or *unattractive girl.*

5. What is the slang term you most commonly use that you would not want your parents to hear you use? Remember that just any vulgar term is not necessarily slang.

6. Following are one hundred slang expressions current in California in the mid-1970's. Your instructor may make various assignments with them. You probably will not know some, or even many of them or will think some are out of date. Your instructor can get a meaning for each from the Instructor's Manual for this text. One exercise you might do is to establish four groupings — such as, for example, disapproval of an individual — and see how many of the expressions will fit under each grouping

baked	(to) boogie
balls	bosco
biffy	bozo
biscuit	buds
bitchen	(to) bug off
(to) blow it	bull jive
(to) burn	(to) hang in there
burned out	heavy
(to) buzz	hipe
a cat nip	hog
cheap shot	honkey
chopper	hot dog

(to) cool it	hot tuna
(to) cook	jacked up
cookie	jail bait
(to) crash	(to) jet
crib	(to) jam on over; *also* to make
(to) dig out	a jam
dork	jock
dudly	juju
fag	loose
faggy	mind rot
far out	number
flaming	pencilneck
fox	plastic
freaky	plucked
frimp	pole
funky	popped
geek	quail
gimpy	rag
(to) gross me right out	(to) (to be) ralph
(to) hang it	(to) rattle your cage
ricky racer	toad
(to) rip off	total bonanza
ripped	trainpuller
roach	(to) trash

(to) roll out	troll
rooting around	tuna
rotifer	turkey
scuzzy chick	(to) turn out
scrotin	turned on
sewer wisp	tuned in
a short	urch
spaced	(to) waste
squirrel	wasted
(to) shuck	whuss
stash	wired
straight	zip
stud	zonked

USAGE
LESSON
17

NONSTANDARD
WORDS
AND
EXPRESSIONS

Though slang terms are nonstandard in the standard dialect, they may, if consciously and carefully used, occasionally enliven the style of semiformal writing. Words and expressions that are nonstandard because they belong to a nonstandard dialect, and are thus avoided by educated people, should not be used in semiformal writing (or speech either, for that matter). Some dictionaries label these expressions **substandard** rather than **nonstandard,** but the prefix *sub* implies inherent badness, whereas in their own dialects these expressions are perfectly suitable. Thus we will continue to use the prefix *non,* which implies that some words and expressions are outside the boundary of the standard dialect but does not imply that they are inherently bad.

Television and other means of rapid communication and transportation are increasing the dominance of a nearly uniform standard dialect and are decreasing socially unacceptable pronunciations, grammatical forms, and so on. Even television announcers quickly learn to rid their language usage of characteristics that cause some people to laugh. For example, when a certain midwestern TV announcer was twitted about his speaking of "aigs" rather than eggs, he quickly modified his dialect. Thus there are not many vulgate expressions that college students need to be warned against.

But also some colloquialisms should be avoided in college writing, for there is a broad spectrum of colloquialisms, and those at the lower end are generally frowned upon when used in semiformal writing. Following is a brief list of common vulgate and low colloquial words and expressions that you should avoid. Remember that these are not slang and do not belong in the category of confused words.

anyways is vulgate for *anyway.*
like should be avoided in favor of *as if* or *as though* in a semiformal situation. (E.g., "He behaved *as if* he were insane.")

at should not be added to a question asking where.

awful, awfully, mighty, plenty, real, and **terribly** are low colloquial intensifiers. Avoid *awful good* and so on; prefer *quite, especially,* and so on.

being as and **being that** are nonstandard for *since* or *because.*

bust is nonstandard for *burst.*

but what should be avoided and *but that* preferred.

can't hardly and **can't scarcely** are vulgate double negatives. Use *can hardly.*

could of, would of, and so on are illiteracies. Use *could have* and so on.

hadn't ought to is inferior to *should.*

hanged is what happens to outlaws; *hung* is standard only for inanimate objects.

hisself and **theirselves** are vulgate for *himself* and *themselves.*

inside of *a week* is low colloquial for *within a week.*

invite as a noun is nonstandard. Use *invitation.*

irregardless is not vulgate but is truly substandard for *regardless.*

kind of and **sort of** *friendly* are low colloquial for *rather friendly.*

learn is vulgate for *teach.*

most is at best low colloquial for *almost.*

nohow is vulgate. Prefer *anyway.*

nowheres and **anywheres** are vulgate. Omit the *s.*

pretty near all is vulgate for *almost all.*

reckon for *suppose* is considered nonstandard.

sure is colloquial for *surely.* Avoid *it sure is cold* in semiformal writing.

sure and is low colloquial for *sure to.* Avoid *be sure and study.*

these kind and **these sort** are nonstandard. Use *these kinds* or *this kind.*

this here boat and **that there** *motor.* Omit *here* and *there.*

try and is low colloquial for *try to.* Use *try to perform well.*

EXERCISE 17.   The following sentences contain not only vulgate and low colloquial words and expressions from the list on the previous pages but also other vulgate constructions that almost all college writers avoid. In the blanks provided, rewrite each sentence to achieve wholly acceptable standard words and constructions.

1. The FEPC don't know but what the Congress ain't going to vote them no money.

   _____

   _____

2. Do you reckon Joe and me will be hung for stealing pretty **near all** them cattle?

   _____

   _____

3. Marvin hisself hadn't ought to go nowheres with Gertie, being as she's awful mad at him.

   _____

   _____

4. I could of did it for Sam, but I can't hardly stand the way he busts up friendships.

   _____

   _____

5. These sort of parties are kind of hard on anyone who wants to try and behave properly irregardless of where he's at.

   _____

   _____

6. I'll learn you not to give no help to them who won't give me an invite to their party.

   _____

   _____

7. Most all the classes I'm taking sure is real hard.

_____

_____

8. They acted like they can't scarcely solve most all their problems, anyways.

_____

_____

9. Pretty near all the miners ain't got no pension nowheres big enough to live on.

_____

_____

10. Them there girls are mighty pretty but sort of strange.

_____

_____

11. Inside of a month Jim and Jane wasn't nothing but enemies theirselves.

_____

_____

12. What would you of done if nobody hadn't given you pretty near all of these sort of collector's items?

_____

_____

13. The Congress sure looks like it will run us into a depression.

_____

_____

14. Rod don't care nothing about grades, but most everyone else will be sure and study to make good grades.

_____

_____

CHAPTER 18

DIALECTS

A **dialect** is a regional or social class variety of a language, distinguished from other varieties of the same language by pronunciation, grammatical forms, or vocabulary. Thus when we speak of a person's having a New England or a Southern accent, we are really referring to his dialect. For example, a person from Massachusetts may say *Cuber* instead of *Cuba* or a Southerner may say *cain't* instead of *can't* or pronounce *pen* and *pin* identically. Or when we take note of a person's habitual use of "bad grammar" or strange words — such as *ain't got none* instead of *haven't any* or *croker sack* instead of *gunny sack* — we are also acknowledging that his dialect is different from ours. Thus everyone without exception speaks or writes a dialect, the **standard** (or educated) **dialect** being considered the norm. However, in pronunciation the standard dialect is really several dialects varying slightly from region to region. In grammar and vocabulary, on the other hand, the standard dialect is mostly uniform throughout the country.

Many people believe that a dialect which departs radically from the standard dialect is a corruption of a once-pure language, but no dialect is a corruption of any other, and in a linguistic sense none is any better than any other. For example, in the year 1200 there were many English dialects in the British Isles. It just happened that the dialect of London — the East Midland Dialect — became standard. Chance could have favored any of several others, which today have descendants among nonstandard dialects. Even now in our Appalachian Mountains there are large remnants of nonstandard dialects once spoken in parts of Elizabethan England other than London.

Many expert linguists love these "Elizabethan dialects" and like to trace their lineage back to sixteenth-century Britain. Thus though the word *non-standard* might seem to mean that a dialect is in some way "bad," it should not be taken to mean "bad," for all dialects are equally good for basic communication. The only superiority of our standard dialect over various nonstandard ones lies in the much greater extent of its vocabulary, and any dialect can increase its vocabulary. Much more important than a person's dialect is the extent of his vocabulary, the fund of information in his mind, and his ability to think rationally.

We must say, however, that some socal prejudice against some nonstandard dialects exists among some speakers of the standard dialect, and that if one wishes to hold a well-paying job of some importance and wishes to circulate in middle- or upper-class society, he usually must make sure that his dialect is at least close to the standard. And, since this is also a composition text, you should remember that in writing there is essentially one standard dialect, not a multiplicity of them (though a few variations in grammatical forms and in vocabulary exist in the standard written dialect).

Dialect, then, should be a neutral word, and for linguists it *is* a neutral word. But human nature being what it is, almost everybody thinks his dialect is the norm and thus superior to others. For example, once an uneducated girl in the mountains of northern Georgia heard a Georgian college student speak a few sentences and then said, "My God, he's a yankee," and laughed in derision. Or, for another example, countless uneducated New York taxi drivers have secretly laughed at the speech of countless educated Texans. And the simple fact that many people laugh at bad jokes just because they are told in Negro, Jewish, Irish, and other dialects is further evidence that people generally consider their own dialect superior to any other. But when a young speaker of a nonstandard dialect becomes educated, he usually no longer considers his native dialect superior. He sees the social and economic advantage of speaking and writing the standard dialect. However, many people who have changed their dialects lapse consciously into their original dialects when they are among old home folks because they do not want to appear different.

The regional aspect of dialects is quite complex, for, though we do recognize large dialect areas such as the South, the Midwest, and New England, small pockets of long-established dialects also exist in many areas such as Brooklyn and a small section of the Virginia–North Carolina border. For example, the narrowly localized pronunciation *toity-toid street* has been good for a laugh for generations, and most people find it difficult to master the pronunciation of *south* and *about* in the Virginia border dialect referred. to — pronunciations something like *sooth* and *aboot*, but not quite that. Also newly established pockets of dialects, such as those of the Okies and Arkies in parts of southern California and of Appalachian hillbillies in small areas of Chicago and Minneapolis, often stubbornly resist assimilation For example, there are housewives in a small section of Chicago who still go to the produce market to buy *ros'n ears* (from *roasting ears,* meaning *sweet corn)* even though the vast majority of Chicagoans would be mystified by the term. Furthermore, regional overlapping of dialects occurs. For example, people in Missouri might be amused by the Southern dialectal *larruping* for *very good* when their own dialect is in many ways similar to the southern and might be mistaken by a Northerner as a Southern rather than Midwestern dialect.

Dialects not only are regional; they also vary according to social class. For example, in a town no larger than Augusta, Georgia, several Southern dialects exist side by side and do not merge into one because economic and social conditions keep them mostly separated. For example, a wholly uneducated Augustan might say *us'ns is gonna git you,* in contrast to an educated Augustan's saying *we'll take revenge on you.* Such dialects merge, if at all, very slowly. The dialect of an uneducated plumber in Augusta, for example, is not much affected by his brief entries into the houses of well-to-do people who speak a cultivated (in their view) Southern dialect. However, minor differences do not keep dialects from merging and generally go unnoticed among those whose dialects are quite similar. For example, in the West a great many speakers of the standard dialect pronounce *for* and *four* identically, while many others pronounce them differently, as in *or* and *ore.* But unless the matter is brought up for discussion, few people are aware of this minor difference in the speech of educated Westerners. Or, for another example, within one dialectal group some may say *stewdent* and others *stoodent* for *student* or some may say *own* and others *ahn* for *on.* Generally they will be unaware of the difference. Many other small differences, such as *care* being pronounced like the first syllable of *carry* by some people and to rhyme with the first syllable of *ferry* by others, are not noticed by people who believe they are speaking identical dialects. As a matter of fact, everyone has an idiolect (see page 156).

You might be wondering at his point, What causes dialects to exist? The answer is that population groups split and that language inevitably changes. For example, though no one knows for sure, the original inhabitants of North and South America may have come across the Bering Strait in just one or a few migrations, with all speaking one language. But over thousands of years different tribal groups established themselves at different points all over the two continents, and language change brought not only new dialects but new languages. It is estimated that at the time Columbus landed in the New World about one hundred language families — not languages, but language families — existed in the Americas, and many individual languages had closely related dialects. Or, for another example, the language of the Australian Aborigines, who are a single people and number only in the thousands, is estimated to have about 500 dialects, some almost mutually unintelligible but still belonging to the master language. The Aborigines probably came into Australia as one people, and the continent's great geographic area caused them to spread and dialects to develop. Not so many dialects originate in a small geographic area. One important point, however is that literacy — writing and reading — inhibits the development of new dialects and promotes the merger of existing dialects. Literacy both slows down certain aspects of language change and also causes some changes to spread rapidly and not remain in a pocket.

In general, dialects have great vitality, and in many countries members of a dialectal group are very proud of their dialect and its differences from the standard (or official) dialect of the country. For example, many Scotsmen, who speak English, lovingly maintain their Scottish burrs and other dialectal characteristics, even if they rise high enough to sit in the British Parliament. American dialects do have vitality and do change slowly, but in general Americans are not vigorously proud of nonstandard dialects and do not actively try to prevent a uniform dialect from eventually establishing itself (though complete uniformity is almost certainly impossible). In fact, no other country of geographic size or population similar to America's has anything like the uniformity of dialects that we have, and this uniformity has to a degree been sought and worked for in various ways. The American desire for uniformity of American English is partly based on our being a young nation made up of many ethnic groups that immigrated and wanted to lose their foreign accents. It is also partly based on our being a nation always on the move; we find it convenient not to have wide dialectal variations. Thus in spite of the general vitality of dialects, there is a slow march in America towards uniformity, and most of us seem willing to accept uniformity. However, recent trends in lexicography, and also the considerable publicity that modern linguistic studies have had, have fostered an amiable tolerance of the pronunciations in nonstandard dialects, so that the march towards uniformity is perhaps slowing somewhat. But in writing, there is still a standard dialect, and it is unlikely that differing written English dialects will develop again for use in newspapers, magazines, business correspondence, and so on.

The study of dialects is quite an interesting aspect of linguistic study. Serious scholars of the American Dialect Society, which was formed in 1889, have for years been preparing linguistic atlases which show geographically the boundaries of various American dialects and also the degree of their overlapping. The atlases take into account pronunciations, grammatical forms, and vocabulary — the three aspects of language that make up a dialect. Eventually a complete atlas will be available, but changes in dialects over the years, even though they are slow, will make the finished atlas partially obsolete. Two important dialect dictionaries are Wright's *English Dialect Dictionary* and Wentworth's *American Dialect Dictionary*. Both treat only the vocabulary of dialects, not variant pronunciations of standard words nor variant grammatical forms. As a supplementary exercise, you might look up six interesting dialectal words in one of these dictionaries (your college library probably has copies of both).

EXERCISES

1. How does your dialect differ from those of strangers you meet?
2. Can you detect any dialectal differences among the students in your class?
3. What dialectal characteristics that do not occur in your dialect can you point out in the following brief selections?

a. Me and pap went back to the house. All that day we worked at the wood tree, and so I never had no good chance until about the middle of the afternoon. Then I taken my slingshot and I would have like to took all my bird eggs, too, because Pete had give me his collection and he holp me with mine, and he would like to git the box out and look at them as good as I would, even if he was nigh twenty years old. But the box was too big to tote a long ways and have to worry with, so I just taken the shikepoke egg, because it was the best un, and wropped it up good into a matchbox and hid it and the slingshot under the corner of the barn. Then we et supper and went to bed. . . .
— from "Two Soldiers" by William Faulkner

b. "Don't you pester wid ole man Noah, honey. I boun' he tuck keer er dat ark. Dat's w'at he wuz dar fer, en dat's w'at he done. Leas' ways, dat's w'at dey tells me. But don't you bodder longer dat ark, 'ceppin' your mammy fetches it up. Dey mount er bin two deloojes, en den agin dey moutent. Ef dey wuz enny ark in dish yer w'at de Crawfishes brung on, I ain't heerin tell un it, en w'en dey ain't no arks 'round', I ain't got no time fer ter make um en put um in dar. Hit's gittin' yo' bedtime, honey."
— from Uncle Remus: His Songs and Sayings by Joel Chandler Harris

c.
God makes sech nights, all white an' still
    Fur 'z you can look or listen,
Moonshine an' snow on field an' hill,
    All silence an' all glisten.
Zekle crep' up quite unbeknown
    An' peeked in thru' the winder,
An' there sot Huldy all alone,
    'ith no one nigh to hender.
A fireplace filled the room's one side
    With half a cord o' wood in —
There warn't no stoves (tell comfort died)
    To bake ye to a puddin'.
— from "The Courtin' " by James Russell Lowell

USAGE
LESSON
18

PAST-TENSE
AND
PAST-PARTICIPLE
VERB
FORMS

The characteristic of nonstandard dialects that probably causes most social prejudice is the use of verb forms considered incorrect in the standard dialect. Aside from subject-verb agreement (see Chapters 12 and 13), verb problems are almost wholly due to confusion of past-tense and past-participle forms. English verbs have five **principal parts,** which can easily be shown in the form of a paradigm (which is a set of related forms). Here is the verb paradigm:

Stem	Third Person Singular, Present Tense	Present Participle	Past Tense	Past Participle
(to) talk	talks	talking	talked	(have) talked
(to) see	sees	seeing	saw	(have) seen
(to) break	breaks	breaking	broke	(have) broken

An English verb is said to be **regular** (or **weak**) when both its past tense and past participle are formed by the addition of *ed.* (Some archaic forms, such as *spelt,* substitute a *t* for the *ed.*) Otherwise, a verb is **irregular** (or **strong**).

The verb forms (except for a very few peculiar verbs, such as *to be*) in slots two and three of the paradigm are always regular (that is, take an *s* in the third person present singular and an *ing* in the present participle) in the standard dialect and usually in nonstandard dialects, though in a few isolated parts of the country one can hear such a sentence as *he talk fast, don't he?* Thus almost all verb problems occur because standard past-tense and past-participle forms are confused or are formed with *ed* when, for the standard dialect, they should not be. Following are typical examples of errors in verb forms; the asterisk means that the grammatical construction is nonstandard. (The correct forms are in parentheses.)

*I **taken** the rock crusher.   (took)
*He **come** at a bad time.   (came)
*It **begun** to rain hard.   (began)
*I was almost **shook** off my skeleton.   (shaken)
*I **knowed** you'd lie.   (knew)
*He **run** like a scared rabbit.   (ran)

Such errors are not due to a person's inherent lack of knowledge of his native language but to his speaking a nonstandard dialect.

For reference, here is a list of the irregular verbs most often responsible for errors in the standard dialect.

Stem	Past Tense	Past Participle
begin	began	(have) begun
bite	bit	(have) bitten
blow	blew	(have) blown
break	broke	(have) broken
bring	brought	(have) brought
burst	burst	(have) burst
catch	caught	(have) caught
choose	chose	(have) chosen
come	came	(have) come
deal	dealt	(have) dealt
do	did	(have) done
draw	drew	(have) drawn
drink	drank	(have) drunk
drive	drove	(have) driven
eat	ate	(have) eaten
fall	fell	(have) fallen
flee	fled	(have) fled
fly	flew	(have) flown
forbid	forbade	(have) forbidden
forget	forgot	(have) forgotten
freeze	froze	(have) frozen
give	gave	(have) given
go	went	(have) gone
grow	grew	(have) grown
know	knew	(have) known
lead	led	(have) led
lose	lost	(have) lost
ride	rode	(have) ridden
ring	rang	(have) rung
rise	rose	(have) risen
run	ran	(have) run
see	saw	(have) seen
shake	shook	(have) shaken

Stem	Past Tense	Past Participle
sing	sang	(have) sung
sink	sank	(have) sunk
speak	spoke	(have) spoken
steal	stole	(have) stolen
swear	swore	(have) sworn
swim	swam	(have) swum
swing	swung	(have) swung
take	took	(have) taken
tear	tore	(have) torn
throw	threw	(have) thrown
wear	wore	(have) worn
wring	wrung	(have) wrung
write	wrote	(have) written

EXERCISE 18A. Without consulting a dictionary, list the past-tense and past-participle forms of the following verbs. Then check them in your dictionary. Discuss your experience with these verbs.

	Stem	Past Tense	Past Participle
1.	cling	_____	have _____
2.	dive	_____	have _____
3.	spring	_____	have _____
4.	bear	_____	have _____
5.	forecast	_____	have _____
6.	lay	_____	have _____
7.	lie	_____	have _____
8.	sit	_____	have _____
9.	deal	_____	have _____
10.	cleave	_____	have _____
11.	lend	_____	have _____
12.	slay	_____	have _____
13.	hew	_____	have _____
14.	fight	_____	have _____
15.	sight	_____	have _____

EXERCISE 18B. If you have access to the *Oxford English Dictionary*, see whether there are archaic forms of the following verbs. Have you ever read or heard one of these old forms?

	Stem	Past Tense	Past Participle
1.	help	_____	have _____
2.	clap	_____	have _____
3.	climb	_____	have _____
4.	clothe	_____	have _____
5.	cling	_____	have _____
6.	buy	_____	have _____

Stem	Past Tense	Past Participle
7. heed	_____	have _____
8. leap	_____	have _____
9. plead	_____	have _____
10. wring	_____	have _____

CHAPTER
19

EUPHEMISMS, CLICHÉS, JARGON

Since the ideas and feelings that we express through language are often very subtle or complex and since we often (sometimes unconsciously) want to conceal the fact that we understand clearly just what ideas or feelings we are expressing, we sometimes distort, abuse, or fail to be direct in our use of language. Though linguists maintain that *linguistically* a language cannot become debased and that any segment of speech or writing that a native speaker accepts without thinking about the language itself is good language, nevertheless language can be debased or in some way be bad in so far as *social* and *artistic* judgments are concerned. Thus without taking issue with linguists, in this and the following chapters we will see some of the ways we manipulate language and fail to be completely clear and direct in our expression. We will also see how we sometimes give language more than average artistic quality.

Euphemisms

A **euphemism** is an inoffensive word or expression deliberately chosen by a speaker or writer as a substitute for a clear, direct term that he thinks may be offensive to his audience or that he fears may prejudice his audience against him. Euphemisms thus are indirect expressions. For example, countless telegrams have contained the expression "So-and-so *passed away* last night" rather than "So-and-so *died* last night." The composers of the telegrams simply feel that the direct word *died* might have a shock effect that can be avoided by the euphemistic *passed away*. Though some people insist on being fiercely direct, such euphemisms do little if any harm as long as they are clear. Thus many people are grateful that they can speak of *natural fertilizer* rather than *manure*, *intestinal flu* rather than *diarrhea*, *perspiration* rather than *sweat*, *paying guest* rather than *boarder*, and so on. In fact, even some of those fiercely direct people are happy to take advantage of the euphemistic qualities of *urine*, *feces*, *nasal discharge*, *fornication*, and other such words so that they can avoid using the so-called four-letter words that offend many people.

Writers of advertising copy and some commercial firms are addicted to euphemisms, and may at times use them to mislead customers. For example, the television ad in which a wife says to a grouchy husband "Is it . . . irregularity?" not only avoids the specific, direct word *constipation* but might give viewers the idea that a laxative can relieve almost any sort of general discomfort. But even when no one is misled, many knowledgeable people scorn the commercial devotion to euphemisms. Once, for example, an undertaking firm posted large billboards showing a pretty, young — but dead — woman with the caption "Beautiful bodies by (name of firm)." Can you imagine the word *corpses* instead of *bodies* being used in the ad? Undertakers also much prefer to be called *morticians* and also often label the part of their establishment where corpses await transportation to the graveyard (naturally called *cemetery* or, more recently, *memorial park*) the *slumber room*.

Sometimes euphemisms are coined or used for the purpose of prestige — to make a menial job sound important. For example, in some places garbage collectors are called *sanitation engineers*. Janitors have become *custodians*. In Germany, not only does the manager of an apartment house sometimes call himself the *Hausmeister* (master of the house) but his wife may take on the grand title *Frau Hausmeister* when she just does cleaning chores. No doubt eventually ditch diggers will become *excavation experts*. Still, little real harm is done by most of the kind of euphemistic language we have discussed.

But sometimes euphemisms are used to deceive and may do harm. For example, when the famous Watergate case broke in mid-1973, the White House issued some statements that were soon shown to be outright lies. When confronted with the evidence, the president's press secretary merely said that those statements are now *inoperative*. For some time the press gleefully used *inoperative* to suggest *lies* in order to show up the misuse of language that had occurred, but no doubt many people did not realize that the press secretary's use of *inoperative* really meant that the statements issued had been lies. For another example, during the Vietnam war the word *pacification* was used to mean imposing an iron military grip on hostile villages, but no doubt many people thought that some sort of peaceful process was going on. The use of deceitful euphemisms should, of course, be strongly condemned.

Clichés

A cliché is a trite, overused, worn-out expression. Lazy, unoriginal writers use many clichés so that they will not have to think. Since most clichés are commonly known because of their frequent use, it is easy for the nonthinking writer just to use them. Some examples are *sly as a fox, depths of despair, a lean and hungry look, love nest, pretty as a picture, our glorious heritage, the heart that beats true, had them rolling in the aisles*, and so on. Such clichés are mostly harmless in that they do not often deceive a reader, but they do deaden a writer's style and in general signal to the critical reader that the piece of writing is probably not worth reading.

Some clichés, however, can be harmful — mostly those used by politicians. The political cliché has the indirectness of a euphemism and may lull some voters into thinking that the politician has said something important and forwardlooking when he has just used worn-out phrasing. For example, if a politician is asked what steps he plans to take to reduce unemployment, he may spin out seemingly impressive statements with such phrases as *every man's rght to work, get this country going again, demand full corporate responsibility*, and so on. The perceptive listener or reader will realize that the politician actually has just used clichés and said nothing, but the gullible may be misled. Or in explaining how he will close tax loopholes a presidential candidate may fill his speech with such phrases as *each man bear his due burden, not allow the wily rich to escape taxation, tax with due regard for incentive to promote growth, use vigilant tax agents*, and so on — saying nothing. Thus clichés sometimes represent a distortion and abuse of language, allowing people who should show responsibility to conceal their real ideas or feelings — or their ignorance.

Jargon

The term **jargon** has several meanings (look them up in your dictionary), but it is most commonly used to mean the specialized or technical language of a profession or field of study that is so full of abstractions and difficult phrasing that it sounds like gibberish to ordinary, reasonably well-educated people. Thus one may refer to *sociological jargon, educational jargon, the jargon of art criticism*, and so on.

Since you are now in the middle of this text's part on language, we will illustrate jargon from writing about language. Consider this passage:

A generative grammar has a syntactic component which generates strings, a semantic component which semantically interprets sentoids, and a phonological component which provides the phonetics of utterances.

Is that a good, clear definition for you? It comes from a text written for ordinary college students. Or consider this passage:

In nonexceptional structures the coordinates that constitute multiple units exhibit essential similitude in grammatical functioning and usually in parallelism of semantic qualities in addition.

Would you like to study grammar using a text written in such a jargonistic style? Or would you rather read this paraphrase of the above example:

Ordinarily, elements in a series in a sentence are alike in grammatical form and usually have some similarity of meaning too.

Many advanced college students, however, become so accustomed to jargon that they are suspicious of any concept expressed in clear, simple terms.

Why does jargon exist? Partly, perhaps, because some scholars become so learned that they lose the ability to write with direct simplicity, and then, since new scholars are trained by old scholars, the old train the new to write jargon, and so such styles are perpetuated. Excessive pride in their learning may also lead some writers into composing jargon.

We should close our comments on jargon, however, by saying that English has and needs a great many "big" and technical words and that words such as *syntactic, semantic, phonetics,* and so on are essential to the language. Jargon is created when the writer uses difficult phrasing when it is unnecessary and when he obscures his meaning by clothing his thoughts in strings of difficult words instead of using them judiciously and striving for clarity. The mere presence in the language of essential "big" and technical words does not make jargon unavoidable. Most well-educated people scorn jargon.

EXERCISES

1. Tell, or write out in three lists, which of the following expressions you think are euphemisms, which clichés, and which both.

according to Webster	laid to rest
pre-owned Cadillac	a tower of strength
company representative (at someone's door)	the crack of dawn
last but not least	planned withdrawal (of an army)
in a family way	powder room
senior citizens	the whole thing in a nutshell
quick as a wink	social disease
substandard residential area	blessed event
the exceptional pupil	disadvantaged student
rest room	father time
rotten to the core	the spur of the moment
indisposed	hard as nails
culturally deprived	career education
at the drop of a hat	fit as a fiddle

2. Can you, your teacher, or anyone you know make any sense out of these opening sentences of a college textbook?

The proper understanding of the transcultural equivalences of all cultures begins with the sociology of knowledge. The sociology of knowledge is concerned not simply with such forms of deception as false dichotomization, the all-or-nothing mistake, by which binary choices between easy extremes obscure the value of contextual clues in the formulation of rational decisions. It concerns itself also with the situational determinants of binary decisions.

USAGE
LESSON
19

MODIFIER
FORMS

A **modifier** is a word or word group in a sentence (or meaningful utterance) that describes, limits, or adds to another word or word group. For example, in *the gang with no headquarters, with no headquarters* modifies *the gang,* since it adds meaning to or describes *the gang.* Similarly, in *a shaggy-dog story, shaggy-dog* modifies *story,* since it describes *story* or tells what kind it is. Modification in our language is hugely complex, but there are only a few troublesome aspects of it that lead to errors. We will concentrate just on the trouble spots.

Though nouns, verbs and word groups may function as modifiers, adjectives (which usually modify nouns) and adverbs (which usually modify verbs). To understand the problem of confused adjectives and adverbs, you should think of modification in terms of *what goes with what.* For example, in

Luis spoke *sweetly* to Carole,

you should see that the adverb *sweetly* goes with (or modifies) the verb *spoke.* But in

Carole is *sweet*

or

This orange tastes *sweet*

you should see that the adjective *sweet* goes with (or modifies) the nouns *Carole* and *orange.* Thus do not misuse adjectives for adverbs, as in these examples:

wrong:	Can Joe breathe *normal* now? (*Normally* is correct.)
wrong:	Sue talks *easy* with strangers. (*Easily* is correct.)
wrong:	Greg runs *different* from Hugh. (*Differently* is correct.)
wrong:	Do your work *careful.* (*Carefully* is correct.)
wrong:	Blow your nose more *frequent.* (*Frequently* is correct.)

Think carefully and you will see that the italicized adjectives go with (or modify) the verbs *breathe, talks, runs, do,* and *blow* and thus should be in the adverbial form.

Be sure, however, not to use an adverb after a so-called linking verb (*to be, to seem, to appear, to become, to feel,* and so on) when an adjective form is needed to modify not the verb but the subject of the sentence. The most common such mistake is the use of *badly* with *feel.* Example:

wrong:	I feel *badly* about your divorce. (*Bad* is correct.)

Would you say

wrong:	I feel *sadly* (or *gladly*) about your divorce.

Except for *feel badly,* such mistakes are not common. However, do not make the error of using *bad* when the word modifies a verb instead of a subject (usually a noun or pronoun). Examples:

wrong:	My car runs *bad.* (*Badly* is correct.)
wrong:	Cheri plays bridge *bad.* (*Badly* is correct.)

In these sentences *badly* should modify the verbs *run* and *plays,* not the noun subjects *car* and *Cheri.* Note that Cheri herself is not bad but that she *plays badly.* When in doubt ask what the modifier goes with, and you will be able to tell whether the modification pattern is *hurts badly, tastes bad,* and so on.

Good (an adjective) is sometimes misused for the adverb *well* to modify a verb. Examples:

wrong:	I did *good* in math. (*Well* is correct.)
wrong:	Are things going *good* for you? (*Well* is correct.)
wrong:	Teaching doesn't pay *good.* (*Well* is correct.)
wrong:	Little Billy can read *good.* (*Well* is correct.)

You should see that the incorrectly-used adjectives really go with the verbs *did, going, pay,* and *read* and therefore that the adverb *well* is needed.

Avoid using *near* for *nearly.* Examples:

wrong:	I didn't earn *near* as much as I expected. (*Nearly* is correct.)
wrong:	I wasn't driving *near* as fast as you. (*Nearly* is correct.)

In such sentences the adverb form *nearly* is needed to modify the adverb clauses that follow it.

Finally, in your college writing avoid *real* and *sure* in such expressions as *real pretty, real intelligent, I sure enjoyed the bash,* and *John sure brags a lot.* Either use *really* and *surely* or express yourself in other words.

EXERCISE 19.

In the following phrases cross out any misused modifiers and be prepared to tell what form is needed. Do not cross out correctly used modifiers.

1. sounded oddly to my ears
2. tasted fresh
3. plays tennis good
4. felt badly about the loss
5. acted careless around his aunt
6. seemed careless to his uncle
7. is real generous
8. talked different when he returned
9. mixes easy in a crowd
10. can see good with his new glasses
11. performed well on the test
12. sure is crazy about you
13. paused frequent to take a swig
14. not near as big as mine
15. felt the bruise gently with his fingers
16. felt gentle in her presence
17. fruit smelled sourly
18. behaved angry
19. peach smelled sweet
20. felt around in the casket uneasily
21. felt uneasily in her presence
22. felt bitter about his loss
23. felt bitterly about his loss
24. sat comfortable in the chair
25. talked indecent to his teacher
26. smiled happy at the thought

27. grinned happily as he won
28. appeared kind to his neighbors
29. behaves more pleasant than Jack
30. seemed more pleasant than Jack

CHAPTER 20

DENOTATION AND CONNOTATION

You may be under the impression, as perhaps most people are, that a word is a word and that if you want to know the meaning of a word, you look it up in the dictionary. But language is not nearly so simple as that. In fact, the most learned linguists even disagree among themselves as to what a word is. We will not step into that briar patch of technical dispute but will just assume that we all know what a word is.

Words vary greatly in the roles they play as we use language to express our ideas and feelings. For example, consider the sentence "Your religion is different from mine." The word *from* is essential in the sentence, but could you even begin to define its meaning? And does it play any part at all in the emotional reactions that this simple sentence could possibly evoke? No, it is just a common structure word (a preposition) indispensable to the language but playing only a very small and uncontroversial role in the hugely complex world of ideas and feelings that our language opens up for us. But many words play a large and often controversial part in that world of ideas and feelings. In this chapter we will briefly explore some of the characteristics of this latter group of words.

Many of the **content words** in our language (nouns, verbs, adjectives, and adverbs) may be said to have **denotative** and **connotative meanings.** The denotative meaning of a word is its literal, surface, dictionary meaning — usually a meaning that it has for everyone who knows the word. Thus one denotative meaning of *liberal* is "a person favoring political change and reform." Or one denotative meaning of *doctor* is "a person trained in the healing arts and licensed to practice medicine." Or, for a final example, one denotative meaning of *justice* is "fair handling and equal treatment."

But when used in various contexts, many words carry more than denotative meaning. They may also carry connotative meaning — which may be defined as the suggestive or associative implications that words may have for individuals or groups because of their experiences with the things the words denote. A connotative meaning, then, cannot be entered in a dictionary because it lies beyond the literal, explicit sense of a word and thus may vary with individuals. For example, to a person with inherited wealth and a conservative background, the word *liberal* might carry the connotation of an undesirable person who would lead the country to ruin if he could. That is, on hearing that a stranger is a liberal, the conservative person mentioned might have the thoughts mentioned run through his mind. The word *doctor* might seem to be neutral, but what might it connote to a young child who has been hurt in clinics by men wearing white jackets and known as doctors? William Carlos Williams wrote a short story entitled "The Use of Force" that admirably demonstrates the unfavorable connotation the word *doctor* can have for a child. Or consider the word *justice*. What thoughts might race through the mind of a poor, rural black man who has been arrested and imprisoned for the simple act of possessing a little bootleg liquor and who perhaps was mistreated by the authorities during the ordeal he underwent for what to him seemed no good reason? To him *justice* might connote favoritism to whites and distortion rather than fair or equal treatment.

Connotation is sometimes wholly private because of an individual's personal and nonshared experiences. For example, there is one person in this world who simply cannot swallow a pill, no matter how sugar-coated or harmless it is. Try as she may, she cannot make a pill go down her throat. To that person the word *pill* undoubtedly has an unfavorable connotation, probably bring fearful thoughts into her mind when she hears it. To her it is a "bad" word, whereas to millions needing relief from distress, *pill* no doubt is a "good" word. Or consider the word *dean*, as in the dean of a college. To most people it connotes learning, benevolent authority, and genteel accomplishment. But perhaps there is one person who almost goes into a rage when he hears the word because he had some unfortunate experiences with an autocratic, ignorant dean. Experience greatly affects our reactions to various words, and we have individual experiences.

There is, however, such a thing as *public* connotation — the suggestive meaning that a word has for a large portion of the population. (If a word has *exactly* the same suggestive meaning for *everyone* who knows it, then that meaning may more fairly be said to be a part of the word's denotation.) We used the word *doctor* above as an example of how a word can take on an unfavorable connotation. But actually for most of our population the word *doctor* has a favorable connotation. "The doctor is coming" or "going to see the doctor" suggests to many relief, security, and reassurance. In fact, a great many people think of *doctor* as almost a godly word, as some of the television series show.

But it is in the areas of politics, religion, social behavior, economics, and so on that many words have public connotations, and most speakers gauge their audiences very carefully to determine which words to avoid and which to emphasize. When, for example, a liberal politician has a wholly liberal audience he might use such words or phrases as *the Pentagon, the military-industrial complex,* and *The National Association of Manufacturers,* secure in the knowledge that the words will produce in his audience the unfavorable connotations he wants them to have. However, if the same politician, perhaps running for high office, had a more general audience he might avoid those terms and talk about *our country's mighty productive capacity, the profit incentive,* and *the military guardians of our democracy,* depending on the connotations not to produce an undesired reaction in voters who have not yet made up their minds. (In the next chapter we will see how both denotative and connotative meanings of words are often used deceitfully.)

As we have already made clear, language may be classified in various ways. One way is to classify a segment of language as **objective** or **subjective** (while recognizing that both types of language may be mixed in a passage). Objective language is mostly free from personal feelings, opinions, prejudices, emotions, self-interest, and bigotry. It is mostly unbiased and detached — the latter term meaning that the writer or speaker is really standing aside from his subject matter. (Purely objective language can, however, sway the emotions of a reader; for example, a completely objective and detached report of famine and starvation can bring tears to the eyes of a reader. But that is because the reader himself adds something to the objective language.)

Objective language usually is composed to make most use of denotative meanings and to deemphasize connotative meanings. We say *usually* and *deemphasize* because connotation generally cannot be avoided completely. Here is an example of objective writing:

> The ribs, whose office it is to give form to the thorax, and to cover and defend the lungs, also assist in breathing; for they are joined to the vertebrae by regular hinges, which allow of short motions, and to the sternum by cartilages, which yield to the motion of the ribs, and return again when the muscles cease to act.
>
> Each rib, then, is characterized by these material parts: a great length of bone, at one end of which there is a head for articulation with the vetebrae, and a shoulder or knob for articulation with its transverse process; at the other end there is a point, with a socket for receiving its cartilage, and a cartilage joined to it, which is implanted into a similar socket in the side of the sternum, so as to complete the form of the chest.
>
> —from John Bell, "Of the Ribs"

It would be hard to find a word in this passage with any degree of public connotation. Some private connotation could be present; for example, an athlete who had suffered torn cartilage might feel a twinge of emotion when he read that word. But mostly this passage illustrates both objectivity and absence of connotation (leaving denotation). The more objective he wants to be, the more a writer will rely on denotation and the more he will define his terms when he uses words which normally carry much connotation. For example, an objective writer will define what he means by *romantic* when he calls a person a romantic, for that word is rife with connotative meanings.

Subjective language is not only *not* free from, but is intended to make use of, the speaker's emotions, interests, feelings, opinions, prejudices, and biases. It is not primarily concerned with objective reality and is for the most part not subject to proof. Subjective language is much more likely to depend for its impact on connotative meanings than is objective language. Thus, since connotation can vary so widely with individuals, subjective language usually evokes many more interpretations and reactions than does objective language. Here is an example of subjective writing:

> I shall choose friends among men, but neither slaves nor masters. And I shall choose only such as please me, and them I shall love and respect, but neither command nor obey. And we shall join our hands when we wish, or walk alone when we so desire. For in the temple of his spirit, each man is alone. Let each man keep his temple untouched and undefiled. Then let him join hands with others if he wishes, but only beyond his holy threshold.
>
> For the word "We" must never be spoken, save by one's choice and as a second thought. This word must never be placed first within man's soul, else it becomes a monster, the root of all the evils on earth, the root of man's torture by men, and of an unspeakable lie.
>
> The word "We" is a lime poured over men, which sets and hardens to stone, and crushes all beneath it, and that which is white and that which is black are lost equally in the grey of it. It is the word by which the depraved steal the virtue of the good, by which the weak steal the might of the strong, by which the fools seal the wisdom of the sages.
>
> — from Ayn Rand, *Anthem*

While the words in this passage carry their denotative meanings, as they must in all language, the author depends much more on their connotative effects. At the very beginning, for example, Ms. Rand expects the words *slaves* and *masters* to evoke suggestive and associative meanings in the minds of her reader, as she does with such expressions as *join our hands*, *walk alone, the temple of his spirit*, and so on. Though subjective language might be thought to be richer than objective language because of its greater reliance on connotation, both kinds of language are very important, and they are quite often mixed.

EXERCISES

1. Discuss the different connotations that
    a. the word *school* might have for a studious, bright youngster and for a disturbed, rebellious child.
    b. the word *welfare* might have for a destitute mother of six whose husband has deserted her and for a well-to-do, conservative person.
    c. the word *liquor* might have for a family who use it moderately and pleasurably for social purposes and for a wife whose husband is an alcoholic.
    d. the word *profit* might have for a radical communist and for a hardworking, capitalistic businessman.
    e. the word *tribe* might have for a well-trained anthropologist studying a particular primitive culture and for a follower of Hitler's racist beliefs.
2. The following passage is a mixture of objective and subjective writing. Point out five instances of connotation that increase the subjectivity of the passage. What sentence in the passage seems to be most objective?

Every man must ultimately confront the question "Who am I?" and seek to answer it honestly. One of the first principles of personal adjustment is the principle of self-acceptance. The Negro's greatest dilemma is that in order to be healthy he must accept his ambivalence. The Negro is the child of two cultures — Africa and America. The problem is that in the search for wholeness all too many Negroes seek to embrace only one side of their natures. Some, seeking to reject their heritage, are ashamed of their color, ashamed of black art and music, and determine what is beautiful and good by the standards of white society. They end up frustrated and without cultural roots. Others seek to reject everything American and to identify totally with Africa, even to the point of wearing African clothes. But this approach leads also to frustration because the American Negro is not an African. The old Hegelian [*from Hegel, a German philosopher*] synthesis still offers the best answer to many of life's dilemmas. The American Negro is neither totally African nor totally Western. He is Afro-American, a true hybrid, a combination of two cultures.

— from Martin Luther King, Jr.,
"Where Do We Go from Here: Chaos or Community?"

USAGE
LESSON
20

SHIFTS
IN
NUMBER

Number is a grammatical term that has to do, obviously, with how many objects or individuals are referred to. English has just two numbers in grammar: singular (one) and plural (more than one). Some languages have more than two grammatical numbers.

A weakness or error that sometimes occurs in writing (or speech) is an **improper shift in number.** That is, the writer starts expressing his idea in the singular and then improperly shifts to the plural, or vice versa. Here is a typical example:

> *wrong:*　When a *person* spends most of *their* time viewing television, *they* often develop televisionitis. (*His* and *he* are proper.)

The hypothetical composer of this sentence began a reference in the singular (*person*) and then without changing reference improperly shifted to the plural (*their* and *they*). Though the reader of such a sentence is not confused, such a shift still lowers the quality of the style because of the inconsistency, and experienced readers generally develop negative feelings about a writer who is so inconsistent in his usage.

There are two reasons why improper shifts in number are rather common. The first is that in English we can refer to people in general in either the singular or the plural. Here is an example:

> *correct:*　A *teacher* should be aware of *his* students' feelings.
> *correct:*　*Teachers* should be aware of *their* students' feelings.

The two statements mean exactly the same thing, though the reference to teachers in general in the first is in the singular and in the second is in the plural. Since a reference to people in general can be made in either the singular or the plural, some writers sometimes begin with one kind of reference and then inconsistently shift to the other. Example:

wrong: A *teacher* should be aware of *their* students' feelings, but *they* should also maintain high scholastic standards.

Such an inconsistent shift from the singular *teacher* to the plural *their* and *they* sometimes is not apparent to a writer because he is used to both singular and plural reference to people in general.

The second reason why improper shifts in number are common is that English just does not have singular third person pronouns (*he, she, his,* and so on) that refer to both sexes. It has been conventional in English for centuries to use the masculine third person pronoun (*he, him, his*) when reference is made to indefinite or mixed sex. Nevertheless, many people, especially since feminist movements have become vigorous, feel uneasy about using the masculine *he, him, his* when sex reference is indefinite. No doubt some of these people are unconsciously uneasy, but nevertheless uneasy. Many who are aware of inconsistency in reference try to solve their problem with the awkward *he or she.* Example:

awkward: If a *musician* becomes deaf, *he or she* may still be able to compose good music.

But in such a construction awkwardness has replaced the inconsistent *they,* with little improvement. Thus many people solve their problem by shifting to the plural pronoun that refers to both sexes. Example:

wrong: A school *counselor* needs special training, but *they* also need a good academic background.

Such a shift in number from the singular *counselor* to the plural *they* may avoid the possible problem of hurting women's feelings, but it produces poor style. Note also in this example sentence that there is only one academic background to go with the plural *they,* anoher inconsistency.

The improper shift in number probably occurs more often with the *everybody, everyone* group of words than with any others. Actually a third cause of the inconsistent shift enters the scene with these words. *Everybody* is grammatically singular in English but carries the concept of plurality. That is, it means *all,* which is plural in many of its references. Thus an untrained person sees nothing wrong with

Everybody grabbed *their* bottles,

since *everybody* means *all.* Yet no native speaker of English would say

Everybody are going,

for the singular verb *is* automatically goes with *everybody.* Thus the word's singular number is obvious. Also note that in the first example sentence with the inconsistent *their* (*his* would be proper), the reader cannot tell whether each person had one or several bottles, whereas

Everybody grabbed his bottle

and

Everybody grabbed his bottles

deliver precise information.

The whole matter of number is a briar patch in English usage. Nevertheless, the careful writer will maintain consistency in number. Thus — at least until English adopts a singular third person pronoun referring to both sexes — our recommendation is that you maintain consistency in number and use the forms *he, him, his* for singular reference to indefinite sex. Examples:

correct: A pro football *player* earns a high salary, but *he* must accept much physical bruising. (Avoid *they.*)

correct: *Everybody* wanted *his* question answered. (Avoid *their.*)

correct: A *freshman* may think that *he* knows almost everything, but *he* always has much to learn. (Avoid *they* and *they.*)

Maintaining such consistency in number is one mark of a careful writer.

A final note: Proper shifts in number do occur. Example:

correct: I found another golden eagle's *tail feather. They* make excellent decorative pieces.

Here the writer is consistent in his shift from singular to plural reference because the *they* does not refer to just the one tail feather mentioned, but to all golden eagles' tail feathers.

EXERCISE 20.   In the following sentences cross out the words that produce inconsistent shifts in number, and in the blanks below each sentence write the words that will produce consistency in number. Sometimes it may be best to change a singular reference to the plural, rather than vice versa. Some sentences may be correct.

1. When everybody had taken their places, the performance began.

   _____

2. A person is responsible for their own adult life, and they should accept that responsibility.

   _____

3. Pine trees flourish in poor soil, but if it is overfertilized it may die.

   _____

4. A dictionary is a student's best friend in college studies, and if they use them diligently their grades will improve.

   _____

5. Will each contestant take their seat? They may be the lucky one tonight.

   _____

6. Will everybody stop their bickering and show me that they will work for the Tory Party's success?

   _____

7. Who cares what a waiter thinks? They may be prejudiced.

   _____

8. A word doesn't have just one meaning. They may have several denotative meanings as well as connotations.

   _____

9. Doesn't anyone know who their partner is, or what they are supposed to do?

   _____

10. I bought another Swentford Christmas plate. They decorate my kitchen's walls prettily.

_____

11. A public entertainer seems always to want to be in the limelight, but they may sometimes want privacy.

_____

12. A TV performer is often out of work. There are so many of them that there are not enough programs to provide full employment for all.

_____

13. Not everybody is a genius. Some of us have only average intelligence.

_____

14. If a mule won't budge, they ought to be swatted on their rear, but they may kick you instead.

_____

15. When they are angry, a preacher will often behave like a layman.

_____

16. Does nobody understand their specific assignments in this formation?

_____

17. A cop who doesn't carry out their responsibilities honestly ought to ask the Mafia to take them in.

_____

18. Since a bartender must be of drinking age, they often drink on the job.

_____

19. A "living companion" often doesn't know what is expected of them.

_____

20. When everybody does their share, a supervisor is often able to do their work easily.

_____

CHAPTER
21

PROPAGANDA

Sometimes language is designed to do something *for* the reader (or listener) — such as to tell him facts about new developments in a national scandal or how to improve his golf game — and sometimes it is designed to do something *to* the reader — such as to touch his heart with a story of human sadness or to cause him to believe that a certain political principle is harmful and should be combatted at all costs. Language intended to do something for the reader is mostly informative and is usually more objective than subjective. Language intended to do something to the reader covers a very wide range — from, say, a poem intended to trigger emotional reactions to a calculated insult about one's personal neatness. In this chapter we will deal briefly with the kind of language known as **propaganda**, which is intended to do something *to* rather than *for* the reader. It is intended to do something *for* its creator.

Propaganda is defined variously in various dictionaries, with one simple definition being "material distributed by those who want to promote a particular doctrine or cause." That definition, however, is rather deceptively simple; it does not express the almost universal pejorative connotation that the word carries in English. For example, when a minister delivers a sermon does he not try to promote a doctrine of the Christian religion? Yet few people think of sermons as propaganda. Thus we are going to use the term *propaganda* in a more restricted, and generally accepted, sense: "language designed subtly or deceitfully to cause its readers or listeners to accept or retain belief in some doctrine or cause when objective, unsubtle, undeceitful language might not lead the reader to accept that doctrine or cause." That's a fairly lengthy definition, but it is the meaning that most people have in mind when they use the word *propaganda*. The implication is that there is something underhanded in the language of propaganda; it might be just subtle connotation, the use of loaded words and slanted diction (see below), distortion of facts, omission of relevant material, hypocrisy, or flagrant lies. Open and full disclosure of objective facts, while it might sway opinions, does not make propaganda in our sense of the word.

Thus we also need a term to describe language that tries to sway opinion in a reasonably honest, openminded, nondeceitful way. **Editorializing** is one such term. Some dictionary definitions of *propaganda* include editorializing, but most writers of editorials and of news reports with editorial overtones — at least those who publish in well-known and respected newspapers and magazines — do not think of themselves, nor do their readers think of them, as propagandists. However, just as an openminded editorialist may be fully sincere, the propagandist may also be (and usually is) sincere in believing his ideas. The difference is that he is not committed to an honest means of disseminating them. Hitler no doubt sincerely believed in his monstrous doctrines but saw nothing wrong with using propagandistic lies to promote them. Also we should note that the line between editorializing and propaganda is sometimes hard to determine.

Though propaganda must — as all language must — make use of denotation (for example, the phrase *political radical* carries enough denotative meaning to serve the purpose of many political propagandists), it relies heavily on connotative meanings. Thus writers of propaganda choose their words carefully to try to achieve the desired reactions in their readers. Objective, openminded writers, on the other hand, choose words carefully to deliver the precise information they have in mind. But propagandists go beyond mere connotative effects and use what are known as **loaded words** and **slanted diction.** Loaded words are those that are so charged with meanings that will produce extremely positive or negative feelings in readers that the writer uses them to manipulate readers. Words like *fascist, communist, darkie, wetback, demonstrator, addict, segregation, ivory-tower, redneck, Zionist, pornography, America-Firster,* and on and on are loaded or charged with meanings that, in certain contexts, serve propagandists to their satisfaction. Of course loaded words will produce a favorable response in some people and an unfavorable response in others.

When loaded words and those with rather simple connotative meanings are carefully chosen to sway emotions and opinions, the language phenomenon of **slanting** occurs. That is, two writers observing and commenting on the same incident can, by slanting, leave widely varying opinions in their readers' minds. Consider these two pairs of statements, each of which might have been written about the same situation:

> The fairminded dean compromised on the issue of establishing more objective standards for grading.
>
> The indecisive dean was manipulated by those who want to trap teachers in a rigid grading system.
>
> In an effort to serve the public better, the customer-oriented Mammouth Supermarkets adopted a new pricing system, lowering many prices and raising a few.
>
> With a public-be-damned attitude, the price-gouging Mammoth Supermarkets sneakily pulled a sharpie in order to raise prices overall.

Thus propaganda often goes beyond merely using connotation in an open and nondeceitful way and uses charged language to sway opinions when objective, honest use of language would not accomplish the writer's purpose.

Following are three passages of propaganda that illustrate a subtle if not deceitful manipulation of language to rouse the ire of the readers. Many of the words chosen for their particular effect (some to which the reader is supposed to react unfavorably and some favorably) are italicized. The first takes an extreme leftist view in politics:

> If Mr. X carries this state by one million votes, we will have *reactionary* control of the state assembly. Our *social insurance* advances will be crushed by the *far right*. Mr. X is *stealing* the *unions' right* of *free* bargaining. He is placing *controls on wages* but none on *soaring profits*. He is *menacing* the future of the Supreme Court by urging the *white supremacy* doctrines of the *dreadful* past. And he belittles the *patriotism* of Americans who disagree with him and flaunts his *cooperation with totalitarian* powers.

Note how such words as *stealing* (unfavorable) and *free* (favorable) are played off against each other.

The second is a piece of religious propaganda:

> There is an *epidemic of dissent* spreading inside our fundamentally *pure* church. The *religious spirit* is unfortunately being replaced by a *humanistic spirit*, and *autonomous groups*, claiming to represent a purer Christianity, drift towards *sociological and political views* that are *humanistic*. These *dissenters* resist *authority* and try to gain *devilish* control over our church to make it *humanistic* rather than *religious*.

Note how such words as *religious spirit* and *authority* (favorable for this group) are played off against such words as *humanistic* (unfavorable for this group, though favorable for many others).

The third passage takes an extreme rightist view of politics, though it cleverly begins as though it is to be liberal:

> I am glad for the Watergate *exposure* of the *debris,* the *filth,* the *bribes,* the *payoffs,* the *shredded documents,* the *solicitations* from the airlines and other *vast corporations,* because only by seeing the *collaborationist* elected leaders *wallow* in such disaster, after their *détente* with *China* and *Russia,* can we as *citizens* stop the march toward American *socialism.*

Note that at first the charged words suggest an extreme leftist position, but then the "bad" words *collaborationist, détente, China, Russia,* and *socialism* show the writer's propagandistic bent. Note how the "good" word *citizens* is played off against the "bad" word *socialism.* Politics, incidentally, is the area of human activity that produces by far the greatest amount of propaganda.

To spot propaganda (as opposed to sensible editorializing) notice the excessive use of loaded words and obvious slanting. For example, if you find an article opening with the sentence

> Well, again we see the fascistic manipulation of the American economy squeeze more profits out of the poor,

you can be fairly certain that the writer intends to propagandize rather than editorialize, in our sense of the words. Also in propaganda there will usually be an absence of objective, sound factual information, or factual information will be distorted. Note that in the three sample passages above no clear, understandable facts are expressed.

The weakness of a passage of propaganda will often be exposed when it is subjected to logical analysis, as explained in the first thirteen chapters of this book. For example, consider the second example of propaganda above. One conclusion in the paragraph is, "Some forces in our church are trying to destroy its desirable qualities." The syllogism for this deductive conclusion is this:

major premise: A religious spirit in a church is more desirable than a humanistic spirit.

minor premise: Some forces in our Church are trying to make it humanistic rather than religious.

conclusion: Some forces in our Church are trying to destroy its desirable qualities.

The question then becomes whether the major premise is true, and that, of course, means defining terms so that you know exactly what the major premise means. Once you examine the logic of a piece of propaganda and get its terms defined, you will very often find that its conclusion is not justifiable.

EXERCISES

1. Decide from the following opening sentences whether you think propaganda will follow. Why do you think so or not?

   a. While farm workers prepare for another round of strikes against the Teamster-grower alliance, the most hostile anti-UFW forces have had their hired goons brought to justice.

   b. Since federal funds for our public schools have been illegally stopped because of alleged segregation, we all must give unstinting support to our effort to maintain quality schools for those of suitable intelligence to profit from the instruction.

   c. A new member of the State Equalization Board has stated that his careful research into the nineteenth century shows that some of the land now owned by the Western Power Company was taken illegally from the Pit Indians.

   d. Standard Oil Company greased the way for anonymous wealthy donors to provide the ready cash that defeated Proposition 16 in the last so-called "free" state election.

   e. The pointed-head "intellectuals" with their bizarre archeological findings have been totally unable to stop the trend of thousands joining our pure, original Christian Church.

2. See whether you can work out some aspect of logical analysis of the following passage.

> Mr. X's constantly rotating forty-member staff of "specialists" is recruited from other federal agencies, Ivy League colleges and from the Council on Foreign Relations. Many of Mr. X's staffers receive three to six months' indoctrination and are then planted in strategic spots in highly sensitive federal agencies. Thus Mr. X is building a bureaucratic empire of "loyalists" instantly responsive to his clandestine orders without going through normal official channels.
>
> — from *Washington Observer*, February 1, 1971.
> (The official's name has been replaced by Mr. X.)

USAGE
LESSON
21

SHIFTS
IN
PERSON

The grammatical term **person** has to do with who is talking, or being talked to, or being talked about. The **first person** refers to the person or persons talking, the pronoun forms being *I, me, we, us, our,* and *ours.* The **second person** refers to those talked to, the pronoun forms being *you, your,* and *yours.* And the **third person** refers to those talked about, the pronoun forms being *he, she, him, her, his, they, them, their, it, its,* and other forms. Also nouns such as *student, counselor, player, musician,* and so on are in the third person. That is we talk *about* a student; if we talk *to* him, we normally say *you.*

The second person pronoun *you* often functions as the so-called **indefinite second person** or **indefinite you.** This means that it refers to people in general, not to a specific individual.

An improper or inconsistent shift in person is almost always from the third person to the second, or, less often, from the second to the third. Example:

> *wrong:* A *student* has a responsibility to *his* studies, but *your* social life in college is also important.

True, the reader of such a sentence is not confused or misled, but the inconsistent shift from the third person (*student*) to the second person (*your*) produces poor style and creates negative feelings in an experienced reader, who will often think that such writing is not worth reading and turn to something else.

Improper shifts in person are fairly common because in English we can use either the third person or the indefinite second person to refer to people in general. Example:

> *correct:* A *gambler* cannot play poker well unless *he* has a good understanding of the odds.

> *correct:* You cannot play poker well unless *you* have a good understanding of the odds.

Here, the second sentence is referring to people in general, not to an individual; thus the two sentences have identical meanings. But the first makes reference to people in general in the third person (*gambler, he*) and the second makes reference to people in general in the indefinite second person (*you*). Since both modes of reference are available and commonly used, some writers unconsciously make inconsistent shifts in person. Example:

> *wrong:* A *gambler* cannot play poker well unless *he* has a good understanding of the odds. *You* have to be able to estimate the chances of certain cards coming up.

In this sentence the idea begins with a reference to gamblers in general in the third person (*gambler, he*) and then inconsistently shifts to the second person (*you*) to make the same general reference. The result is poor style.

Here are some other examples of faulty shifts in person:

> *wrong:* A *student* often has to decide between going on a date or studying. *You* should always choose studying unless *you* know *you* will have sufficient time later to get the work done. (*He, he,* and *he* would be proper.)
> *wrong:* A good *Christian* doesn't just go to church on Sunday. *You* must practice Christian ethics during the week. (*He* would be proper.)
> *wrong:* A *person* shouldn't donate to a charity unless *you* know *your* money will reach the charity that is supposed to get it. (*He* and *his* would be proper.)

Though some people object to the use of the indefinite second person, inconsistent shifts can be avoided if the indefinite *you* is used throughout a passage. For example, in the first example sentence, *student* could be replaced by *you*. But in any case, consistency should be maintained.

Sometimes a shift from the third to the second person is proper and consistent. Example:

> *correct:* A *musician* can make a good and enjoyable living, but if *you* enter that profession *you* should avoid the drug scene that many musicians get hung up with.

Here the reference of *musician* is to musicians in general, but the refernnce of the indefinite *you* is to people who may consider becoming musicians. Thus the shift is not only proper but necessary (though the indefinite third person *one* could be used instead of *you*).

EXERCISE 21.   Most of the following sentences have improper shifts in either number or person. Strike out the words that produce improper shifts and in the blanks below the sentences write the words that will produce consistency. Some of the sentences may be correct.

1. Like a fool, I bought still another Paperlover pen. They are expensive and not very reliable.

    _____

2. A person may stay in a line for an hour to buy a ticket, and then you may just give up, having wasted your time.

    _____

3. A track star can't make nearly as much money as a football star, but they may love their sport just as much.

    _____

4. If a person is arrested, he may be released on bail immediately. But you may have to spend a night in jail.

    _____

5. A young student usually dreams of getting a perfect job, but you may wind up with a job you don't like, for polls show that 48 percent of the people do.

    _____

6. A teacher is thought to have a great deal of vacation time, but if you become a teacher you will learn that much of that "vacation" time must be spent in preparation for teaching.

    _____

7. At first a college freshman is a little frightened, but as time passes you learn there is nothing to fear in college.

    _____

8. An appliance repairman usually charges a great deal for his work, but you have no choice but to pay them unless you can repair the appliance.

    _____

9. A good TV program is hard to find, but they are well worth watching when you find them.

   _____

10. A full-time college student should spend at least twenty hours a week studying out of class, but you seldom do that.

    _____

11. You can't expect society to support you always. One must be at least a little responsible for their own welfare.

    _____

12. One who plays an amplified guitar doesn't need to know much about music. You can get by just by learning to strum a few chords.

    _____

13. Anybody who loses their shoes in a theater deserves to step on stale popcorn.

    _____

14. The giant sequoia tree makes a person realize how insignificant you are.

    _____

15. When a person is traveling, they should try to visit all nearby historical sights, but you often just pass it by.

    _____

16. Often a person must go against their best interests. For example, sometimes you have to lend money to an unreliable friend.

    _____

17. Taxi drivers often receive insults, but he should just ignore it.

    _____

18. Don't ridicule another person's mistake, for if one does they may make the same mistake themselves.

    _____

CHAPTER 22

IRONY AND SATIRE

A passage of language is **literal** when it means just what it says on the surface, that is, when it should be taken at its face value. Of course connotations may cause different people to react differently to, or make different interpretations of, a literal passage. But when we say something such as "I literally mean he will cheat his mother," we mean exactly what the words say. However, language is such a marvelous vehicle of communication that it often takes various nonliteral forms. That is, a nonliteral passage does *not* mean exactly what it says on the surface.

One of the most common forms of nonliteral language is **irony,** in which the intended meaning is the opposite of — or at least in sharp contrast to — what is literally said. There is also such a thing as irony of incident, in which what happens is in sharp contrast to what could normally be expected to happen. For example, if a boy scout starts to help an old lady across the street and both are run over by a truck, that is irony. Life in general is full of irony of incident, and thus literature that depicts life is full of such irony. We, however, will restrict our brief discussion to irony of language.

Irony in various forms is very common in language of all sorts. For example, you as a student use irony frequently in your conversation when you make sarcastic remarks to friends or enemies. That is, if you say to your boy (or girl) friend "Oh, you're so sweet to me" in a sarcastic tone, you have used irony, for you mean your comment not to be taken literally but to mean the opposite of what it says on the surface. Or irony can appear in the most serious and advanced writing. For example, Theodore

Spencer, a noted professor at Harvard who became disgusted with the obscurantism of much modern literary criticism, once wrote a supposedly learned essay entitled "How to Criticize a Poem," *criticize* here meaning "how to extract meaning from and evaluate the worth of." The poem he analyzed was "Thirty days hath September, etc.," a rather clear clue at the outset that the article was to be ironical. He used all sorts of high-sounding phrases, such as "fundamental *dynamic*," "prose-*demand*," "*proto-response*," "two varieties of mensual time," and so on. He was being ironical in that he meant what he said to be meaningless, absurd, and ridiculous — in short, he meant for his readers to understand that his meaning was the opposite of what he seemed literally to say. Yet about 75 percent of bright college freshmen who are given the essay to read with no clue that it is ironical take it seriously and try to learn something from it. The ability to detect irony is, in fact, the surest sign of a reader's intellectual maturity.

Much of the ordinary reading public is sometimes taken in by an ironical letter-to-the-editor, and some respond angrily because of their literal misinterpretation of the writer's intent. For example, a letter to the editor of a daily newspaper, written under a pseudonym before the current popularity of small American cars, began this way:

Sir:
The present clamor for increases in teachers' salaries shows how a segment of the population can lose its reason and make demands no sane person could accede to. Teachers don't need raises. Look at all the advantages they have for saving money and their not needing large expenditures, as we businessmen do. For example:
1. Since teachers work with children all day, they need no children of their own and are thus spared the expense of raising a family.
2. Teachers must spend their evenings grading papers and thus can't watch TV. So they are spared the cost of buying that item.
3. Teachers, apparently being radicals, are addicted to cheap foreign cars and thus need little money for transportation.
4. Since teachers must spend their vacation time preparing lesson plans for the future, they don't need vacation money.

[Eight more such reasons followed.]
Thus I believe I have clearly demonstrated that teachers not only don't need a raise but could get along nicely with smaller salaries.

Well, for weeks letters — many from teachers — poured into the paper berating the writer of the letter for being so antiteacher. A few letters tried to tell the paper's readers that the letter was just ironical and really supported raises for teachers, but most people remained irate. The writer of the letter, enjoying his success, then wrote another to the effect that night-school classes for older people were a waste of money, citing such reasons as that the old people would be dead soon anyway and their education thus wasted. Again, failure to detect irony brought blasts from the literal-minded public. The writer finally ended his private literary party by writing a letter commending the high quality of the letters that berated him — quoting only the most illiterate sentences that had appeared in the letters. The lesson here is that even blatant irony is often misunderstood by those without a good deal of reading experience.

Serious literature often makes use of ironical language (as well as irony of incident), and detecting little ironical touches often greatly increases one's enjoyment of a piece of literature. We will give just one example. The great American poet E. A. Robinson's "Mr. Flood's Party" is about a man who has outlived his time and is completely friendless because all of his former friends are now dead. Here is the first stanza of the poem:

> Old Eben Flood, climbing alone one night
> Over the hill between the town below
> And the forsaken upland hermitage
> That held as much as he should ever know
> On earth again of home, paused warily.
> The road was his with not a native near;
> And Eben, having leisure, said aloud,
> For no man else in Tilbury Town to hear:

Do you detect the delectable bit of irony that improves an excellent poem otherwise without irony of language? It is the phrase *having leisure*. The point is that old Mr. Flood has nothing but leisure, and thus the poet's speaking as though Mr. Flood just happens to have a moment of leisure is ironical. Understanding such irony is not only a sign of a mature reader but also increases the reader's pleasure.

Satire is language that ridicules, usually with sharp wit or derision or mock soberness, what the writer considers to be the foolishness, wrongheadedness, or wickedness of some individual or group. The sharp wit and derision are important. For example, an article that seriously in flat tones attacks a politician or political policy is not satire but just condemnation, debate, or vilification. To be satire, a passage of language must jibe or ridicule with some kind of nonliteral use of language. We are entering a brief discussion of satire in this chapter on irony because a large proportion of satire makes use of irony, and some satire is all irony, though some is not ironical at all.

As a first example of satire, we will quote a passage in which there is not any irony of language. In his later life Mark Twain, who had become anti-religious, wrote a series called *Letters from Earth*, which satirize man in general. The letters are written by Satan to the Archangels Michael and Gabriel, telling them of man's follies. Here is a passage from Letter II:

1. First of all, I recall to your attention the extraordinary fact with which I began. To wit, that the human being, like the immortals, naturally places

sexual intercourse far and away above all other joys — yet he has left it out of his heaven! The very thought of it excites him; opportunity sets him wild; in this state he will risk life, reputation, everything — even his queer heaven itself — to make good that opportunity and ride it to the overwhelming climax. From youth to middle age all men and all women prize copulation above all other pleasures combined; yet it is actually as I have said: it is not in their heaven; prayer takes its place. . . .

2. In man's heaven *everybody sings!* The man who did not sing on earth sings there; the man who could not sing on earth is able to do it there. This universal singing is not casual, not occasional, not relieved by intervals of quiet; it goes on, all day long, and every day, during a stretch of twelve hours. And *everybody stays*; whereas in the earth the place would be empty in two hours. The singing is of hymns alone. Nay, it is of *one* hymn alone. The words are always the same, in number they are only about a dozen, there is no rhyme, there is no poetry: Hosannah, hosannah, hosannah, Lord God of Sabaoth, 'rah; 'rah! siss! — boom! . . . a-a-ah!''

Irony of language is absent in this satire because there are no sentences the true meaning of which is the opposite of the literal meaning. Irony of incident, however, is present because Mark Twain is saying that man has invented for himself a heaven the opposite of what he could normally be expected to invent.

The master writer of ironical satire in English was Jonathan Swift. His "Modest Proposal" has baffled or enraged countless students because they did not detect the irony. Swift seriously wanted to improve the status of the hapless Irish but knew that just a serious plea would have no effect. Therefore he made his "Modest Proposal." He begins with a discussion of the plight of the poor Irish, but drops hints of bland irony from the beginning. He says the Irish need to "find out a fair, cheap, and easy method of making [their] children sound, useful members of the commonwealth." Then, after more subtle ironical clues, he drops his bombshell:

I shall now therefore humbly propose my own thoughts, which I hope will not be liable to the least objection.

I have been assured by a very knowing American of my acquaintance in London, that a young healthy child well nursed is at a year old a most delicious, nourishing, and wholesome food, whether stewed, roasted, baked or boiled; and I make no doubt that it will equally serve in a fricassee or a ragout.

Then Swift continues blandly to give statistics as to how many infants can be sold for food and how many kept for breeding stock, to explain how gourmets will be pleased, and so on. Then he ends in this way:

I profess, in the sincerity of my heart, that I have not the least personal interest in endeavoring to promote this necessary work, having no other motive than the public good of my country, by advancing our trade, providing for infants, relieving the poor, and giving some pleasure to the rich. I have no children by which I can propose to get a single penny, the youngest being nine years old, and my wife past childbearing.

The ironical effect, especially since the irony is so bland, is absolutely devastating, and the satire is of the highest order. With this and some other satiric pieces, Swift did bring about an improvement in the status of the Irish, who were being bled white by the English colony masters.

EXERCISES

1. In your college library (or elsewhere) find a copy of Jonathan Swift's "Argument Against Abolishing Christianity in England" and find instances of ironical satire in the first page.
2. Since the 1960's the columnist Art Buchwald, whose work appears in newspapers throughout the country, has been famous for his satiric and ironic articles on issues of the day. Find a column by Buchwald and note instances of satire and irony in it.
3. Think of some weakness in your college's operations and explain how a piece of ironic satire about it might bring about an improvement.

USAGE
LESSON
22

SHIFTS
IN
TENSE

Tense in grammar is the information in a verb form that indicates time of occurrence. Tense as a whole is enormously complex in English, and many of the names given to tenses are inaccurate. For example, in

Brad goes by Brock's on his way to work,

goes is called the simple present tense, but obviously in the sentence it refers to both past and future times of occurrence and not necessarily to the immediate present at all (Brad might be on vacation when the sentence is spoken). But in considering **improper** or **inconsistent shifts in tense** we need only concern ourselves with past and present tenses and need not differentiate between varieties of those.

An inconsistent shift in tense, and resulting poor style, occurs when a writer begins an account of some past action in the past tense and then improperly shifts to the present tense, or vice versa. Example:

> *wrong:* At the beginning of the novel Flem Snopes *was* very poor, but he *uses* all the dirty tricks he can and soon *is* well off.

The shift from the past-tense *was* to the present-tense *uses* and *is* is inconsistent and would cause a negative reaction in an alert reader.

The reason inconsistent shifts in tense are fairly common is that in English we can talk about the past — as in summarizing the plot of a novel or discussing an historical event — in either the past tense or in the so-called **historical present tense.** Example:

> *correct:* By 1570 Queen Elizabeth I *was* in solid control of her government but *knew* that she *would* always have to remain alert and occasionally execute opponents.

correct: By 1570 Queen Elizabeth I *is* in solid control of her government but *knows* that she *will* always have to remain alert and occasionally execute opponents.

Though the first sentence is in the past tense and the second in the historical present, the two are identical in meaning, because writers and speakers of English commonly use either tense to summarize the past. Since both modes of expression are commonly used, some writers fail to see that they inconsistently shift from one to the other. The error seldom misleads anyone, but it does annoy experienced readers. To avoid inconsistent shifts in tense, almost all writers must be careful when they compose long passages summarizing periods of history or pieces of fiction.

Here are some other examples of improper shifts in tense:

wrong: The Civil War *is* in its third year. General Lee *is* still somewhat confident, but he *began* to see that without supplies the Confederates *could* not win. He *called* a summit meeting. (*Begins, can,* and *calls* would be proper; or *was* and *was* would be proper.)

wrong: By the middle of the novel Eugene *was* a gangling teenager. He *went* off to college, where he *begins* to develop a great interest in writing. He *sees* the future he *wants*. (*Began, saw,* and *wanted* would be proper; or *is* and *goes* would be proper.)

Even experienced writers slip into this kind of inconsistency easily. Alertness and careful proofreading will assure consistency.

Sometimes a shift in tense is consistent and proper. Example:

correct: The great earthquake and fire of 1906 utterly *destroyed* San Francisco, but the city *was* rebuilt in a remarkably short time. We *know* now from seismological studies that another great earthquake in that area *is* almost certain to come before another century passes and maybe within a few years.

The shift from the past-tense *destroyed* and *was* to the present-tense *know* and *is* is not only proper but necessary, for, unlike the references in the example wrong sentences, the references of the past- and present-tense verbs in this sentence are completely different from each other.

EXERCISE 22.   Most of the following sentences have improper shifts in either tense or person or number. Strike out the words that produce inconsistency, and in the blanks below the sentences write in words that will produce consistency. Some sentences may be correct.

1. In Hawthorne's "Birthmark," Aylmer at first thinks Georgiana is perfect, but then he began to let her tiny birthmark keep him upset.

   _____

2. Everybody did their share of the work.

   _____

3. A person's responsibility to God comes first. You fulfill your responsibility to man next.

   _____

4. At the beginning of 1713 Queen Anne is thoroughly under the domination of the Tories, but before her death in 1714 she foresaw that the Whigs would quickly regain power.

   _____

5. Nobody does their best all the time. Sometimes you just feel like letting things slide.

   _____

6. A forest ranger's job is pleasant, but if you plan to go into that line of work you should be sure you like to live close to nature.

   _____

7. At the beginning of the story old Scrooge is as stingy as they come, but by the end he was a generous Christian.

   _____

8. A drug addict doesn't like their kind of life, but you get caught up in the scene and they can seldom break the habit.

   _____

9. It is 1779. Washington seems unable to make progress in any of his campaigns. But soon breaks came his way and by 1781 he had the Revolution won.

   _____

10. Why should a contest winner report their winnings when the income tax people don't know about it?

    _____

11. Thoreau was clearly a radical, but when we study Emerson's life carefully we find that he is not nearly so radical as he pretends to be.

    _____

12. Today a man likes their wife to be feminine but they also want them to have the same opportunities as men.

    _____

13. The ancient mariner is at first condemned for killing the albatross, but when the ship began to move northward, the sailors forgave him. Later he is condemned again for shooting the albatross.

    _____

14. Doesn't anybody know their part in the play? A good actor seldom forgets their lines.

    _____

15. A lawyer must pass the bar exam in order to practice law, but you do such things as being marriage counselors if you fail the bar exam.

    _____

16. A person should establish regular social habits just as they do work habits, for your social life is as important as your work life.

    _____

17. In the story Jonathan pretends to be an undercover agent, but everybody knew he was just faking.

    _____

18. A medical doctor's work is hard, but if you decide to enter that profession you can count on a high income.

    _____

19. A medical doctor's work is hard, but they make a high income.

    _____

20. Lincoln was deliberating about Sherman's military advances when General McClellan comes storming in to complain.

    _____

CHAPTER
23
FIGURES
OF
SPEECH
AND
SYMBOLS

Irony is only one variety of nonliteral language; in other ways we use language so that our true or complete meaning is not what the words literally say on the surface. One large area of such language use is called **figurative language** or **figures of speech.** Classical rhetoricians (scholars of long ago who studied the nature of language usage) identified about 250 different figures of speech, many of them being mere oddities in the use of language but the most important of them requiring the reader (or listener) to make some sort of transfer of meaning in his mind as he reads the nonliteral passage. In other words, the most common figures of speech seem to say one thing on the surface but actually convey another meaning. The user of a figure of speech, then, tells a literal untruth in order to express a truth or idea beneath the surface or literal meaning of the language.

As an example of the mere oddities of language usage that rhetoricians classified as figures of speech we will choose the **oxymoron,** which is the use of contradictory terms in a single phrase, such as "a mournful optimist." Many writers have delighted in creating oxymorons, occasionally with signicant meaning. For example, Shakespeare, who apparently amused himself by playing with language even in serious passages of his plays, occasionally created oxymorons. In *Romeo and Juliet,* for instance, he has Romeo, who is woe-striken, say

> O brawling love! O loving hate! . . . .
> O heavy lightness: serious vanity!
> Misshapen chaos of well-seeming forms!

Feather of lead, bright smoke, cold fire, sick health!
Still-waking sleep . . . .

Piling up ten oxymorons in one passage was just a virtuoso performance by Shakespeare, who probably chuckled over his out-doing his contemporaries.

As an example of one of the less frequently-used figures of speech that require a transfer of meaning in the reader or hearer's mind, we will choose **synecdoche** (pronounced see-*neck*-duh-key), in which a part of an object is used to mean the whole object, or vice versa. Here are some examples:

Has Mike got *wheels?* (meaning a car or motorcycle)
Look at that *skirt!* (meaning a fully-clothed girl)
I'm running 200 *head* on my ranch this year. (meaning whole cattle)
Well, here comes the *army.* (meaning one soldier)
Can you spare your *wallet?* (meaning some money from your wallet)

In the first three examples, each italicized word is a part used to mean the whole, and in the last two, each italicized word is a whole used to mean just a part. Many infrequently-used and seldom-noted figures such as oxymorons and synecdoches occur in our language. Sometimes, apparently new ones occur, such as Sam Goldwyn's famous line, "An oral agreement isn't worth the paper it's written on," which can only be called a Goldwynism.

But by far the most important and common kind of figurative language is called **metaphoric,** which includes the two figures of speech known as **metaphors** and **similes.** Metaphoric figures directly identify two dissimilar things as being the same or express a comparison between two unlike things. But there is always some supposed (that is, figurative and not literal) similarity between the two, and the reader's mind perceives that supposed similarity, makes a transfer of meaning, and understands the figurative truth or idea the writer is expressing. For example, consider the common expression "He is hard as nails," which is usually applied to a person's will or determination to be unyielding. Now literally an aspect of an individual's personality cannot be as hard as nails; in fact, it can have neither physical hardness nor softness. Yet our minds perceive a kind of similarity between the hard steel of nails and the unyielding determination of a strong-willed person. Thus our minds make a transfer of meaning and the expression becomes metaphorically meaningful.

The difference between a simile and a metaphor as figures of speech is merely technical and unimportant. A simile makes the comparison between the two essentially dissimilar things with the use of a comparative word, such as *like* or *more than.* Here are some examples of similes:

Thou [West Wind], from whose unseen presence the leaves dead
Are driven, like ghosts from an enchanter fleeing . . . .
— *Shelley*

I wandered lonely as a cloud . . . .

— Wordsworth

How like a winter hath my absence been
From thee . . . .

— Shakespeare

Sin, like a barn fowl, comes home to roost.

— proverbial

The comparative words *like* and *as* make these figures of speech similes, though their language may be called metaphoric. In the similes, leaves are compared to ghosts, a person's loneliness to the loneliness of a cloud, a person's absence to a winter, and sin to a barn fowl. These things are of course in reality not at all alike, though a kind of similarity between them is perceivable to the human mind. However, when such a comparative word as *like* or *as* is used to compare things which really are very similar, no figure of speech is created. For example, in

Julie's eyes are as blue as her mother's,

no simile is created, for the comparison is literal.

The figure of speech known as a metaphor directly identifies one thing as another without the use of a comparative word. The two things, of course, are usually completely different but have a suggestion of similarity so that the reader's mind can make a transfer of meaning and understand the idea the writer wishes to convey. Here is a famous passage of metaphors, spoken by Macbeth when he hears that Lady Macbeth is dead:

> She would have died hereafter . . . .
>   Out, out, brief candle!
> Life's but a walking shadow, a poor player
> That struts and frets his hour upon the stage
> And then is heard no more: it is a tale
> Told by an idiot, full of sound and fury,
> Signifying nothing.
>
> — Shakespeare

Shakespeare directly identifies life as a briefly burning candle, a walking shadow, a performing actor, and a tale told by an idiot. Life is none of these things, but the suggestive correspondence between life and each of the phrases is such that the reader gets a meaningful and powerful message. To do so he must make a transfer of meaning in his mind from the literal to the figurative. Our language would be dull indeed if it did not provide for endless metaphors of this sort.

Language is also metaphoric when an object is described in a nonliteral way. Examples:

Ross told the *naked* truth.
Alberto has nerves *of steel*.
Cheri's mind is *clouded*.

In these examples two dissimilar things, such as life and a burning candle, are not identified as being the same; instead, *naked, of steel,* and *clouded* are adjectivals modifying *truth, nerves,* and *mind.* But since truth cannot literally be naked, and so on, the language is metaphoric.

Language is also metaphoric when something is said to behave in a way that is not literally possible. Example:

> Tomorrow, and tomorrow, and tomorrow,
> Creeps in this petty pace from day to day,
> To the last syllable of recorded time;
> And all our yesterdays have lighted fools
> The way to dusty death.
> — *Shakespeare*

Since tomorrow does not literally creep, the language is metaphoric, though one thing is not being directly identified as another, different thing. As a brief exercise, point out other instances of metaphoric language in this passage.

In spite of the large number of figures of speech that classical rhetoricians identified, it will be sufficient for us to mention and illustrate the four that, after metaphor, are most common in our language.

Hyperbole (pronounced hy-*per*-bo-lee) is a figure of exaggeration, telling more than the truth about size, number, or degree without intending to deceive. Example:

> And I will love thee still, my dear,
> Till a' the seas gang dry.
> — *Burns*

The poet exaggerated openly to make clear his point — his faithfulness in love. We cannot literally believe that the mortal poet will still be loving his mortal lover when all the seas on earth have gone dry.

Understatement — variously called meiosis (pronounced my-o-sis) and litotes (pronounced *lie*-tuh-teeze), terms which are not often used — tells less than the truth about size, number, or degree to emphasize a point. Example:

> . . . and yet thy [Milton's] heart
> The lowliest duties on herself did lay.
> — *Wordsworth*

Since Milton did not perform lowly duties but was the equivalent of secretary of state in Cromwell's regime, Wordsworth understated the situation greatly to achieve emphasis. He did not intend his readers to take him literally.

Personification is a figure that attributes human qualities to nonhuman objects or beings. Example:

> Wake, melancholy Mother, wake and weep!
> — *Shelley*

The Mother in the line is the muse of astronomy, with human qualities being attributed to her in the words *melancholy*, *Mother*, *wake*, and *weep*. The meaning is thus figurative, not literal.

Metonymy (pronounced muh-*tahn*-uh-me) is a figure in which something or someone is called by the name of something associated with or suggested by it rather than by its own name. Examples:

> His campaign was overshadowed by headlines about "gas prices going up, milk prices going up, half the White House indicted."
> — quoted in *Time*

> The Oval Room was alleged to be the source of the order to "get" Ellsberg.
> —The Los Angeles *Times*

In these examples, *White House* means the officials in the White House, and *Oval Room* (the president's main office) means the president himself. No reader would believe the writers literally meant the physical White House and Oval Room. Such use of metonymy often has a certain euphemistic quality; that is, the reporter who wrote the second example was perhaps happy not to have to use the president's name itself.

A **symbol** is anything, such as a letter of the alphabet, that represents something else (a speech sound in the case of the letter of the alphabet). In language, particularly in imaginative literature, symbols as words or phrases are often used to suggest a nonliteral meaning additional to the literal meaning, or a meaning entirely different from the literal meaning of the word or phrase. Like irony, symbolism has something of the nature of figurative language, for a transfer of meaning from the literal to the nonliteral must take place in the reader's mind if he is to understand the writer's intended meaning. Symbols enrich literary language. Here is an example:

> My mother bore me in the southern wild,
> And I am black, but O! my soul is *white*;
> White as an angel is the English child:
> But I am black as if bereaved of *light*.
> — *Blake*

A reader of this first stanza of "The Little Black Boy," written in 1789, badly misunderstands the poet if he thinks the word *white* is being used to indicate that being white is more desirable than being black. Instead, Blake is using *white* and *light* as symbols of Christian innocence and purity and of God's love for all mankind. The words carry some literal meaning, but an understanding of their symbolic significance is necessary for a full understanding of the poem.

Sometimes literary symbols seem to bear little relationship to the meaning they are supposed to convey. For example, here is the opening of a poem entitled "Gerontion":

> Here I am, an old man in a *dry* month,
> Being read to by a boy, waiting for *rain*.
> — *Eliot*

The poet intends the word *dry* to be a symbol meaning lack of virility and the word *rain* to be a symbol of fertility or virility. In other words, the old man is waiting for his sexual powers to return. But unless a reader, no matter how intelligent, has been told about these symbolic meanings, he is quite unlikely to understand the writer's intent. Some readers love literature with such obscure symbolism; others care little for it. These latter generally feel that unless the symbolic words or phrases also carry some literal meaning which is enriched by the symbolic meaning, symbols are of little interest or value. You will, of course, develop your own attitude toward literary symbolism, but now you at least know basically what it is.

EXERCISES

1. In the following soliloquy from *Hamlet*, the usurping king speculates on his crime of killing his brother, the previous king. Identify as many figures of speech in it as you can.

> O, my offence is rank, it smells to heaven;
> It hath the primal eldest curse upon't,
> A brother's murder! Pray can I not,
> Though inclination be as sharp as will;
> My stronger guilt defeats my strong intent,
> And, like a man to double business bound,
> I stand in pause where I shall first begin,
> And both neglect. What if this cursed hand
> Were thicker than itself with brother's blood,
> Is there not rain enough in the sweet heavens
> To wash it white as snow?

2. The following poem was published by A.E. Housman in 1896. Explain as well as you can its use of figurative language. You should identify an instance of hyperbole in it.

> Think no more, lad; laugh, be jolly:
>   Why should men make haste to die?
> Empty heads and tongues a-talking
> Make the rough road easy walking,
> And the feather pate of folly
>   Bears the falling sky.
>
> Oh, 'tis jesting, dancing, drinking
>   Spins the heavy world around.
> If young hearts were not so clever,
> Oh, they would be young for ever:
> Think no more; 'tis only thinking
>   Lays lads underground.

3. Try to create a figure of speech to express the literal language in each of the following situations. For example, a situation might be "trying to understand a disorganized teacher" and you might say, "Trying to follow Professor Snerd's lectures is like searching for the bathroom in a strange house in complete darkness."
   a. standing in a long registration line
   b. taking a test without being prepared for it
   c. going on a blind date with someone who is a social drag
   d. describing a student who is trying to flatter a teacher
   e. blundering into the wrong restroom

4. In his poem "Credo" the American poet E. A. Robinson expresses his inability to find any meaning in life or in the universe. With that information to go on, explain how symbols are used in these opening lines of the poem:

> I cannot find my way: there is no star
> In all the shrouded heavens anywhere;
> And there is not a whisper in the air
> of any living voice . . . .

USAGE
LESSON
23

SHIFTS
IN
VOICE

In grammar, the verb of a sentence (or the whole sentence) is said to be in the **active voice** if the subject performs the action expressed in the verb. Example:

A cold wind buffeted the cavorting nude.

As the subject, *a cold wind* is performing the action expressed in the verb *buffeted*. The verb of a sentence (or the whole sentence) is said to be in the **passive voice** if the subject receives the action expressed in the verb. Example:

The cavorting nude was buffeted by a cold wind.

As the subject, *the cavorting nude* is receiving the action expressed in the verb *was buffeted*. In the passive voice, a *by* phrase is always expressed or understood, and the object of *by* (even if the prepositional phrase is omitted) performs the action expressed in the verb.[1]

Generally, good writers use the passive voice only when the doer of the action is unknown or unimportant or when they want to put the receiver of the action in the conspicuous subject position and the doer of the action in the less conspicuous *by* phrase. Examples:

The victim had been decapitated.
The president was relentlessly pursued by the reporters.

---

[1] Some verbs (or sentences) do not have voice because they express no action. Example: *Toby is off the strong stuff.* Such a sentence cannot be made passive with a *by* phrase and thus does not have voice.

In the first sentence, who did the decapitating is unknown and so the *by* phrase is suppressed. In the second, the writer wanted to focus more attention on the president than on the reporters and thus used the passive voice with the doer of the action named in the *by* phrase. When good writers do not have one of these reasons for using the passive voice, they generally use the active voice, for it usually produces a stronger sentence. For example, the middle clause of the preceding sentence, if it were written

the active voice is generally used by them,

would be stylistically weak. And that brings us to our lesson — inconsistent and awkward **shifts in voice.**

As in shifts in number, person, and tense, inconsistentcy is the culprit in improper shifts in voice. Here are two examples of the faulty shifts, with corrections:

poor style: Something *warned* me that our trip would not be successful, and some kind of unfortunate occurrence *was experienced* by each of us.

    correct: Something *warned* me that our trip would not be successful, and each of us *experienced* some kind of unfortunate occurrence.

poor style: And last, you *must teach* children about sex so that it *will not be learned* by them in the streets.

    correct: And last, you *must teach* children about sex so they *will not learn* about it in the streets.

In each example of poor style, the writer began properly with the active voice but then inconsistently shifted to the passive voice.

The reason such inconsistent shifts are rather common is that English often allows us to say exactly the same thing in either the active or the passive voice. Examples:

    correct: The cheerleaders boosted the morale of the players.

    correct: The morale of the players was boosted by the cheerleaders.

There is no difference in meaning between the two sentences, the first being in the active voice and the second in the passive. Since both modes of expression are common in our language, careless writers sometimes weaken their style by inconsistently shifting voice. (You might note that a passive-voice verb form always has a form of *to be* as an auxiliary: *was shot, is praised, had been robbed,* and so on. Also in a passive-voice sentence a *by* phrase naming the doer of the action is always grammatically possible, though often suppressed.)

Sometimes a shift in voice is proper and not inconsistent. Example:

    correct: At last the police *discovered* the mobster's corpse, which *had been mutilated* with an ax.

The reason that the shift from the active-voice *discovered* to the passive-voice *had been mutilated* is proper here is that two different doers of action are involved, and since the latter (the one who did the mutilating) is not known, a passive-voice verb with the *by* phrase suppressed creates the best style.

Inconsistency in shift of voice usually occurs when the doer of two actions is the same, but is the subject in one clause and the object of the preposition *by* in a following clause. Example:

poor style: Parents *should* not only *provide* a suitable home for their children, but the children *should be loved* by them too.

correct: Parents *should* not only *provide* a suitable home for their children but *should love* them too.

Since the parents are doing both the providing and the loving, the two verbs should, for consistency, be in the same voice, preferably the active.

EXERCISE 23. All of the following sentences have inconsistent shifts in either voice, number, person, or tense. Strike out words that produce inconsistent shifts, and in the blanks below the sentences write in words that will produce consistency. In the case of inconsistent shifts in voice, you should indicate the subject and verb needed to produce consistency.

1. The streaker paused a second, and the gaping on-lookers ~~were jeered at by him.~~ *pointed at him*

   _____

2. A student should have ~~their~~ *his* share of social life and not let studies dominate them entirely.

   _____

3. A freshman is usually scared during the first few weeks, but soon ~~you learn there is nothing to fear.~~ *mostly* *you can relax.*

   _____

4. Policemen are taught to be courteous to those they arrest, but sometimes those arrested are treated discourteously by them.

   _____

5. The story opens as Julio is plotting his escape. Several of his attempts fail, ~~and~~ *but* then he ~~seemed to give up.~~ *succeeded.*

   _____

6 The Pioneers made a tremendous comeback in the second half; ~~and they game was won by them by two points.~~ *however,* *lost the game* *by two points.*

   _____

7. Why will a woman who vocally supports the Women's Lib not give ~~any of their time working for it?~~ *to* ~~any~~ *work for it?*

   _____

8. The houses were not damaged by the storm, but it left flooded areas and impassable streets.

   _____

9. The repairman spent twenty minutes working on the washer, but then it was just left unplugged by him without any of us knowing of that bit of stupidity.

   _____

10. We are leaving for college soon, and a lot of decisions must be made.

_____

11. Nobody raised their hand when volunteers were asked for by the professor.

_____

12. I have just got out of the hospital, and there are a thousand things to do.

_____

13. When a family stays together, life is enjoyed by them more than if they split up.

_____

14. A person has to decide how to provide for themselves; you can't always lean on someone else.

_____

15. The wind blew strongly, and our shutters were rattled by it until we thought they would surely blow off.

_____

16. Don't make fun of someone else's handicap; instead, one should show compassion for the suffering of others.

_____

17. The bear rushed the hunter, and he was somewhat mauled by the bear.

_____

18. As President Harding is attending to the girls who slipped into the White House by the back way, some members of his cabinet are secretly meeting. They decided they could trust Harding not to find out about their schemes.

_____

19. Nobody is better than their own opinion of themselves.

_____

20. A young sudent is usually not capable of much independent study; you need a well-informed teacher to guide you constantly.

_____

CHAPTER 24

FUN WITH LANGUAGE: AMBIGUITIES, PUNS, SPOONERISMS, AND PARODIES

Learning to use your native language well is a serious matter, for our civilization grows more and more verbally oriented. Even if that were not true, language would still be all-important because human beings use it to perpetuate their cultures, even when those cultures do not change. But there is also a light side to language, and in many ways we have fun with it. Taking delight in language begins in early childhood, with children hardly yet able to read or write creating new "lyrics" for metrical and rhyme patterns they learn at an early age. For example, in the now dim past the children of a certain neighborhood for a time took great delight in shouting at certain cars the metrical phrase "STUDEBAKER! STUDEBAKER! STINK, STINK, STINK!" They had earlier used the same metrical pattern for other phrases that intrigued them. As a matter of fact, one doctoral dissertation at UCLA is a collection of and commentary on the metrical patterns and words of young children's joyful shouting-singing creations.

Adults, too, take delight in playing with language in various ways. For example, the great Jonathan Swift, one of the most learned and dignified writers in London from 1710 to 1714, created a playful "little language" which he used in letters to two women in Ireland whom he supported. Some people even go so far as to give their children ridiculous names, just, apparently, because they think they are funny. For example, a couple with the last name Hogg actually named their twin daughters Ima and Ura. Another couple with the last name First named a son Safety. When he became an adult he thought about legally changing his name but then decided that, since he had so much fun when traffic officers and other such people stopped him, he would continue to answer "Safety First" when asked his name. The same family had a daughter named June. And a lady who married a man with the last name Sippy kept his name when she divorced him because she wanted to be known as Mrs. Sippy.

An **ambiguity** is a passage of language that has two possible meanings, and often the reader or listener cannot be sure which meaning the writer or speaker intends. Sometimes ambiguities — usually when they are deliberate — are humorous and good not only for a laugh but also for an interesting discussion of why the language is ambiguous. For example, consider this question:

How would you like to see a model home?

The grammatical explanation of the ambiguity is rather complex: If the meaning is to see a new house, then *see* has its normal meaning and *model home* is a compound noun functioning as the direct object of *see*. But if the meaning is to escort a lady to her home, *see* takes on the meaning of *escort, model* is the direct object of *see*, and *home* is a noun functioning as an adverbial modifying *see*. Few people can understand that explanation, but everyone can enjoy the humor of the ambiguity.

Here is another example, with the ambiguity being only potential but with humor involved nevertheless. You make two sentences using each of of the verbs in parentheses and see whether you can explain why the meanings are different and why there is humor of ambiguity.

Bathing beauties _____ fun.
(is *or* are?)

The ambiguity would be real rather than just potential if such a verb form as *can be* were used, though in speech one's tone of voice would divulge his his meaning.

Ambiguities can also be produced by one's manipulation of the tone of his voice. Here is one such vocal ambiguity that is so old that it may be new to you. Someone asks this question:

What is that down the road (*pause*) ahead?

In addition to the pause (called *juncture*), the pitch of the speaker's voice also rises at the end of the question to produce the effect he wants. As is the case with much of the playing with language we do (especially with puns), most hearers of this intonational ambiguity would hoot in derision while probably enjoying the humor.

Humorous ambiguities occur in various other forms. Advertising copy-writers, for example, love to lace their ads with ambiguities in order to attract the readers' attention. Here is an example that appeared in magazines for some months:

People who drink Old Fitzgerald don't know any better.

And here is one from a TV ad for dandruff shampoo:

Don't wait until you're itching to get at it.

The grammatical explanations of these ambiguiies are quite complex. In other cases the grammatical explanation may be simple. For example, a man named Joe once established a shop for repairing automobile bodies. At his place of business he put up a large sign reading

JOE'S BODY WORKS

Also a man with the last name Child started a company manufacturing bearings for motors. Naturally he called his company The Child Bearing Company. Our language seems to have an infinite capacity for the creation of humorous ambiguities.

A **pun** is usually defined as "a play on words," but various manipulations of language produce puns. Perhaps the most common source of puns is the substitution of one *phoneme* (a speech sound) for another, with the resulting phrase having some sort of meaning. Examples:

Many people cringe when they are forced to hear a pun. Thus someone who hears puns where he works has cringe benefits.

During the time of the college fad of streaking, a student ran naked through the House of Representatives in Lansing, Michigan. He wanted to be the Streaker of the House.

Just the substitution of a *k* sound (spelled *c*) for *f* and of a *t* for *p* produces these puns, which no doubt make groan men.

Sometimes the substitution of a *homophone* (a word pronounced like but spelled differently from another) produces a pun. Examples:

A new building designed to house optometrists' offices is under construction. Obviously, it will be a site for sore eyes.

"The Duke of Buckingham is dying. He has no heir."
"No air? No wonder he's dying."

English has hundreds of homophones such as *site, sight,* and *cite,* which provide rich ore for the punning minor (as well as adult).

Sometimes just a close resemblance of sounds produces a pun. Examples:

A Czechoslovakian in trouble with the Communist authorities was fleeing from policemen. He ran into a shop and asked the shopkeeper, "Can you cache a Czech?"

A woman planted some fronds and anemones for a spring garden party, but only the fronds came up. Her friends consoled her by saying, "With fronds like these, who needs anemones?"

Puns of this sort are often as much visual as they are aural and thus are best printed.

Sometimes puns are produced by a reversal of words in a well-known phrase or sentence. Examples:

A chiropractor examined a pretty girl's sore elbow and asked, "What's a joint like this doing in a pretty girl like you?"

The great Walt Kelly, originator of *Pogo*, went to elaborate lengths to produce this pun: Some of the denizens of the Okefenokee Swamp found Georgia on a map of the USSR and concluded that the Communists had stolen the Georgia of the USA. A bear dressed as a Santa Claus began to worry that they had stolen his native Virginia too. Eventually the other characters assured the bear, "Yes, Santa Claus, there is a Virginia."

Kelly was punning on the famous editorial of some decades ago that began, "Yes, Virginia, there is a Santa Claus," after a little girl named Virginia had written the columnist asking if there really was a Santa Claus.

Finally, some puns depend on seeing an unexpected meaning in an ordinary word. Here are a few original examples:

debater:	"a clever fish"
desire:	"to kill one's father"
deceit:	"to defeat a candidate up for re-election"
discontent:	"to empty a bottle"
exceed:	"a sprouting plant"
exit:	"a cat whose sex has been determined"
promote:	"a medieval swimming pool for professionals"
remember:	"to put on an artificial limb"
submit:	"a second-string catcher's glove"
uncanny:	"without a bathroom"
unstable:	"to evict a horse"

The pun is often called the lowest form of humor, and most people groan when they hear one. Yet every day countless people enjoy this phenomenon of language.

A **spoonerism** results from a transposition of speech sounds in a phrase or sentence, as in

Let me sew you to your sheet.

for

> Let me show you to your seat.

Here the sounds *s* and *sh* (which is a single sound) are transposed. This speech phenomenon is named after William A. Spooner, an English clergyman who unintentionally sprinkled his sermons with such slips of language as

> As I look out over these beery wenches,

when he meant weary benches.

Here are some more examples of spoonerisms:

spoken about stock market losses:	I was dealt a blushing crow.
spoken to farmers:	You noble tons of soil. . . .
spoken to a student:	You have hissed all my mystery lectures.
spoken to a student:	You have tasted the whole worm.
spoken in church:	Sir, you are occupewing my pie.
a reference to Queen Victoria:	The queer old dean. . . .
spoken at a lively party:	We have a hem of a ghost.
spoken at a cycle repair shop:	Thats a well-boiled icicle.
order given in a restaurant:	I'll have a stare rake and wed rine.
shopowner to sign painter:	I want it to read "Leer, Bine, and Wicker Sold Here."

Most spoonerisms are, of course, unintentional (countless teachers have experienced such language slips in class, such as saying Kyron, Belly, and Sheets for Byron, Shelley, and Keats), but an imaginative person can create them for the amusement of his friends.

A **parody** is an imitation of a literary work or of an author's general style which exaggerates or mimics certain characteristics of the work or the author's style with ridicule as its intention. Many readers greatly enjoy parodies, even, sometimes, when they like the work or author being parodied. Our first illustration is just a part of a parody of Edgar Allan Poe's "The Raven." First, here are the opening stanzas of the poem:

> Once upon a midnight dreary, while I pondered, weak and weary,
> Over many a quaint and curious volume of forgotten lore,
> While I nodded, nearly napping, suddenly there came a tapping,
> As of someone gently rapping, rapping at my chamber door.
> " 'Tis some visitor," I muttered, "tapping at my chamber door —
> Only this and nothing more."
>
> Ah, distinctly I remember it was in the bleak December,
> And each separate dying ember wrought its ghost upon the floor.
> Eagerly I wished the morrow — vainly I had sought to borrow
> From my books surcease of sorrow — sorrow for the lost Lenore —
> Nameless here for evermore.

The characteristics of the poem that the parodist ridicules are its singsong rhythm, its internal rhyme, its lavish use of alliteration and assonance, and its general romantic trappings. Here is the first part of the parody:

RAVIN'S OF PIUTE POET POE

Once upon a midnight dreary, eerie, scary,
I was wary, I was weary, full of worry, thinking of my lost Lenore,
Of my cheery, airy, faery, fiery Dearie — (Nothing more).
I was napping, when a tapping on the overlapping coping, woke me grapping,
    yapping, groping . . . towards the rapping. I went hopping, leaping, . . .
    hoping that the rapping on the coping
Was my little lost Lenore.
That on opening the shutter to admit the latter critter, in she'd flutter from the
    gutter with her bitter eyes a-glitter;
So I opened wide the door, what was there? The dark weir and the drear
    moor, — or I'm a liar — the dark mire, the drear moor, the mere door
    and nothing more!

— *C. L. Edson*

As in all parodies, the humor of this one, which can be enjoyed even by those who like Poe's poetry, lies in the exaggeration of some of the characteristics of the original.

The next example is a parody of T. S. Eliot's "Love Song of J. Alfred Prufrock" and also of certain literary critics who find arcane and esoteric symbolism in modern poetry. We do not have space to print the original, but your teacher will tell you something about Eliot's "Love Song of J. Alfred Prufrock" and "The Waste Land" and also something about the obscurity of the poetry of Wallace Stevens.

THE LOVE SONG OF WALLACE STEVENS

Let us go then you and I
When the moon is spread over the sky
Like a mildewed cantaloupe[1] tossed in the garbage.

Let us go, nor hide our shame
That, like a flame,
Scorches the dust[2] that forms the cartilage

Of our souls. Oh, do not ask, "How soon?"
Let us go and rent a room.[3]

On the street the foxes meet,
Treat the fleet with gastric heat.

---

[1] In Abyssinian mythology, a symbol of the Earth Mother.
[2] Cf. *Antigone,* III, 62.
[3] See Basler, *Sex Symbolism in Literature.*

The grey-green bug[4] crawled jealously
Along the crinoline serpentine,
Ate the carrion callously,[5]
And joyfully stalked off the scene.

But you and I were at a trot;
I remembered, you forgot.[6]

But I have known the ayes already, known them all —
The ayes girls speak, the ayes that caused the fall,
Ayes hedged with noes too feebly whispered,
Transparent ayes, crossed with eglantine.[7]

I have known them all — *Anonymous*

[4] When crawling, a symbol of voracity.

[5] This beautiful image first appeared in Shakespeare's *Canterbury Tales*, Canto VI.

[6] The reader should ignore this deliberate attempt to confuse him.

[7] In oriental poetry, a symbol of infertility. Hence, this line refers to W. S.'s Narcissism, already hinted at in line six. So the meaning of the whole poem becomes clear.

EXERCISES

As an exercise for this chapter, create (or find) some humorous ambiguities, puns, spoonerisms, or parodies of your own, according to your teacher's directions.

USAGE
LESSON
24
COMPARATIVE
CONSTRUCTIONS

A **comparative construction** is of course one that compares two things. Three kinds of errors in the use of comparative constructions are rather common.

Pronoun Forms after *than* and *as*

A very common comparative construction in English is one that ends with *than* or *as* followed by a pronoun, and in such a sentence some writers are not sure whether to use the pronoun *I* or *me, he* or *him, they* or *them,* and so on. (When a noun follows *than* or *as,* there is no problem.) Example:

> Joe dated Fran more often than _____ .
> (I *or* me?)

Testing for the correct pronoun form in such a comparative construction is very easy, for a part of the sentence is almost always understood and not expressed. If you mentally supply the understood part, the correct pronoun form will be clear. Examples:

> *correct:* Joe dated Fran more often than *I* (dated Fran).
> *correct:* Joe dated Fran more often than (he dated) *me.*

As you can see, the pronoun form used can radically alter the meaning of some sentences, though in general readers are seldom misled even if the wrong pronoun form is used.

Here are other examples to show you how to choose proper pronoun forms in comparative constructions. The parts of the sentences in parentheses would normally be understood and not expressed, but mentally supplying them provides an easy test for choosing the correct pronoun form. All of these examples are correct:

Luis just isn't as nearly committed to the cause as *I* (am committed).
I'm sure I earn more money than *he* (earns).
George treats his pets better than (he treats) *me.*
George treats his pets better than *I* (treat my pets).
Nobody else is as ignorant about politics as *they* (are ignorant).

The test for the proper pronoun form is simple and seldom fails.

Omitted Comparative Words

One type of faulty comparative construction puts one of the two things being compared in both parts of the comparison through the omission of a comparative word and thus produces an illogical statement. Example:

wrong: Seagram's sells more whiskey than anybody.

Since the Seagram company is an "anybody" too, the sentence really says Seagram's sells more whisky than Seagram's, which is nonsense. Regardless of the penchant of advertising copy writers to omit comparative words, the careful writer will use the comparative words needed to make his sentences logical. Examples, with the comparative words in italics:

correct: Guido was caught with more contraband than anybody *else.*
correct: GM makes more cars than any *other* company.
correct: I'd rather live in Fort Hays than anywhere *else.*
correct: No *other* quarterback completed as many passes last year as our quarterback.

Note how illogical the sentences become if the words in italics are omitted.

Illogical Comparisons

Some writers occasionally write faulty sentences by comparing two things that cannot logically be compared. Example:

Durham's traffic is just like New York.

Now New York is a city and traffic is moving vehicles, and thus they can hardly be logically compared. The sentence should read

correct: Durham's traffic is just like New York's.

Now *traffic* is understood after *New York's* so that traffic in one city is compared with that in another — a logical comparison. Here are other examples of illogical comparisons:

wrong: I'm trying to find some scrimshaw just like the Eskimos. (*Eskimos'* is correct.)

wrong: This course is just as difficult as Harvard. (*Those given at Harvard* is correct.)

wrong: I like my beds to be firm just like the hotel. (*Hotel's* is correct.)

Even when he is not misled, an experienced reader is annoyed by such illogical comparisons.

EXERCISE 24. Most of the following sentences have faulty comparatve constructions. Strike out the words that cause the errors and write in the correct words in the blanks below the sentences. Or, if no word should be changed, write in the blanks any additional words needed to make proper comparative constructions. Some sentences may be correct.

1. I made some arrowheads just like the American Indian.

   _____

2. Nobody is as good at handball as Steve.

   _____

3. Nobody donated more of his time to the project than me.

   _____

4. Organized crime in Los Angeles is just like Chicago.

   _____

5. Did you make a higher score than her?

   _____

6. Did Bruce date Jane more than her?

   _____

7. We fly more people to Hawaii than anybody.

   _____

8. Did you find Hawaii like the Fiji Islanders?

   _____

9. Professor Snool praised Cheryl more than me.

   _____

10. José has a memory like an elephant.

   _____

11. I don't think anyone is more tolerant of junkies than me.

   _____

12. Our city dump stinks just like Milwaukee.

   _____

13. Who behaves in a Christian manner more than we?

   _____

14. Whom did Dean Harris insult more than me?

   _____

15. My bartender can mix more different kinds of drinks from memory than any bartender.

   _____

16. Don't pretend that you can chug-a-lug better than him.

   _____

17. No one brews beer as good as ours.

   _____

18. These admissions standards are just like Yale.

   _____

19. Who is as friendly to strangers as me?

   _____

20. No airline fles to as many cities as United.

   _____

PART THREE

COMPOSITION

CHAPTER 25

THE WRITER AND HIS READERS

Though there are innumerable kinds of writing — fiction, biography, history, poetry, textbooks, philosophical treatises, factual news reporting, editorializing, friendly letters, business letters, memos to superiors and subordinates, notes to the milkman, and on and on — some basics of composition apply to most kinds of good writing. In the chapters that follow we will explain and illustrate some of the most important basics. We necessarily must limit our discussions since this text is designed for a one-term course that also includes some study of logic, language, and usage; but the chapters that follow will give you a thorough grounding in the fundamentals of composition.

Though as noted above, writing occurs in manifold varieties, the classical rhetoricians mentioned in Chapter 23 (which you undoubtedly have not studied yet) classified writing and speech into only four **forms of discourse,** *discourse* meaning simply the expression of ideas. The first of the four forms of discourse is **narration,** or story-telling, either fictional or factual. This kind of writing involves characters passing through a series of events in a particular setting. Though we will not discuss narration, your teacher may at the beginning of your course have you write a theme of personal narrative, for that is the kind of writing students find easiest, and it can help them overcome their apprehension as they begin their composition course. The second form of discourse is **description,** which is writing that tells how something looks, sounds, feels, tastes, or smells. It is mostly used in narration to provide setting and help establish characterization.

Compositions of pure description may of course be written, but our text will not give separate analysis of that kind of writing, mostly because it, too, is an easy kind of writing for most students.

The third form of discourse is **exposition,** or **expository writing,** which is informative writing designed to explain or clarify facts and ideas. It is the kind of writing most often required of college students and of people holding jobs that require a college education. Its composition is usually difficult for most students. The fourth form of discourse is **persuasion,** the purpose of which is to induce readers to accept the opinions of the writer even though no proof of the validity of the opinions can be adduced — or even though there is no good reason at all to accept those opinions. Exposition, then, is intended to inform, persuasion to persuade. Sometimes the term **argumentation** is used instead of persuasion, but technical distinctions between the two lie beyond our course of study. (Chapters 20 and 21 deal somewhat with persuasion, though as a matter of language study and not specifically composition.)

Though there is much validity in the four-fold classification of the forms of discourse, in actuality most writing is an intricate mixture of all four, and the four terms are used mostly for convenience and not to set rigidly the boundaries of any piece of writing. For example, let's consider a business letter, a kind of writing you may be called upon to produce many times. Such a letter can easily involve all four forms of discourse — and those not in discrete units but in a mixture. The letter may state certain facts (exposition), urge its recipient to take a certain action (persuasion), narrate some events that led to its composition (narration), and describe a product the writer is concerned with (description). And so it is with most other kinds of writing. For example, you would be hard pressed to find an article of medium length in, say, a news magazine like *Time* that does not have some mixture of the forms of discourse.

We, however, will in the following chapters mostly limit ourselves to a discussion of some of the basics of exposition and persuasion, for those are the basics most useful to college students.

You may be, or may come to be, interested in imaginative writing — or creative writing, as it is often called. But to be a good college student and to function well in the workaday world you must be interested in the utility of writing. Though there obviously are exceptions, from the time a college graduate writes his first letter of application until he retires from his (obviously) important job, he will need to *use* writing, and the better he knows how to use it, the more likely he is to be successful. As the famous writer and former English teacher James Michener once wrote,

> The American who can write a competent sentence is rare. Those who can are in an enviable position, because if they also have something to say, they are sought for the finest jobs. . . . Their first business reports will probably be rushed right into the head office with the notation: "We've hired a genius!"

Actually, Michener also meant that the writer of a competent sentence must also know how to combine competent sentences effectively. But the sentence must come first. Let's consider just the sentence and your first letter of application. In it you want your sentences to be clear and effective, but some people even get advanced college degrees while still lacking the ability to write clear, effective sentences. For example, not long ago an applicant for a teaching position in a college English department opened his letter with this sentence:

This concerns a possible teaching position in composition or literature.

The department chairman immediately asked himself mentally, "What? Where? Who?" The sentence is so vague and indirect as to annoy anyone charged with finding a suitable employee. How much better it would have been for the writer to open his letter with such a direct and simple sentence as

I wish to apply for a position teaching composition or literature, or both, in your English department.

Or he might have been even more direct and effective if he had imitated another applicant, who opened his letter with this sentence:

I am a superior teacher who would like a job teaching any level English in your department.

The first applicant mentioned did not seem to realize that his letter *would have a reading audience* and that he should be very conscious of who that audience would be.

Writing clear, effective sentences is so important in composition that more illustrations like those above are in order. The first applicant referred to in the preceding paragraph also wrote the following sentence:

I coauthored the anthologies of poetry and fiction with the collaboration of James M. Coleman.

The chairman of course wondered whether Coleman collaborated with the applicant but not with his coauthor. The sentence is foolishly redundant. You may think that this discussion is mere nit-picking, but you can be sure that persons in a position to employ others are very aware of the quality of letters of application, especially since such letters presumably show the applicants at their best.

Another applicant for a similar (or the same) job opened his letter with this sentence:

You may be interested in the summary of studies in the humanities on the enclosed sheet.

The chairman at first thought that some sort of annotated bibliography was enclosed and that a pitch was being made to sell a book or journal of some sort. Only at the third or fourth sentence did he realize that the writer was applying for a job to teach composition and humanities. Even changing the phrasing of the opening sentence to "the summary of *my* studies in humanities" would have improved the sentence greatly. Again, the writer was not conscious enough of his reading audience.

So, you should think of the future *usefulness* to you of your study of composition and you should realize that the clarity and effectiveness of your writing will have a great bearing on its usefulness. You should also realize that your writing will have a reading audience and that you should suit your writing to its audience. What is appropriate for one reading audience may not be appropriate for another. For example, one of your business correspondents might want you to go into much detail, while another might want you to be brief.

In a composition course the student cannot easily get a feeling of writing for a particular audience, for he knows that his audience is merely his teacher, and that realization is unlikely to be inspiring. But if as a student you can *pretend* that you have a wider audience, and keep in mind the *usefulness* of writing, you may be surprised at how much a one-term course can do for you, even though your study is limited to a few basics.

EXERCISES

Following are some fabricated opening sentences of letters of application. Rewrite each to make it more direct and effective and to make it appeal to its probable reading audience. Remember that it is not wrong, nor is it in bad taste, to open a letter with the pronoun *I*.

1. *Letter applying for a job as a lab technician:* There may be a need for the kind of services I can perform.

2. *Letter applying for a job as a legal secretary:* The legal profession is fascinating, aside from knowing all the technicalities of secretarial work.

3. *Letter applying for a job as a law clerk:* With the bar exam passed, the time has come for entering the legal profession.

4. *Letter applying for a job as a pharmacist:* The attached data sheet shows the degree of pharmacological training.

5. *Letter applying for a job as a teacher's aide:* Experience in the classroom offers many advantages for service to your district.

USAGE
LESSON
25

COMMAS IN A SERIES AND IN COMPOUND SENTENCES

Proper punctuation of writing is a great aid to rapid reading and comprehension; conversely, incorrect punctuation hinders the reader, for it often makes him pause to think out the word relationship in a sentence. For example, this sentence appeared in a newspaper:

> The White House, which had earlier issued a denial did not respond to the senator's question.

The careless omission of a comma after *denial* probably caused many readers to stumble and reread the sentence, for an experiencd reader is used to assuming that a short passage of language has unity unless a mark of punctuation tells him that one unit has ended and another is beginning. In other words, a comma is needed after *denial* to show that *which had earlier issued a denial* has unity and is to be read rapidly without pausing, and that *did not respond* . . . is not a part of that unified construction but of another. (Unified constructions are of course sometimes interrupted with a construction that could be lifted out.)

Of course any reader can rather quickly understand the meaning of the above example sentence. It's just that the careless omission of the comma reduces his reading speed and annoys him. But punctuation can radically change the meaning of a sentence. First consider this sentence:

> Woman without her man is nothing.

It expresses one clear meaning. But without changing the words, add this punctuation:

> Woman — without her, man is nothing.

Now an entirely different meaning is clearly expressed. Note that the dash (or a colon but not a comma,) is necessary. Otherwise the sentence would read

Woman, without her, man is nothing.

the punctuation of which means that *without her* can be removed from the sentence and still leave some clear meaning (see Chapter 28). But

Woman man is nothing,

is meaningless.

Thus careful punctuation of sentences is always necessary to aid the experienced reader and to keep from annoying him, and it is sometimes necessary to establish the writer's desired meaning. Modern English punctuation is based on sentence structure, and thus the better one understands sentence structure, the more correctly he will punctuate his sentences.

The simplest rule of punctuation is **that commas are used to separate three or more similar sentence constituents in a series,** with a comma before the *and* that connects the last two constituents being optional. Examples:

> **After being thrown out of the game, fired from the team, and sued for taking bribes, Grompski decided his future in organized baseball was over.**

> **My favorite drinks are milk, root beer, cider, and orange juice and vodka.**

Almost any kind of sentence constituent can be used in a series of three or more. In the first example, past-participial phrases (*thrown out of the game,* and so on) are in a series. The comma before the *and* in that series is considered optional, but the most careful writers would use it. In the second example, the constituents are nouns. Again, the comma after *cider* is considered optional, but note that its omission could lead to confusion. Whether or not you use the comma between the last two constituents in a series, be sure each is unmistakably separate from the others.

The connectives *and, but, or, nor, for, yet,* and *so* are called **coordinating conjunctions.** In English when one of these conjunctions connects two independent clauses (i.e., really two sentences), a comma is used before the conjunction unless the clauses are short. Examples:

> **In 1973 the vice president of the United States resigned because of admitted criminal acts, and two former cabinet members were indicted on charges of conspiracy.**

I agreed to prepare a lengthy explanation, for the dean felt that I might otherwise be expelled.

Joe invited me to the dance but I didn't go.

In the last example, the two independent clauses are too short and simple to require a comma before the *but*. Always use a comma before *for* as a conjunction, for otherwise the reader might take it for a preposition and stumble in his reading (e.g., *a lengthy explanation for the dean . . .*) Never put a comma directly after a coordinating conjunction unless you use two commas to set off a sentence constituent.

EXERCISE 25. Enter commas where needed in the following sentences. If a comma is optional, give an explanation in the blank below the sentence, like this: *Series of compound sentences*

A comma after <u>books</u> is optional.

1. Since we needed four more for another bridge table, we invited the twins, George, and Humphrey.

2. We prepared some special drinks, for the Johnsons are finicky drinkers.

3. With the birds singing, the breeze sighing, the brook babbling, and the pines exuding pleasant odors, we were enjoying our mountain vacation thoroughly. *optional*

4. We could choose from gin and tonic water, scotch and soda, vodka and tomato juice, and bourbon and water.

5. Beware of shills, chills, frills, and Jills.

6. We had our choice of leaving in the early morning, just before noon, in midafternoon, or late at night.

7. I declined to speak, for the minister had already told the whole truth.

8. We pushed with all our strength, but the car remained stuck. *optional*

9. We were fed eggs, bacon, and dry cereal and fruit.

10. Strong and healthy but immature, Joel undertook tasks he was not suited for, often embarrassed his friends, and was a constant problem for the school authorities.

11. The trial continued for six months with dozens of witnesses testifying, yet the jurors obviously were little better informed than when the trial began.

_____

12. The Harrises, the expected couple, and Joan and Alice appeared, to the Davises' dismay, since they were not prepared to feed six more people.

_____ *optional* _____

13. Little girls are made of energy, enthusiasm, creativity, and sugar and spice.

_____

14. Cross your t's, dot your i's, and watch your p's and q's.

_____

15. I'm surprised Oral exchanged his wife, for the indications were that they were happy.

_____

16. With the kite in the air, the wind blowing strong, and endless time on our hands, we decided to try for a two-mile distance.

_____

17. What is English as a part of a college's curriculum: literature, composition, usage, and various other aspects of language study.

_____

18. We tried harder but the opposition won.

_____ *correct* _____

19. We had a choice of cherry pie, mocha ice cream, peach cobbler, or strawberries and cream.

_____

20. The defense attorney screamed like a banshee when the prosecution introduced Exhibit A, yet the judge made no attempt to maintain order in the court.

_____

CHAPTER
26
INTRODUCTION TO INFORMATIVE AND PERSUASIVE WRITING

Most of the writing done in college and in various professions and occupations is either informative or persuasive or a mixture of the two; thus we will deal with the important basics of these kinds of writing in the next ten chapters. This chapter, like the preceding one, is introductory. To repeat what we said in the last chapter, the most important point for you to understand, perhaps, is that the focus of the basics we will discuss is on the *usefulness* of writing (though much of what you learn here can also apply to personal or imaginative writing not intended to have utility). Every experienced composition teacher has heard hundreds of students say, "I know what I want to say but I don't know how to say it." The following chapters will help you learn how to say it. And knowing how to say clearly and effectively what you mean can have a great bearing on your success in college, your holding a job and getting promotions, and your influence on other people. Therefore, approach your composition course as though you expect to learn how to use an important tool better than you now do.

Though we are limiting our instruction to informative and persuasive writing, we should acknowledge at the outset that bits of narration and description can do much to help clarify exposition and persuasion. For example, here is a paragraph from a student theme entitled "How to be a successful door-to-door salesman":

The door-to-door salesman's job, at least in selling most products, is made much easier if he can flatter a lonely housewife without appearing to be playing up to her. When I started selling Kirby vacuum cleaners, my supervisor gave me a lesson. We rang the doorbell of a deserted-looking house. The lady who answered greeted us coldly, but my supervisor introduced us and immediately asked about the variety of some potted plants in the front entrance. The lady eagerly answered the questions, but turned a little cold again when we urged her to let us demonstrate the Kirby. My supervisor very shrewdly asked if she kept potted plants in the house, too. That question got us in easily, and then the supervisor spoke learnedly about how much better house plants do if the house is kept free of dust. He admired one of her African violets but rather sneakily pointed out how the dust on its leaves was stunting the plant's growth. By this time the lady had taken the bait, hook, line, and sinker, and the supervisor was ready to show me how to make a sale.

The student's paper was, overall, an informative one exposing some of the shady methods used in door-to-door selling. In the paragraph quoted, however, he narrated a little story to make one point clear. He could have stated his point in factual terms, such as

First find some way to attract the housewife's attention. For example, appear interested in some aspect of her house and flatter her while at the same time subtly suggesting that not everything is right in the care of her house. [And so on.]

But the bit of narration the student used helped clarify his factual point. Such use of narration or description as an aid to factual writing should not be confused with the writing of wholly narrative papers about personal experiences. The point here is that narration and description are themselves ofen useful in composing useful writing.

The usefulness of some of your future writing may depend on your properly mixing exposition and persuasion. For example, here is a paragraph from a student composition entitled "The desirability of the British parliamentary system over the U.S. system."

Another advantage of the British system is that it provides for variable terms for prime ministers and for irregularly spaced elections. The U.S. system, of course, provides for rigidly fixed terms for presidents and for regularly-spaced elections. We should change our system to one like that of the British in order to prevent such calamities as happened with President Nixon. With the British system an election could have been called early in the Watergate scandal, and the people's will could have been carried out without strong demands for the impeachment or resignation of the president. Nixon, if he lost the election, could even have remained head of his party if it continued to want him. The advantages of such a system are obvious. We should, I think, have another Constitutional Convention and prepare a partially new Constitution that would allow for national elections any time the president is in or has caused a grave crisis that threatens the stability of the country. A system that forces the country to keep a president for, say, three years after he has lost the ability to govern is a bad system.

Part of this paragraph is factual and thus is informative writing, and part is opinion with the writer urging others to accept his opinions, which makes the writing persuasive. Of course this example paragraph comes from a composition written for a college course, but the *training* that the student received will undoubtedly be helpful to him in future real writing situations, on which the degree of his success may depend. That is, he may have been trained so that he could write a memo that *would* be rushed right to the head office (see the quotation from Michener in the preceding chapter). The exercises and compositions required of you in this class are intended to train you for future real tasks of written communication.

The example paragraph just given shows how easily informative and persuasive writing can be mixed. Much writing of course is wholly factual and informative, but persuasive writing usually includes passsages of exposition. Thus in the following chapters we will not make a distinction between the two forms of discourse. We will simply try to teach you how to organize a composition and develop it with unified, coherent paragraphs, well-formed sentences, and properly chosen words.

We need to make one other point in this introductory chapter: you should be aware of the logic of what you write. You perhaps have not yet got far in your study of logic as presented in Part I, but you should develop as best you can the ability to use sound logic. For example, here is the opening paragragh of a student paper entitled "Why superior students should not be placed in special classes that exclude average and below-average students":

> Many elementary and high schools set up special classes for superior students, or so-called rapid learners, on the grounds that it is advantageous to give such students the best opportunity for a superior education. But the disadvantages of educational aristocracy outweigh its advantages, and, in my opinion, students should be assigned at random to their classes. One disadvantage is that the superior students are likely to develop an inflated opinion of their worth and thus to develop undesirable psychological traits. The student who learns to sneer at his less talented peers is likely to be an undesirable member of a democracy. Being constantly told that he is superior, he is likely to think that he deserves rights and considerations denied to other citizens. In rare cases, such students may come to think that they are above the law. The Leopold and Loeb case comes to my mind. On a lesser level I have seen acquaintances of mine swagger and boast their way out of friendships. It is not good to lead people to believe that they deserve undemocratic special considerations.

The main syllogism (see Chapter 7) of the paragraph is this:

major premise: We do not want to harm students psychologically.

minor premise: Segregating superior students into special classes often harms them psychologically.

conclusion: Superior students should not be segregated into special classes.

The student writer intended his paragraph to show the truth of the minor premise. Did he use sound logic? As is so often the case, definite proof of his point cannot be demonstrated. However, the writer makes a good case for his point and certainly does not fall into any of the logical fallacies discussed in Chapters 9 through 13. He is probably sound in his point that if a person is constantly told that he is such and such, he is likely to believe that he is. Also the writer gave a sound example to illustrate his point: Some very bright people, such as Leopold and Loeb, have come to think that they are above the law. Thus the writer could easily defend the logic of his paragraph, though he could not *prove* his point. Since many or most ideas are not subject to absolute proof, it is sufficient for a writer to use logic that seems sound to many of his readers and this is not flawed with fallacies. (You should, of course, avoid propagandistic writing of the sort discussed in Chapter 21.)

EXERCISES

1. Here is the opening sentence of a paragraph; finish the paragraph by making up a little story (narration) that supports its main point:
   The jury system for criminal trials in America can lead to verdicts harmful to the public, verdicts that could be avoided if a trained panel of three judges were substituted for the jury. For example, ...

2. Here is another paragraph from the composition quoted from above. Discuss whether the student used sound logic in making his point.

   Our democratic educational system must be concerned as much with average and below-average students as with bright ones. Since what students do or say in a classroom, as well as what the teacher says or does, can have an educational effect, it seems only fair than the average students deserve to have bright students among them so that they can learn from the bright students. A classroom full of nothing but dummies is wholly dependent on the teacher for educational advancement, and the teacher is not likely to be able to provide sufficient educational opportunities. Even a sparkling teacher can't make a completely dull class sparkle. Segregation of bright students is simply unfair to the other students. And besides, the bright students will probably learn as much in a mixed class as in a segregated one. It's quite possible that segregation does little for bright students and harms dull ones.

USAGE
LESSON
26

COMMAS
TO
SET
OFF
INTRODUCTORY
CONSTITUENTS

Most writers begin some, or even many, of their sentences with various kinds of unified constituents that are not a part of the subject that follows. Example:

> Before Wayne had left, the manager of the night club had already called for police to be sent to his aid.

The subject of the sentence is *the manager of the night club*, which is preceded by the **introductory constituent** *before Wayne had left*.

When such an introductory constituent is short, is not followed by much of a voice pause, and does not produce momentary ambiguity if the reader passes rapidly from it to the sentence subject, it need not be set off by a comma. Examples:

> *correct:*   With rain imminent we headed for shelter.
> *correct:*   Of course no one believed the professor's threat.
> *correct:*   If the test is hard I'll pretend to get sick.

Commas after *imminent, course,* and *hard* are not necessary, for their absence does not impede the reader. The use of a comma after these words, though, would not be wrong.

However, commas are often needed after introductory constituents to prevent the reader from stumbling or from having to pause unnecessarily to understand the sentence structure. Normally, a comma should be used after any introductory constituent when a significant voice pause occurs between it and the following sentence subject. Examples:

> *correct:*   However, the stock market declined sharply instead.
> *correct:*   After I hemmed and hawed for some time, the professor called on another student.

correct: Wherever Rual may be, at least three pretty girls are sure to be with him.

correct: Why, I have never said such a thing.

The distinct voice pauses after *however, time, be,* and *why* call for commas to separate the introductory constituents from the sentence subjects. Their presence is an aid to the reader.

Aside from the voice-pause rule, two more specific rules need explanation. Always use a comma after an introductory verb phrase and after an introductory adverb clause unless the clause is short. Examples:

correct: Having lost all my money, I had to hitchhike home.

correct: To be very truthful, I had no intention of honoring my promise.

correct: The fracas being over, we slowly dispersed.

correct: Whenever a number of highly placed politicians are shown to be crooks, most people resort to saying, "They're all crooked."

Not only the voice pause after the introductory constituents but also their structural nature makes commas after them a great aid to the experienced reader.

Also, regardless of whether voice pause exists, use a comma after an introductory constituent when its absence would at first seem to produce an ambiguity. Examples:

wrong: While Terry was fighting Alberto was trying to be a peacemaker.

wrong: Below the steerage decks were awash with bilgewater.

wrong: Though we were forced to leave the theater manager assured us no charges would be filed.

wrong: Though angry at no time did I charge Nancy with deliberate dishonesty.

Without commas after the introductory constituents, the reader will at first mistakenly think the constructions are *Terry was fighting Alberto, below the steerage decks, forced to leave the theater,* and *though angry at.* The careful writer will not treat his readers so impolitely but will aid them by using proper punctuation.

NAME _____   DATE _____

EXERCISE 26.   Enter commas where needed in the following sentences. In addition to commas needed to set off introductory constituents, some commas may be needed to separate constituents in a series and clauses in compound sentences. If there is a place where a comma is optional, indicate the precise option in the blank below the sentence, like this:

A comma after <u>crazy</u> is optional.

_____

1. Having really been taken, there was nothing I could do but suffer my loss.

_____

2. My favorite old comedy actors are Buster Keaton, Harold Lloyd, the Marx Brothers, and Laurel and Hardy.

_____

3. If it snows, we'll go to the ski slopes.

   optional
_____

4. After giving a great deal of conflicting testimony about his role in the bribery scheme, Mordaunt was indicted for perjury.

_____

5. I swore never to leave my wife, for another woman held no attraction for me.

_____

6. Though Ray seemed to agree, with so many other opponents holding firm, we did not count on his vote.

_____

7. Hundreds of persons pledged $5.00 each to the campaign, yet we actually collected only $220.00.

_____

8. We invited the Turners, Joan, and Ted, which gave us another full table for bridge.

_____

9. Overall, we earned a bare 2% on our investment.

   optional
_____

Introduction to Informative and Persuasive Writing   271

10. Instead of James, Scott was chosen to scout the opposition.

_____

11. With no regrets, we returned to our jobs in the strawberry fields.

_____ *Optional* _____

12. The nature of the course having been explained to us, we eagerly enrolled.

_____

13. By squeezing, Joan was able to pass through the aperture.

_____

14. Never one to underestimate the opposition, Coach Wooden scheduled extra practice sessions.

_____

15. Reading books, playing bridge, hiking in the mountains, and collecting stamps are all my hobbies.

_____ *Optional* _____

16. Since I was ready to eat, the steaks looked particularly appetizing.

_____

17. However we behave, let's give the appearance of being humble.

_____

18. If the Republicans win, taxes may be reduced.

_____

19. If the Republicans win control of the Senate, the president may be in trouble.

_____

20. Wherever you go, to be there first should be your goal.

_____

CHAPTER
27
PLANNING
A
BASIC
ORGANIZATION

Any piece of writing of much length needs to be organized, and that usually means that the writer must plan his work, at least to a degree, before he begins writing. Different kinds of organization are suitable for different kinds of writing, but the simplest and most effective way to organize most informative and persuasive writing in composition courses is to state the topic fully and clearly and then to derive from it three to five **main points,** each of which will be developed into one paragraph in the finished paper. Actually, deriving a few main points from a topic is the beginning of the process of outlining. However, the outlining process discussed in this and the next chapter produces a **scratch** or **working outline** for the writer's use, not a formal outline for the reader's use. Thus we will think of our process as organizing, not outlining.

One of the reasons why your topic should be expressed fully and clearly is that it will then often contain a clear clue to the main points that can be derived from it. In its simplest form this clue is a **plural noun** that can be divided ino a few main points. For example, in the topic

Discuss what you think are the most important *duties* of parents to their children,

the plural noun *duties* is a clear clue to organization on the basis of main points. You as the writer just need to think of three to five general duties of parents to their children and you will have main points that can be developed into paragraphs. As you think of your main points, jot them down in this way:

1. to provide their children with the necessities of life

2. to develop in their children a feeling of security

3. to demonstrate love for their children at all times

4. to teach their children to be moral and honest citizens of the community

Now you have four main points, each of which can be developed with details and explanations into a full paragraph. After you have jotted down three to five main points for your topic, you should decide the order in which you will discuss them in your composition, for you will not always think of the points in the most desirable order. For example, in the basic organization above you might want to develop point 3 about love as your second paragraph and to use point 2 about security after that.

As you prepare a basic organization for a topic as illustrated in the preceding paragraph, it is important for you to understand that you want to jot down main points that can be developed into full paragraphs, not specific points that do not call for development. In other words, your main points will be **generalizations** (see Chapter 2), not specifics. For example, the following list would *not* be a suitable basic organization for the topic expressed above:

1. to provide their children with food

2. with shelter

3. with clothing

4. with toys and other personal belongings

Such specific points could hardly be developed into interesting paragraphs. Thus you should always try to think of general main points that just beg for paragraph development.

(Many students find that just a basic organization of main points is enough to guide their writing of an entire composition. Other students like to jot down details under each main point so that they can be more closely guided in their actual writing. The next chapter will discuss the expansion of basic organizations.)

Now we should mention that many instructors like their students to compose a **thesis sentence** for each of their themes. A thesis sentence states the overall main idea of the paper; thus it is a phrasing of the topic in a well-formed sentence. For example, here is a thesis sentence for the first topic discussed in this chapter:

This theme will discuss the most important duties of parents to their children.

Since we are emphasizing the need for stating your topic fully and clearly, we do not really need to emphasize thesis sentences also. However, if your instructor wants you to provide a thesis sentence for each theme, compose it by converting your topic into a well-formed sentence that summarizes the main idea of your paper, just as your topic does.

Here is another example of deriving a basic organization from a plural noun in the fully stated topic:

Topic: If you belong to a minority race, discuss some of your attitudes towards the white majority.

Plural noun: Attitudes

Basic organization:
1. My resentment because whites accept celebrities of my race but not ordinary members of it

2. My resentment because we are not really given equal opportunity

3. My gratitude to many whites for trying to eradicate inequalities

4. My friendly attitude towards many individual whites that I like

Once you focus on such a plural noun as *attitudes* in such a topic, you should find it relatively easy to prepare a basic organization of three to five main points. Of course you *still* have your actual writing to do, but without a plan of some sort you are almost certain to write a poor paper.

Many fully expressed topics, however, do not contain plural nouns to serve as clues to organization. But, when not stated, such a plural noun will usually be **implied,** and you should learn to examine a topic closely to see what plural noun is implied. For example, consider this topic:

Some people claim that if a person is poor it is his own fault.

Write a composition either attacking or defending that idea.

First, we'll say, you plan to attack the idea. Now you must think hard to see what implied plural noun will guide you in preparing a basic organization. You should see that *reasons why* is such an implied plural noun, and you might jot down these general reasons (main points) why a person is not necessarily to blame for being poor:

1. A person can't choose either the family or the country he is born into.

2. A person may not be responsible for mental or physical handicaps that keep him poor.

3. A person can't be responsible for depressions or other political or economic situations that keep him poor.

4. There simply isn't enough wealth for everyone to be well-to-do.

Once you see that you are explaining the *reasons* why you are taking a particular stand on a question, it should not be hard for you to think of several main points, each of which will be one reason that can be developed into a full paragraph.

Here are some other examples of topics with implied plural nouns:

Topic:	Describe the personality of your best friend
Implied plural noun:	Characteristics *or* traits
Basic organization:	1. Her friendly, outgoing nature
	2. Her sense of humor
	3. Her respect for the rights of others
	4. Her latent high temper that shows itself when she sees injustice

Topic:	Explain how your college could improve academically.
Implied plural noun:	Methods *or* ways
Basic organization:	1. By requiring more general education courses for graduation
	2. By raising its standards for hiring faculty and gradually weeding out incompetent teachers
	3. By devising means, such as awards, to cause students to want to achieve a high academic ranking
	4. By having frequent cultural and out-of-class academic events

Topic:	Explain some task that you are particularly good at, such as overhauling a car's engine.
Implied plural noun:	Steps
Basic Organization:	1. Disassembling the engine
	2. Renewing the cylinder sleeves and rings
	3. Repairing damaged valves
	4. Reassembling the engine

If you always state your topic fully and clearly, you will often find in it a stated plural noun that will serve as a clue to organization. But if your topic has no stated plural noun, careful thought will usually expose an implied plural noun that is just as helpful as a stated one. The most common implied plural nouns in fully stated topics are *reasons, characteristics, methods,* and *steps.*

The foregoing explains an elementary method of organizing a composition or an essay test question. But if you master this simple mode of organization, you will later find it easy to organize other kinds of writing in other ways.

EXERCISES

1. For each of the following topics find an implied plural noun that will guide you in preparing a basic organization. Prepare a basic organization for one of the topics.

   a. Discuss whether you think "victimless" crimes — drunkenness, gambling, and possession of small quantities of marijuana — should not be punished by jail sentences but only by citations, like traffic offenses.

   b. Discuss how best to choose a car to buy and how to choose a repair shop to service it.

   c. Imagine that you are an employer. Describe what you think makes an ideal employee.

   d. Discuss how you would deal with the problem of runaway teenagers.

   e. Discuss why you think Americans are so addicted to watching professional football games.

2. Add three or four more main points to complete each of the following basic organizations. The plural nouns in the topics are italicized.

   a. *Topic:* Discuss the most important *characteristics* of a good TV program series.

   Basic organization: 1. A really new and interesting situation for each program.

   b. *Topic:* Discuss the chief *reasons* why you think some students do not do as well in school as others.

   Basic organization: 1. A poor home environment often kills motivation.

   c. *Topic:* Discuss the *advantages* of a society in which there is little discipline and restraint on behavior.

   Basic organization: 1. Citizens are less likely to have guilt feelings and other neuroses.

   d. *Topic:* Discuss the *advantages* of being just average in intelligence.

   Basic organizaiton: 1. You have more in common with more people.

USAGE
LESSON
27

COMMAS
TO
SET
OFF
PARENTHETIC
CONSTITUENTS

A constituent is a unified part of a sentence. A **parenthetic constituent** is one that interrupts the flow of the sentence for the purpose of giving an additional bit of information that is not part of the sentence proper. It can be called an **interrupter** since, though it is a part of the sentence, it interrupts the flow of the basic sentence. The interruption, of course, does not damage the sentence but allows the writer to put in an addition to the sentence, such as a connective word or phrase, at just the place where it will be most meaningful to the reader. Example:

correct: Your attempt to sabotage my plans, you may be sure, will only result in failure.

The comment *you may be sure* is parenthetic because it stands aside from the basic sentence, but it is placed just where it will add emphasis to the writer's basic comment. **The general rule is that parenthetic expressions or constituents are set off by commas.**

Phrases of personal opinion, as in the example above, are parenthetic and should be set off. However, they do not often appear in the kind of writing you are studying but mostly in personal writing, such as letters. Examples:

correct: Our sales for August, I believe, will be higher than for any previous month.
correct: Your opinions, I'm sure, will be highly valued by our director.

Words in direct address, which are either names or substitutes for names spoken directly to a person or group, are parenthetic and should be set off by commas. Examples:

    correct: It would seem, Aunt Martha, that Julius has won the argument.

    correct: And my reply to you, sir, is that I will redouble my efforts to put you out of business.

Explanatory phrases and phrases that parenthetically name examples should be set off. Examples:

    correct: I found, as too often has been the case, that I was not properly prepared for that college course.

    correct: Birds of prey, such as the bald eagle, are slowly becoming extinct.

Words and phrases that provide transition between sentences, or serve as connectives, should be set off when they are parenthetically used. Examples:

Treated as separate category by Conlin

    correct: The price of silver, for example, doubled within a space of three months.

    correct: The price of mining stock, nevertheless, continued to decline.

The transitional phrase *of course*, however, is often not set off by commas. Example:

    correct: The dean of course refused our request to turn the dormitory into a commune.

But commas separating *of course* would not be wrong.

    Parenthetic constituents, as you have probably noted, almost always have distinct voice pauses before and after them, and these pauses guide most writers in punctuating properly. In Chapter 30 you will learn that occasionally parenthetic constituents may be set off with dashes instead of commas. And when a writer wants a constituent to be fully separated from its basic sentence, he uses parentheses. Example:

    correct: Alcohol (not to be confused with hallucinogenic drugs) is now legally sold almost everywhere in the world.

Parentheses should be used only when the parenthetic constituent has something of the nature of a footnote.

    Parenthetic constituents of the sort discussed in this lesson may also come first or last in a sentence though then they may be called *introductory* or *concluding constituents*. At any rate, they are then set off by one comma. Examples:

    correct: For example, lithium is lighter than oxygen.

    correct: I returned from Las Vegas broke, as is usually the case.

EXERCISE 27.   Enter commas where needed in the following sentences, which cover rules from Chapters 25 through 27. If a comma is optional, state the option in the blank below the sentence.

1. The president of the United States, in my opinion, should be allowed to serve more than two terms.

_____

2. When I'm finished with this customer, Madam, I will wait on you.

_____

3. Whether I'm hungry, sated, or just nervous, I often bite my fingernails.

_____*optional*_____

4. The kind of novels I'm talking about, such as *The Return of the Native*, are timeless in their appeal.

_____

5. When you have your degree in hand, I will give you several gifts, including a new car.

_____*optional*_____

6. The way to get a job, as you explained to me, is to impress the personnel officer with your reliability.

_____

7. As I was talking, about a dozen strangers, including some weirdos, joined our little group.

_____

8. Of course, no one except possibly Aunt Alice will object to the subject of this movie.

_____*all optional*_____

9. The nation with the most powerful arms, however, may not win a nuclear war, since a surprise attack can wipe out any nation.

_____*optional*_____

11. The thing to do in any case is to report the loss in hopes that your insurance will cover it. *or not, depending on meaning*

---

12. Since Easter I have not touched a drop of alcohol, including the weakest beer.

---

13. Since I was not involved, in no way could I contribute to the "conscience fund."

---

14. Years of work, endless patience, and total dedication will be necessary for you to become a medical doctor. *optional*

---

15. Just bring various odds and ends such as church keys, sieves, and pocket flasks. *optional*

---

16. Why, Josie didn't even tell me, much less her mother, about her little escapade.

---

17. In the process of dreaming, about 40 percent of human beings twitch their leg, arm, and body muscles.

---

18. My term paper, such as it is was, at least turned in on time establishing a precedent for me.

---

19. The book of Ecclesiastes, for example, illustrates how ancient texts became corrupt through additions to the original by scribes, a point most people don't understand.

---

20. We had our choice of watermelon juice, fruit punch, and ale. *optional*

CHAPTER 28
EXPANDING THE BASIC ORGANIZATION

Many students, after they have jotted down the main points they will discuss in their composition (or essay test question), can proceed with their writing without putting more organization (or scratch outlining) on paper. They are able to think of and keep in their minds the details and explanations that will turn each main point into a full paragraph. They usually do some of their thinking as they write. Other students prefer to jot down details under their main points to guide them more closely in writing their paragraphs. Thus we will briefly show how a basic organization, as discussed in the preceding chapter, can be expanded before the writer begins composing his sentences. You must be your own judge whether such additional organizing in preparation for writing is useful to you. You need not maintain the consistency of form required by a formal outline.

Here is an example of how a basic organization can be expanded so that a writer will not forget minor points and explanations that fit into his main points. Since this is *scratch* outlining for your own use, you need jot down only the words that will help you remember your specific or minor ideas.

topic:	Discuss the reasons why personal advice columns, such as Ann Landers', have such wide appeal.

basic organization:	1. The letters all concern problems that people are most interested in.
	    a. Divorce
	    b. Infidelity

    c. Parent-child relationships

    d. Sexual matters

    e. Mean behavior of husbands, parents, and so on

2. People are interested in "human interest" stories.

    a. Columns are really like soap operas and true confession stories.

    b. Readers can identify with the letter writer.

    c. Readers are interested in "solutions" to problems.

3. People look for parallels to their own problems.

    a. Advice might be useful to the reader.

    b. Feel more comfortable knowing others have same problems

    c. Like to see a problem expressed clearly when they can't express it

4. People secretly like to know that others have worse problems than theirs.

    a. Pretend to sympathize but enjoy others' problems

    b. Get psychological relief from others' problems

    c. Like to feel morally superior

    d. Like to blame people's problems on their not having true religion

By the time a student has prepared as expanded an organization as this, he can, if he knows how to compose good sentences, write his paper quickly. But even if a writer prefers to work from just a basic organization of main points, he must, in order to produce a good finished paper, *think* carefully prior to writing, though he can do some of his detailed thinking as he writes.

EXERCISES

Prepare an expanded organization for each of the two following basic organizations.

        1. *topic:* Discuss the chief benefits you expert to get out of your college career.

basic organization: 1. Skills and knowledge for a good-paying job

                  2. More social polish

                  3. Ways to enjoy my future life more

                  4. College fun

        2. *topic:* There is a saying that "money is the root of all evil." Write a composition on the topic "Lack of money is the root of most evil."

basic organization: 1. Causes most crime
2. Causes many divorces and family disharmony
3. Causes people to behave unethically in trying to get a promotion or better position
4. Prevents many people from having equal opportunity for an education and other such things.

USAGE
LESSON
28

COMMAS
TO
SET
OFF
NONESSENTIAL
CONSTITUENTS

The parenthetic sentence constituents discussed in the preceding chapter are to a degree just incidental to their sentences. Indeed, the term comes from Latin meaning "to put in beside"; thus they are constituents just incidentally placed in their sentences, though the writer wants them and they may be important to the total meaning. There are other sentence constituents known as **essential** and **nonessential,** with the nonessential ones being a little like parenthetic constituents in that they need to be set off from the basic sentence by commas. Example:

> *correct:* The Women's Liberation Movement, *waxing and waning as the years pass*, has improved the lot of women a great deal.

The italicized phrase is not parenthetic and yet it is a nonessential constituent and must be separated from the basic sentence by commas. Perhaps the most understandable difference between parenthetic constituents and essential and nonessential ones is that the latter carry the meaning of full sentences and thus could be written as separate simple sentences. Example:

> The Women's Liberation Movement has been waxing and waning as the years pass. It has improved the lot of women a great deal.

Good writers, however, do not write only such short, simple sentences but use essential and nonessential constituents in order to compose mature, well-formed sentences.

Essential and nonessential constituents are modifiers; for example, in the first example sentence above the italicized phrase is modifying *Women's Liberation Movement.* The difference between the two kinds of constituents is that essential ones are **necessary to identify** the word or phrase (usually a noun, noun phrase, or pronoun) they modify and nonessential ones just give additional information about nouns (and sometimes whole ideas) already fully identified. The essential constituent is **not** set off by commas because it is necessary to the sentence; the nonessential constituent **is** set off because it is not necessary to the sentence. Examples:

essential: The student *who chug-a-lugs the most* will receive a prize.

nonessential: Vincent, *who chug-a-lugged the most*, received a case of empty beer bottles.

If the italicized essential constituent is removed from its sentence, no fully meaningful sentence will remain, for *student* is then not identified. But if the italicized nonessential constituent is removed from its sentence, a fully meaningful sentence will remain, for *Vincent* is identified by name. Thus the essential constituent is not set off, but the nonessential one is set off by commas. (In Chapter 30 we will see that nonessential constituents may sometimes be set off by dashes.)

Adjective clauses, which are introduced by the relative pronouns *who, whom, whose, which,* and *that* (which in essential clauses may sometimes be omitted), are among the most common essential and nonessential constituents. The following example sentences are correctly punctuated, and the essential or nonessential adjective clauses are italicized.

essential: A test *that is unnecessarily hard* discourages students.

nonessential: Professor Snolly's last test, *which was unnecessarily hard*, discouraged me.

essential: A lawyer *whose income is over $100,000 a year* usually has his work done by law clerks.

nonessential: My lawyer, *whose income is over $100,000 a year*, pays less in taxes than I do.

The essential constituents are needed to identify which *test* and which *lawyer* are meant, and thus they are not set off. In the examples of nonessential adjective clauses, however, *test* is identified by *Professor Snolly's last* and *lawyer* is identified by *my;* thus the nonessential clauses must be set off by commas. (If the commas were removed from the last example sentence, the meaning would be that I have more than one lawyer and am identifying the one I mean.)

When an adjective clause introduced by *which* modifies the whole idea of a sentence or of a large sentence constituent such as a verb phrase, it is always nonessential and must be set off. Examples:

correct: I finally got a date with Shelley, *which is hard to do.*

correct: Getting a date with Shelley, *which is hard to do*, is worth whatever effort it takes.

The italicized nonessential clauses are modifying whole ideas, not single nouns.

Also a good tip to remember is that whenever the *which* that introduces an adjective clause cannot naturally be changed to *that*, the clause is alway nonessential; when the *which* can be naturally changed to *that*, the clause is always essential. Examples:

correct: The wine *which you gave me* was like vinegar.

correct: The wine *that you gave me* was like vinegar.

correct: Goofing off, *which is my favorite pastime*, does not lead to riches.

unnatural: Goofing off, *that is my favorite pastime*, does not lead to riches.

The fact that *that* cannot be naturally substituted for *which* proves the clause to be nonessential. Also whenever a relative pronoun can be omitted, the adjective clause is *always* esssential and never gives any trouble in punctuation. Examples:

The course *I like best* is The Psychiatry of Encounter Groups.

The coed *we elect Queen* must be more than physically beautiful.

In the first example, *that* is understood after *course;* and in the second, *whom* is understood after *coed.*

Verb phrases also function as essential or nonessential constituents when they modify nouns. The following example sentences are correctly punctuated, with the verb phrases italicized.

essential: The girl *talking so animatedly* is really trying to recruit revolutionaries.

nonessential: Sally Chase, *talking very animatedly*, entranced all the boys.

essential: Anyone *to be executed by a firing squad* can wear a blindfold at execution time.

nonessential: The last spy captured, *to be executed by a firing squad on Friday*, has declared he will not wear a blindfold.

In the essential examples, the italicized verb phrases are necessary to identify *girl* and *anyone* and thus are not set off. But in the nonessential examples, *Sally Chase* and *the last spy captured* are fully identified without the italicized phrases, and thus these verb phrases, being nonessential, must be set off.

Adjective phrases which follow the nouns or pronouns they modify, either directly or at a distance in the sentence, are usually nonessential and thus need to be set off. Examples:

correct: The bride, *happy as a lark*, stood in stark contrast to the groom.

correct: I just stood there, *completely oblivious of the crime being committed*.

The nonessential italicized adjective phrases modify *bride* and *I*.

An appositive (which may be a word, phrase, or clause) is a construction that renames a noun (and occasionally other constructions) in different words. It is a kind of definition. Some appositives are essential and some are nonessential. The following examples are correctly punctuated and the appositives are italicized.

> *nonessential:* The pit viper, *a close cousin of the rattlesnake*, "sees" by sensing heat waves.

> *nonessential:* England, *once the most powerful nation in the world*, is now one of the poorer nations of Western Europe.

> *essential:* The suggestion *that we picket the cafeteria* was enthusiastically accepted. *not relative adjective* No - has no gram. role in sub. clause

In the first two sentences *pit viper* and *England* are identified by name, and thus the appositive phrases, which just give additional information, are nonessential. In the third sentence the italicized noun clause identifies *suggestion* and thus is essential and not set off.

Most errors in punctuating appositives occur when essential appositives in the form of titles or names are incorrectly set off. Examples:

> *incorrect:* Faulkner's novel, *Sanctuary*, shocks many readers.

This sentence could be correct ony if Faulkner wrote just the one novel mentioned. Because he wrote many, the appositive title *Sanctuary* is essential to identify which novel and must not be set off by commas.

> *incorrect:* The reporter, *Jack Anderson*, was responsible for exposing the scandal.

As punctuated, this sentence means that there is only one reporter in existence. The appositive name *Jack Anderson* is necessary to identify which reporter and thus is essential and must not be set off.

Conversely, punctuation is incorrect when a name appositive is not set off by commas when it is nonessential and should be set off. Examples:

> *incorrect:* Don's wife *Carol* is expecting again.

Since the appositive *Carol* is not set off, it is essential, and that means the writer is identifying which of Don's wives he is talking about.

> *incorrect:* The company's board chairman *Paul O'Connell* reported a 79 percent increase in profits over last year.

Without commas setting it off, the name appositive *Paul O'Connell* is essential, which means that the company has more than one board chairman, the one doing the reporting being identified. In sentences like these, commas should set off *Carol* and *Paul O'Connell*, since it is not essential that *Don's wife* and *board chairman* be further identified. Undoubtedly Don has only one wife and the company only one board chairman. Similarly, in

> Fred Cushing's son, Albert, has an IQ of 140,

one can only conclude that Fred has just one son. And in

> Jack Neill's daughter Karen goes to Vassar,

one can only conclude that Jack has more than one daughter. Thus punctuation can greatly affect meaning.

Adverb clauses introduced by *when* and *where* may, when they modify nouns, be essential or nonessential. The following examples are correctly punctuated and the adverb clauses italicized.

> *essential:* On the day *when you pay your debts* hell will freeze over.
> *nonessential:* On Easter Sunday, *when we all went to church*, our house was burgled.
> *essential:* I often dream of a place *where money lies in the streets.*
> *nonessential:* Disneyland, *where oldsters have as much fun as youngsters*, contains many technological wonders.

In the two essential examples, the clauses are necessary to identify *day* and *place* and thus are not set off. (A comma could come after *debts* to set off an introductory constituent.) In the two nonessential examples, *Easter Sunday* and *Disneyland* are identified by name, and thus the nonessential clauses are set off.

Sometimes adverb clauses that are introduced by such connectives as *because, since, as, if, though, as if, so that, while, before, after, until,* and a few others may sometimes be classified as essential or nonessential, but usually only when they specify time. The following examples are correctly punctuated and the adverb clauses are italicized.

> *essential:* I haven't seen you *since our last caper.*
> *nonessential:* Come at about 7:00 PM, *after I've had time to prepare the witching equipment.*

The essential and nonessential nature of these two clauses is clear, but generally adverb clauses introduced by the connectives mentioned above must just be punctuated by ear or feel, for no clear rules govern their punctuation.

EXERCISE 28. Essential and nonessential constituents in the following sentences are italicized. Set off the nonessential ones by commas. When a sentence has two blank lines below it, explain how punctuation or lack of it can produce two different meanings.

1. Centerfolds, *which sell magazines by the millions,* were first made popular by *Playboy*.

2. The police informer *giving testimony now* was once a con himself.

3. Bertrand, *giving his wife the keys to his car,* signaled to Aubrey that he woud be free.

4. *Time's "Essay"* writer, *Stefan Kanfer,* really wants to be a freelance writer.

   _____

   _____

5. On the Sunday *when you attend church* I will donate $100 to the church fund.

6. On Sunday, *when I will be sleeping late,* do not phone until after 10:00 a.m.

7. Lima beans, *often called butterbeans in the South,* are rich in protein.

8. My brother, *who is a butcher,* lets me buy meat at below wholesale prices.

   _____

   _____

9. The British writer *John Wilson* is another one of those lushes who can write only a few weeks out of the year.

10. Professor Snurf, *turning his back on the class,* said he would allow the cheaters to harm themselves.

11. My sister, *Eileen,* is still looking for a millionaire to marry.

    _____

    _____

12. The poice arrived *before we could get the junk stashed safely away*.

13. Carlos called for me at 8:00 p.m., *before I had had time enough to get dressed.*

14. I was sent to interview Tony Yakker, *who had been acquitted at his murder trial.*

15. My job, *which prevents me from studying enough,* does let me support a new car and a girl friend.

16. Blue whales *the largest living animals,* sometimes grow to 150 tons.

17. Carole, *to be honored at the Sophomore Brunch,* has a GPA of 4.00.

18. Burns's poem *"To a Mouse",* is one of the finest lyric poems of the late eighteenth century.

19. I stole the silverware again, *which I had promised not to do.*

20. Another war in Indochina *which has now been wracked with wars for decades* seems inevitable.

21. My stepmother, *Betty* is very rapidly spending all my father's wealth.

22. Cepheid variables *which are stars that pulsate in their brightness,* can be used to determine the distance of other stars.

23. Greer Sneely's article *"On the Value of Alcohol",* caused ripples of laughter in the academic community.

24. I flew to Shannon Airport, *where I was greeted by members of the IRA.*

25. I know of no liquor store *where you can buy 151 proof rum.*

26. I managed to get the autograph of Henry Aaron, *who holds the world's record for most home runs hit.*

27. Molly Snubb, *a champion on the tennis courts,* refuses to allow a man to enter her apartment.

28. Freddie's novel *Tomorrow and Tomorrow and Tomorrow* was finally published by Alfred A. Knopf.

_____

_____

29. We all gathered on the platform, *waving goodbye as the train pulled out.*

30. Herman Melville's novel *Moby Dick* is considered by many to be the greatest American classic of the nineteenth century.

_____

_____

CHAPTER
29
INTRODUCTIONS
AND
CONCLUSIONS
TO
THEMES

The introduction and conclusion of a theme (or of an essay test question) are part of its organization and not a part of the development of the main points. Usually the introduction and conclusion of a 400-500 word paper should not be separate paragraphs but should be a part of the paragraphs that develop the first and last main points. You perhaps should make it a rule of thumb not to have your introduction stand as a separate paragraph unless it consists of at least three medium-length or two long sentences. One-sentence openings are generally sufficient for composition-course themes, and that sentence should be a part of the first paragraph.

The introduction to an informative or persuasive paper should lead clearly and directly into the topic and should not be folksy, startling, cute, teasing, or indirect. It should, at least to a degree, tell the reader what the fully expressed topic tells the writer. It should be as stylistically pleasing as you can make it and not flat and dull, but it should be direct and clear. Here are some examples. Note not only the directness of the introduction but also note how the beginning of each second sentence shows that it will move directly to the first main point of the basic organization. (The next chapter will discuss how main points should be turned into topic sentences.)

> *topic:* Discuss several of the most important duties a teenager owes his parents.
>
> *introduction:* By the time a child reaches his teens it is time for him to be aware of his responsibilities to his parents, not just theirs to him. First of all, he should . . . .

topic:	Discuss the differences in personality between you and one of your brothers or sisters and try to account for the differences.
introduction:	Though we share the same parents, and even the same bedroom, my brother and I are poles apart in personality. He is a frequently morose person who . . . .
topic:	If you belong to a minority race, discuss some of your chief attitudes towards the white majority.
introduction:	The whites that I go to school with and rub elbows with on the street do not really know my secret attitudes towards them. I give the appearance of . . . .

As is proper for informative and persuasive writing, these openings let the reader know immediately the general subject matter he is to read about. Articles in our best magazines usually have such direct openings. Example:

topic:	Five Myths About Your IQ
introduction:	Standard IQ tests purport to measure "intelligence," which is widely viewed as the key to adult success. — *Harper's*

Note that the writer did not beat about the bush to get his article started but began right off with a direct expression of his subject matter.

However, narrative or descriptive openings for informative papers need not always be avoided. A student with a literary flair may use his imagination to make his introduction colorful. Example:

title:	Discuss the proper procedures of a Fairness Committee which hears student complaints about teachers.
introduction:	Professor Snerl snorted and slashed a big red F on the paper. "You can't fool me," he cried. The student immediately thought of the Fairness Committee.

Such an entertaining opening for an informative paper is not out of place, yet most expository compositions should have simple, direct introductions as illustrated in the preceding paragraph.

But whether or not you open a paper with literary flourish, you should **NOT** refer to your title in your introduction, make your opening sound like an assignment of the topic, begin by apologizing for your ignorance, be wishy-washy by implying in your opening that you are not sure which side of an issue to take, nor overuse direct quotations and rhetorical questions as introductions.

The conclusion of a 400–500 word composition should *not* be a summary of the paper but should just be a statement that sounds a note of finality so that the reader feels a sense of completion. Usually the ending should in some final way refer to the total subject matter of the paper, but it should not be repetitious. Also a conclusion to a short paper should just be the last sentence of the paragraph that discusses the last main point. Example:

topic: Discuss what your consider to be the differences between the ideals of your generation and those of your parents' generation.

conclusion: . . . have at that point a meeting of minds. Thus I perceive that though our ideals differ, neither generation is really better than the other.

Note how a simple sentence that *sounds* like a conclusion can be attached to the paragraph that discusses the last main point.

Here is another example of a simple but effective conclusion:

topic: Discuss some of the disadvantages of rural life.

conclusion: . . . about its only desirable qualities. I have been watching the area I grew up in before I went into the Navy, and I see people searching for the ideal rural life giving up very quickly and returning to the city. "Back to the country" is not working out.

The last sentence both sounds a note of finality and also alludes to the total subject matter of the paper.

EXERCISES

Write introductions for two or more of the following topics.

1. Discuss several reasons why it is disadvantageous to be highly intelligent.

2. Discuss the possibilities of democracy being saved without fighting wars against the Communist nations.

3. Discuss the ecological damages caused by one kind of industry.

4. Discuss the merits or demerits of requiring all college students to study a foreign language.

5. Discuss the methods one must follow to become expert in some intellectual game.

USAGE
LESSON
29

AVOIDING
INCORRECTLY-USED
COMMAS

English punctuation is based on sentence structure. In addition to being used to separate constituents in a series and long clauses in a compound sentence, commas are used to set off constituents that are in some way not a part of the basic sentence or that for clarity or proper meaning need to be separated from the basic sentence. If such a constituent comes at the beginning or end of a sentence, one comma sets it off, but if it comes within a sentence two commas are needed to set it off. There is almost always a voice pause where a comma is needed, but often voice pauses occur where commas should not be placed. Following are explanations of the most common misuses of commas.

Do **not** separate a subject from its verb with a single comma. Examples:

incorrect: The main trouble with Cory's racer, was that the cams were not exactly balanced.

incorrect: That Professor Sneel could be wrong, never entered our minds.

Also do **not** separate a verb from its complement (direct object, predicate noun, and so on) with a single comma. Examples:

incorrect: The most important issue before the public is, what to do about a do-nothing Congress.

incorrect: My chief concern was, where to find a joint where I could get a joint.

Only when a constituent is being set off on both sides should a comma be used in these positions.

Do **not** set off essential appositives with commas. Examples:

incorrect: The suggestion, that we call the FBI, brought cries of anguish from the oldest members of the club.

incorrect: Ernest Conine's editorial, "The Road to Impeachment," was full of errors of fact.

incorrect: The German writer, Hermann Hesse, is very popular with young people.

As punctuated, these sentences would have to mean that there was only one suggestion, one Conine editorial, and one German writer. Also do **not** set off essential adjective clauses. Example:

incorrect: Students, who are inattentive, learn nothing.

Such punctuation makes the sentence mean that all students are inattentive and that no students learn anything.

Do **not** separate two constituents in a series joined by a conjunction unless they are two long predicates with one subject and with a distinct voice pause between them. Examples:

incorrect: The mayor, and the councilmen all voted against closing the Follies Burlesk Theater.

incorrect: Professor Sneilly entered the classroom, and began lecturing.

correct: The lieutenant waded into the muck to help his soldiers push the truck free, but became stuck himself as his boots sunk into unyielding mire.

Only when two predicates (*waded* . . . and *became* . . . .) are long should a comma separate them, but such a comma is optional. The last example sentence would also be correct without a comma after *free*.

Do **not** separate two noncoordinate modifiers in front of a noun. If the modifiers sound natural with *and* between them, they are coordinate and should be separated by a comma. Example:

correct: The beautiful, sweet-tempered girl smiled. (*Beautiful and sweet-tempered* sounds natural.)

If *and* between the modifiers sounds unnatural, they are noncoordinate. Examples:

incorrect: I've always wanted to live in a red, brick house. (*Red and brick* does not sound natural.)

incorrect: Mr. Snoally is an honest, elected official. (*Honest and elected* does not sound natural.)

EXERCISE 29.   In the following sentences enter commas where needed and strike out commas incorrectly used. This exercise covers Chapters 25 through 29. Be prepared to comment on any optional use of commas and on how meaning might change according to whether commas are used or not.

[handwritten: semi-colon?]

1. I collect stamps, coins, corks .and bottles, and whisky labels; but my collecting is so diversified~~,~~ that I have only a few items in each category.

2. When the sound of the sirens got close enough to disturb my dogs, I knew that I had better vacate the premises if I wanted to stay out of jail.

3. My wife, Carole, seemed to understand, that I was not going to give up my girl friend, Lucy. *[handwritten: optional]*

4. The greatest need, however, was for blankets and clothing, which were soon furnished by the Red Cross.

5. Faulkner's best known novel, *The Sound and the Fury,* owes a debt to James Joyce's novel *Ulysses.*

6. The worst aspect of my study habits~~,~~ is that I delay studying~~,~~ until it is too late, which many students do.

7. The stock market, for example, which I never invest in, always declines in times of inflation.

8. My left arm, which is broken, doesn't know what my right arm, always up to something, is doing.

9. We arrived at O'Hare Airport, where we picked up the wrong luggage, a case of smallpox, and a lost little dog.

10. I received my report card, and tore it up; some other students, who made good grades, lorded it over us dumb bunnies. *[handwritten: I'm not convinced these commas shouldn't stand.]*

11. Marya Mannes' article, "Last Rights," attracted a lot of attention, which was of course her aim. *[handwritten: optional]*

12. Then Joseph made the boast, that he would drink all that was left, including the beer.

Introductions and Conclusions to Themes   301

13. The Japanese novelist, Osho Nikito, toured California where he gave a dozen lectures, all well attended.

14. When we were leaving the cafeteria manager rushed to apologize, as he should have done.

15. The belief that black cats bring bad luck seems to be true for me, since I have bad luck every time I set one on fire.

16. On holidays when my Uncle Schnur always goes to the beach I like to stay at home drinking Coke orange juice or even bourbon and water.

17. The poem "Tyger! Tyger!" was revised many times by its author, William Blake.

18. Reading *Scientific American* is all the intellectual enjoyment I allow myself being mostly a hedonist.

19. The entire faculty, which took a stand against Proposition 14, struck for a day in protest against the president's actions.

20. "Whatever Happened to Baby Jane?" is the title of the old movie I'm watching on the Friday-Night-at-the-Movies series.

21. Barry, my boy friend, showed up at 1:00 a.m., when all the doors to the dorm are locked, as they should be for maximum protection.

22. The President in a manner of speaking, is responsible for the acts of his subordinates, who sometimes act illegally.

23. The great English poet John Milton was blind when he wrote his greatest poems, *Paradise Lost, Paradise Regained*, and *Samson Agonistes*.

24. An important question is what to do with our obsolete weapons which are still usable under certain conditions.

25. All I know is what I read in the newspapers, which often are inaccurate in their news reporting.

26. My brother Charles often takes advantage of our youngest brother, Bill.

27. According to Hoyle, Scott was wrong when he ruled against me in the bridge tournament which we just finished.

28. The greatest English poet, William Shakespeare, became rather wealthy as an actor and playwright, though he has been said by some to have been a frontman for Francis Bacon or some other notable.

29. Platonism, which is an idealistic philosophy, is to many people absolutely incomprehensible.

30. With the manager so angry, at least half of the players plan to quit, but then they may change their minds.

CHAPTER
30

THE
BASIC
ORGANIZATION
AND
TOPIC
SENTENCES

Different kinds of writing call for different paragraphs, and the only inclusive definition of *paragraph* is that it is a segment of writing that is indented (or set off from other segments in some other way, such as double spacing in typewriting). For example, in news reporting a new paragraph indentation usually begins every two or three sentences; indeed, one sentence often stands as a paragraph in news reports. On the other hand, in some kinds of advanced philosophical writing paragraphs often cover more than one page of a book, or even two occasionally. In narration, one paragraph may be quite long and the next an extremely short piece of dialogue, such as " 'No,' he said." In fact, in most kinds of writing true **topic sentences** do not exist.

However, in the kind of informative and persuasive writing you are studying, it is usually best for each paragraph to have a topic sentence, which may be defined as the statement of a generalization which expresses the subject matter (or topic) that will be developed in a paragraph. In the kind of writing we are discussing, each main point in the basic organization contains the subject matter that should be transformed into a well-composed opening sentence of the paragraph (except for the introduction to the theme that begins the first paragraph).[1]

---

[1] Some composition texts say that a topic sentence may come last in a paragraph, but actually such a sentence is one of restatement and serves as a conclusion to a paragraph. If no specific topic sentence opens the paragraph, there is usualy an implied one that the reader just understands.

Here is an example of how to proceed from topic to basic organization to topic sentences (paragraph development will be discussed in the following two chapters):

topic: Discuss the reasons why our era should be called the "aspirin age."

basic organization:
1. Pace of living
2. Separation from nature
3. Mobility destroying roots
4. Permissiveness replacing strong moral code

introduction to the theme and the first topic sentence: Every era of the past seems to have had its troubles, but our era is so plagued with what figuratively may be called headaches that we have been called the "aspirin age." One of the chief causes of our maladjustment is that the pace of living has quickened so drastically that it keeps most people in a state of tension and stress.

second topic sentence: Another cause of widespread stress is the fact that the large majority of our population lives sealed off from nature in cities made of cement, asphalt, steel, and glass.

third topic sentence: Also, more than any other people in the world, Americans are always moving to new cities or neighborhoods, thus destroying the roots that once gave people a sense of belonging.

fourth topic sentence: Finally, the breaking down of the strong moral code that used to characterize America and its replacement with an anything-goes permissiveness has caused millions of Americans to lose their orientation to a society that they (or their parents) once understood.

Each of these topic sentences establishes a generalization that the writer would develop with details and explanations.

Though such explicit topic sentences are not frequently used in informative articles in such excellent magazines as *The Atlantic* and *Scientific American*[1], they are very useful in college in the composition of themes, terms papers, and essay test questions, as well as in much report and memo writing done in various business occupations. In fact, the ability to grasp a general idea, or main point, and to give it clear expression is an extremely valuable talent for all writers to have. Thus we urge you to develop your

---

[1] The reason they are not is that the long articles is such magazines are not just briefly developing three to five main points. True topic sentences in such articles usually occur in every four to eight paragraphs.

skill in composing topic sentences. Such training will greatly increase your skills in most other kinds of writing.

Also note in the above example how the words *another, also,* and *finally* tie the topic sentences (or paragraphs, if they were developed) together. Chapter 33 will discuss transition and coherence, which have to do with tying sentences together, in more detail.

EXERCISES

Compose a one-sentence introduction and a topic sentence for each of the main points in the basic organization of the following two topics. Imitate the example given above and try to give the main points full and stylistically pleasing expression.

> *topic:* Discuss the personal values that you expect to gain from a college education.
>
> *basic organization:* 1. To be a more competent person socially
>
> 2. To increase my capacity for aesthetic appreciation
>
> 3. To develop a better understanding of and tolerance for people different from me
>
> 4. To do the same for cultures different from mine

> *topic:* If you belong to the Anglo white majority, discuss some of your attitudes toward minority races.
>
> *basic organization:* 1. The remnants of my former tendency to assume that all members of a minority, such as Jews, are alike
>
> 2. My developing ability to judge minority people as individuals rather than as types
>
> 3. My admiration of the great achievements some minority Americans have made such as Orientals in theoretical physics
>
> 4. My occasional lapses into prejudices that were instilled in me when I was young.

USAGE
LESSON
30

THE
DASH
AND
THE
COLON

The **dash** is a mark of punctuation and should not be confused with the hyphen, which is a mark used in spelling. The dash is twice as long as a hyphen, and in typewriting is made by two hyphens (--), even though there is a small space between them. The dash should **not** be used as a mark of end punctuation.

In its main uses the dash functions much as a comma does but suggests more voice pause and more separation of a constituent from the basic sentence. A dash or dashes should be used to set off a parenthetic or non-essential constituent (1) that is especially emphatic or (2) that has commas of its own or (3) that is a complete sentence by itself. Examples:

emphatic constituent: The most important person in our college's administration — the president's secretary — is one of the lowest paid.

constituent with commas: The theater-goers — arty Bohemians, staid businessmen and their wives, out-of-work actors, innocent youngsters — all wildly applauded the author as he stepped onto the stage.

complete sentence: As I considered possible careers for myself — this was several years ago — I never dreamed that I would become a skid-row mission worker.

In example one, commas would not provide the proper emphasis; in examples two and three, commas instead of dashes would probably confuse readers. In example three, parentheses instead of dashes could set off the interpolated sentence.

A dash may also be used to set off a terminal constituent that has the tone of a delayed afterthought. Example:

correct: The minister continued his exhortation — like a mother hen clucking to her chicks.

A comma in place of the dash would produce a correct sentence but the slightly longer pause that the dash calls for produces the afterthought effect that the writer wants.

A **colon** is a mark of punctuation chiefly used to indicate that some constituent or longer piece of discourse is being introduced. The use of a colon after the salutation in a letter implies a formal relationship between the correspondents. Examples:

formal usage: Dear Mr. Gonzales:
informal usage: Dear Matt,

A colon is also used after a label that introduces an example. Example:

standard usage: You're richer than I.

A colon is used after a complete sentence to introduce a long or formal direct quotation. Example:

correct: I like what Emerson said: "The healthy state of mind . . . ." [The quotation could be of any length.]

After such tags as *Emerson said,* a comma is generally used instead of a colon. And after such tags as *Emerson said that,* no punctuation is used before the quotation marks.

A colon is used after a noun that introduces a series. Example:

correct: Professor Snilly emphasized three causes of the recession: an increase in public savings, an influx of cheap imports, and tight-money policy on the part of the FRB.

A dash in place of the colon in such a sentence would represent more informal usage. A colon is also used to introduce an explanation. Example:

correct: I knew what the dean's wife wanted: whiskey.

Also a dash is acceptable in this position but represents more informal usage.

EXERCISE 30. In the blanks below the following sentences indicate the options available for proper punctuaton: dashes, colons, or commas.

1. The stranger at the door—the Veep himself—wanted only to make a phone call.

   _____

   _____

2. There are three possible courses of action: surrender, a fight to the death, or suicide.

   _____

   _____

3. That's what you are—yellow.

   _____

   _____

4. The main inhabitants of this forest—foxes, chipmunks, bobcats, skunks, and porcupines—all live in delicate balance.

   _____

   _____

5. I'm sure that Professor Snelly—I don't know about his colleagues—will join us on the picket line.

   _____

   _____

6. Carlos associates with some peculiar characters—like astrologers and palmists.

   _____

   _____

7. I think it was Thoreau who said, "The mass of men live lives of quiet desperation."

   _____

   _____

8. I know this quotation is from the Bible: "When two lie together, then they have heat, but how can one be warm alone?"

   _____

   _____

9. I like to collect odd things—medicine bottles, corkscrews, bird feathers, and so on.

_____

_____

10. This is my advice, join 'em since you can't beat 'em.

_____

_____

11. Everyone—literally everyone—booed the candidate's speech.

_____

_____

12. Everybody—students, teachers, administrators, and janitors—immediately left the campus.

_____

_____

13. I like the ring of this verse from Ecclesiastes: "The race is not to the swift nor the battle to the strong . . . but time and chance happeneth to them all."

_____

_____

14. Whitney's discovery, which certainly wasn't original, brought many curious people to the laboratory.

_____

_____

15. There's not a sober person—not a sane one, at any rate—in the room.

_____

_____

CHAPTER
31

PARAGRAPH DEVELOPMENT THROUGH ILLUSTRATION

Once you have a basic organization of main points for your theme and have converted a main point into a topic sentence, you face the task of developing a paragraph that will be informative or persuasive or both. Though, as we said in the previous chapter, paragraphs vary widely in widely varying kinds of writing, for the kind of writing we are studying — the intent of our study being to give you an understanding of the important basics of writing — there are two broad methods of paragraph development: (1) **development through illustration** — that is, with specific details and examples — and (2) **development through a logical sequence of ideas** — that is, with explanations. Of course there are varieties of both methods, and both can be combined in one paragraph. But we will separate the two and just concentrate on basics.

Topic sentences that call for development through illustration generally imply the question "What?" rather than "Why?" (though some topic sentences imply both questions, as well as "How?"). Example:

Some TV programs provide educational experiences for preschool children.

The reader naturally expects to be told what some of these programs are and how they are educational. If he is not given specifics to support the generalization of such a topic sentence, he will be uninterested and will have a low opinion of the writer. He has no reason to believe the writer unless the writer supports his generalization. (Chapters 2 through 5 of this text are applicable here.)

Thus one simple method of developing a paragraph is to present a number of **specific details** that will make the generalization of the topic sentence believable. Here is an example paragraph from the middle of a theme:

> Traffic accidents would also be reduced in number if highway signs were improved. Visual signs should accompany verbal signs that give such information as "no left turn" or "slippery when wet." Then drivers who don't read English would be properly informed. Any time that a traffic light is coming up after a long stretch of highway without traffic lights, a prominent sign should announce that the driver is approaching a stop light. Also on heavily travelled freeways, signs should announce long in advance which lane a driver should be in if he is taking a much-used exit. Many accidents have been caused by drivers trying too late to get into the necessary lane for an exit. Certainly an improvement in highway signs would reduce the traffic toll.

This writer used three specific details to make his topic-sentence generalization believable. He did not *prove* the generalization scientifically, but he gave it an aura of truth. Note also that the paragraph has a general sentence of conclusion. Such a final sentence that gives a paragraph a sound of completion is known as a "clincher sentence." It is a kind of restatement that reinforces the topic sentence; it is not useless repetition.

Sometimes the generalization of a topic sentence can be made believable and interesting through development with just one extended example rather than with several short examples or specific details. The principle of development is the same: illustration. But the specific is an *extended* example. Usually it is a little story and thus fits into the four forms of discourse as *narrative*. Earlier we explained that spots of narration and description may often be effectively used in informative and persuasive writing. A little story used as an extended example not only will help the writer make his point clear but may also enliven factual writng.

Here is an example of a paragraph developed with an extended example; the first two sentences are the introduction to the theme.

> A minister's job, I know from observing my father, consists of much more than just preaching sermons. Ministers get entangled in all sorts of community affairs. Sometimes they are even the object of bribery attempts. My father once noticed that our local (small town) banker was looking continuously worried and was out of town frequently on weekends. Wanting to play the mother hen, my father made a point to talk to him after services he attended and eventually decided that he should give him a long visitation some night. Within twenty minutes the banker was spilling his story like milk through a sieve. Embezzlement, women, gambling — these told his whole story. His solution to the problem? For my father to accompany him to the bank one night on business and for them to report a holdup. Everyone would believe my father, and his share would be a fat $5000. That's enough excitement for a cop, much less a minister.

The third sentence of the paragraph is its topic sentence, which is followed by one extended example for illustration. The little story is interesting and also makes the generalization of the topic sentence believable.

A specific kind of extended example is one employing **comparison** or **contrast,** which can be used to explain an idea unfamiliar to the reader in terms of something he is familiar with. Such a comparison is known as an **analogy.** Though an analogy can never really prove a point, it can make the point clear and believable. You should, however, be wary of false analogies, such as comparing the Communist block of nations to a neighborhood street gang (see Chapter 11). Here is an example, from the middle of a theme, of paragraph development through comparison:

Selling by telephone is something like making friends with a watchdog when you are trying to make house-to-house sales. First you must attract the dog's attention without annoying him. That is, you must initiate your telephone call in such a manner that the person will continue listening after he learns you are a salesman. Then you should offer the dog a lure, say a dog biscuit. That is, you make the person on the phone think he will get something free or at least a very good bargain. Then you get friendly with the dog, perhaps petting him. That is, you insinuate yourself into your listener's confidence and try to put the call on a personal basis. With the dog you are now ready to ring the doorbell without fear, and with your listener you are ready for him to take the bait and either place an order or agree to a sales visit. The whole process is one of changing antagonism into cooperation.

This writer developed his analogy step by step, making the unknown understandable by comparing it with something known. Also note that the paragraph has a good concluding sentence.

Less often, an example involving contrast may be used to develop a generalization that calls for illustration. Here is an example from the middle of a theme:

Training a wife is not at all like training a pet. With the pet you must at all times exert firm discipline. With a wife you must conceal the discipline, making her think that your ideas are really her own. You must make the pet think he is pleasing you. You must make your wife think you are pleasing her. You can punish a pet openly and he will understand. You must punish your wife in subtle ways, such as purposefully forgetting her birthday or neglecting to give her her weekly dinner out. Your pet must be given constant praise as he learns his tricks. Overpraise for your wife will spoil her rather than make her more obedient. In fact, you must not make your wife a pet at all, for that will lead to divorce. You must make her your knowing servant.

Such paragraph development through contrast, as through comparison, helps clarify an idea and also adds interest to informative writing.

EXERCISES

1. Choose one of the main points from the following basic organization, convert it into a topic sentence, and develop a paragraph for it using several specific details. Try to give your paragraph a clincher sentence.

> *topic:* Discuss some of the most important functions of a church.
> 1. To provide worship services for the faithful
> 2. To provide consultations to help people with their personal or social problems
> 3. To teach young people the fundamentals of their religion
> 4. To provide social events of various sorts for the membership

2. Choose one of the main points from the following basic organization, convert it into a topic sentence, and develop a paragraph for it using one extended example. Use comparison or contrast if you wish.

> *topic:* Describe several ways to win a girl friend or a boy friend.
> 1. Be a sports hero or a campus queen
> 2. Have a lot of money and a house with a swimming pool
> 3. Be socially charming and the life of the party
> 4. Have a hobby that many people are interested in

USAGE
LESSON
31

THE
SEMICOLON

The **semicolon** is a mark of punctuation that indicates a voice pause of longer duration than a comma indicates, but of slightly lesser duration than a mark of end punctuation indicates. It is always used between constituents that are coordinate, or equal in rank.

Good writers often use a semicolon between two independent clauses (which are, in effect, sentences) that are not joined by a conjunction or connective word or phrase. The writer's intent is to show that the clauses are too closely associated to be separated by a period. Examples:

correct: Bogardo has lessened the authority of the military and increased that of the bureaucracy; now civilians feel more secure and not in daily fear of a military coup.

correct: My family is the biggest part of my life; we're a complete unit.

No connective would sound natural between these independent clauses, and yet the writer wants the two statements to be more closely associated than if they each had end punctuation. Remember that commas instead of semicolons in sentences like those just illustrated produce unacceptable **comma splices** (see Chapter 11).

Unless end punctuation is used, a semicolon rather than a comma must separate independent clauses joined by one of the conjunctive adverbs: *however, nevertheless, therefore, furthermore, consequently, thus, hence, accordingly, then, later, afterwards, moreover,* and a few others. When the writer wants both clauses to be in the same sentence (that is, to have just one mark of end punctuation), he separates the clauses with a semicolon whether or not the conjunctive adverb is shifted to the interior of the second independent clause. Examples:

correct: The play *Thorns on the Rose* closed in New York after six showings; the producer, nevertheless, intended to try to revive it in Boston.

> *correct:*   The registration in this district heavily favors the Democrats; therefore we must plan our campaign to make Republican ideas appeal to Democrats.

Again, the use of a comma instead of a semicolon in this position produces an unacceptable comma splice. One good tip to remember is that when the connective can be shifted to the interior of the second clause (as in the first example), a semicolon is always needed between the clauses unless they both have end punctuation. A few of the conjunctive adverbs, however, — chiefly *hence* — cannot be readily shifted.

The third chief use of the semicolon is to separate constituents in a series that have internal commas of their own. Examples:

> *correct:*   Police departments in Madison, Wisconsin; Miami, Florida; Dayton, Ohio; and Kansas City, Missouri, are some that are reforming.

> *correct:*   We visited the Whist Club, 242 42nd Street; the Cavendish Club, 414 Central Park South; and Abie's Bridge Club, 463 Madison Avenue.

Semicolons in these positions are simply an aid to clarity; the reader might become confused if commas replaced the semicolons, for then many commas would be used in a short space for two different purposes. Also long constituents in a series may be separated by semicolons rather than commas even when they contain no internal commas. Example:

> *correct:*   Professor Silver has demonstrated that very large amounts of dielden can cause cancer in mice; that the descendants of those diseased mice are more than normally subject to cancer of all sorts; and that mice that are not affected by dielden have descendants that are freer from cancer than the general mice population.

Semicolons in this position are just a slight aid to clarity; commas in their place would not be wrong.

Caution: Do **not** separate a dependent clause from an independent clause with a semicolon. Example:

> *incorrect:*   I invested my money in oil stocks; since the oil companies seemed to be on the road to great prosperity.

The two constituents separated by the semicolon are not coordinate, or equal in rank. Remember that semicolons only separate coordinate constituents. Also do **not** use a semicolon after the connective *such as.* Example:

> *incorrect:*   I wanted to put my wealth in tangibles, such as; real estate, gold, and silver.

No punctuation should be used after *such as,* but a comma should be used before it.

EXERCISE 31. In the blanks below each of the following sentences indicate the options for proper punctuation: semicolons, dashes, colons, and commas.

1. Gandy dancer John Henry planted spikes at the rate of one a second; the automatic track layer, however, was gradually overtaking him.

  _____

  _____

2. These were our points of destinaton: the Haberfeld Building, 719 Yvonne Street; the Renegade Ballpark, 400 N. Chester; and Martha's Bistro, 999 Turk Street.

  _____

  _____

3. These were his direct orders: proceed to the suspect's hideout, establish three stakeouts, and wait for further orders.

  _____

  _____

4. The attempt to get a dog elected senior class president was a lost cause, since the student body was tired of stupid pranks.
  optional

  _____

  _____

5. I had practiced on my trombone eight hours a day for weeks; thus I felt I had an excellent chance to make the band.

  _____

  _____

6. I had brought all my equipment—jimmy-bars, plastic explosives, stethoscope, and all—my nerve, however, I seemed to have left behind.

  _____

  _____

7. My last comment, that I would under no circumstances support Huey's candidacy, angered the committee; it seemed best then to leave.

  _____

  _____

8. The Institute for Advanced Study is now racked with dissention; the nation's best brains cannot agree on who has the best brains.

_____

_____

9. The power of the White House is now lessened, the presidential scandals of the early 1970's having taken their toll.

_____

_____

10. We recommended the following: that the right of students to quality instruction be guaranteed · that a student representative sit on all advisory boards · that the administration be reorganized to devote more administrative time to student affairs.

_____ *or commas, since items in a series* _____

_____

11. The vice president realized that the case against him was airtight; he therefore entered into plea bargaining and resigned his office.

_____

_____

12. Not a faculty member—not a single one showed up for graduation ceremonies; they said no one deserved to graduate.

_____

_____

13. Our smuggling venture into Canada was a valuable experience for us; we learned that the threat of large fines is a deterrent to crime.

_____

_____

14. Only one person—Jeff—can handle this job, the rest of us not having had enough experience.

_____

_____

15. Ray Gonzales won the primary with a majority vote; moreover, he polled 59 percent of the vote in the November election.

_____

_____

CHAPTER
32
PARAGRAPH
DEVELOPMENT
THROUGH
ANALYSIS

Though specific details or examples may help develop paragraphs in almost any kind of informative or persuasive writing, many topic sentences call chiefly for development through **analysis, explanation,** or **a logical sequence of ideas** rather than just specific details. For example, when a reader encounters such a topic sentence as

Industrialism has produced a decline in individualism,

he will not expect an answer to the question "What?" or "Which ones?" but to the question "Why?" or "How?" or both. He will expect the paragraph to explain why or how with a progression of related ideas, not just examples (though examples may be used too).

There are closely related varieties of paragraphs developed through analysis. The general variety is developed with a logically related sequence of ideas, or a progression of ideas, with each sentence growing out of the previous one, not with each sentence being an illustration of the topic sentence. Here is an example:

Maintaining regular study habits and hours may greatly improve a college student's grades. The human mind, as well as the body, operates in such a way that regularity increases its efficiency. For example, one sleeps best if he has a regular time for going to bed. Also one learns a skill, such as playing a piano, better if he has regular lessons and practice sessions rather than irregular ones. This response of the body and mind to regularity applies to

321

studying academic subjects. For example, the student who sets aside, say, the period from 10:00 to 11:00 each weekday night for studying German will retain what he learns much better than the student who simply picks up his German book at any odd hour and studies erratically. Regularity increases learning potential.

Note that the topic sentence chiefly calls for an answer to the question "Why?" Examples simply reinforce the sentences of development that explain why. Note also that the paragraph has a clincher sentence of restatement for a good conclusion to the paragraph.

Here is another example:

Conforming to the thought patterns of the majority also weakens a person's creative powers. Being creative is generally considered to be the most desirable characteristic of a human being, but to be creative one must be free and independent. If a person just falls in with the thought patterns of the masses, he will bind and restrict the parts of his brain that produce creativity. He will become less imaginative and less aware of his potential. Even if such a person were an artist and simply conformed to the thinking of the majority, his paintings would just reflect conformity and not be really creative. Nonconformity increases one's creativity.

The sentences in this paragraph could not be rearranged, as they often can be when the development consists only of specific details. In this kind of paragraph development, a line of thought is established, not a series of illustrative details. It is a difficult kind of paragraph to write and calls for hard thinking; but once you have a clear topic sentence and recognize the need to answer the questions "Why?" or "How?," you can develop an effective paragraph of analysis or explanation.

Another variety of paragraph development through analysis is one that explains **cause and result,** the result usually being expressed in the topic sentence and the cause of the result being explained in the sentences of development. Here is an example:

Another result of the starvation wages paid many workers is that the cost of their production is actually greater than it would be if they were paid better. Workers who are very much underpaid know it and resent it. Because of this they take no pride in their work and have no incentive to do good work or a lot of work per hour. With the inevitable slowdown in their work, what they produce actually costs more per hour than what they would produce if paid enough to make them take pride in their work. I have seen janitors in this school working at a snail's pace. The work could be done with half the men if the pay were raised 50 percent.

The topic sentence expresses a result; then the progression of ideas explains the cause of the result. Note that an example is also given in the paragraph, which is often the case in development through explanation.

The paragraph does not have a clincher sentence of conclusion. It might have been a stronger paragraph if the writer had closed it with this sentence:

> Thus employers who pay unjustly low wages are actually costing themselves money.

Such a clincher sentence would in essence be a restatement of the topic sentence, but not useless repetition.

Another variety of paragraph development through explanation is one that expresses **steps in a process**; it most commonly appears in the "how to" kind of writing. In composing such a paragraph the writer must keep his sentences of development in a workable order. He may of course include examples. Here is an example:

> The first step in writing a term paper, after you have a topic, is to prepare a working bibliography. First check the main general encyclopedias and their yearbooks to see if there is a general article that touches on your topic. Next investigate the special encyclopedias and reference works, such as the *Catholic Encyclopedia,* for other general articles that might give you useful information. Now you are ready to search the card catalogue for books that pertain to your topic. You must check subject headings, such as "Astronomy," and you must check cross references. You will also check the card catalogue for pamphlets. Finally you are ready to search the periodical indexes for magazine articles pertaining to your topic. First investigate the *Reader's Guide to Periodical Literature,* using subject headings and cross references, and then see if there is a specialized periodical index, such as the *Art Index,* that might list articles about your topic.

If the writer really knows his subject matter, he has little trouble keeping his sentencs in a proper order in using steps-in-a-process development.

Students are often asked on tests to define terms, such as *irony, a parochial school,* or *astrology.* Sometimes a one-sentence definition is sufficient, but often an **extended definition** consisting of a full paragraph is called for. Such a paragraph, though it will usually give examples, calls for development through analysis or explanation. Usually a paragraph of definition will employ four steps: (1) classification, which means identifying the larger classification the term belongs to and differentiating it from other terms belonging to that classification; (2) explanation of the chief characteristics of the concept or thing being defined; (3) a limited definition of any special term used that might not be familiar to the reader; and (4) an example of the concept or thing defined. Steps 3 and 4 may, of course, not be necessary. Here is an example of a paragraph of extended definition:

> Syntax is the level of structure of a language that has to do with word arrangement to produce meaningful sentences [classification]. A sentence is an

independent, meaningful utterance, though it may have reference to a previous utterance [limited definition of a special term]. The chief aspects of the syntax of a sentence are predication, or the fitting of a subject to a predicate; complementation, or the completion of a meaning initiated in a verb; and modification, or the restriction of the meaning of a word or word group by another word or word group [special characteristics]. For example, here is an ordinary English sentence:

The sophomores elected a beautiful coed class president.

The predication consists of *the sophomores* as the subject and the remainder as the predicate. The complements are *coed* as a direct object and *president* as an object complement. And the modification consists of the adjective *beautiful* modifying the noun *coed* and the noun *class* modifying the noun *president* [example of the term defined].

Of course a very great deal more could be said about syntax, but this is a good example of clear, compact extended definition using the four important steps.

EXERCISES

1. Choose one of the main points from the following basic organization, convert it into a topic sentence, and develop it through analysis or explanation.

> Explain some of the reasons why so many teenagers run away from home.
> 1. Irreconcilable conflicts with parents
> 2. Desire for thrills and excitement
> 3. Maladjustment in their peer groups
> 4. Emotional immaturity

2. Write a paragraph defining one of these terms: *satire, a junkie, spring fever, parental pressure, hard rock music, love, freshman jitters, egotism, inferiority complex, a social misfit,* or any other term of interest to you.

USAGE
LESSON
32

QUOTATION
MARKS
AND
UNDERLINING

In addition to being used to enclose direct quotations, such as segments of dialogue in fiction, **quotation marks** are also used to enclose certain other kinds of sentence constituents. These constituents are usually integral parts of their sentences, though they may be nonessential, such as titles used as nonessential appositives. These uses of quotation marks are discussed below; first we need to consider the use of other marks of punctuation in conjunction with quotation marks.

A comma or period directly following material enclosed in quotation marks is put inside the quotation marks, even when it is not a part of the quoted unit. Example:

correct: I didn't like the way he said "Do your share."

The period closes the whole sentence and is not a part of the quoted phrase; nevertheless it is placed within the quotation marks. The reason why periods and commas are placed inside quotation marks is that early printers thought the line of print looked better that way.

A mark of punctuation that belongs to the quoted unit is placed inside the quotation marks. Example:

correct: Sam asked, "Can you spare a fifth?"

The question mark is a part of the quotation and thus is placed wthin the quotation marks. Note that even though the whole is a sentence and not a question, a period is not used in addition to the question mark. When a mark of punctuation other than a period or comma is not a part of the quoted unit, it is placed outside the quotation marks. Example:

correct: Why did Professor Snailly say this class is an "enigma"?

The question mark belongs to the whole, not just the quoted word, and is thus placed outside the quotation marks.

When a quoted unit comes within another quoted unit, the longer unit is enclosed in the usual double quotation marks and the unit within is enclosed in single quotation marks. Example:

correct: Professor Snaul said that "the best nineteenth century American short story is Poe's 'Fall of the House of Usher.' "

Note that a space comes between the single and the double quotation marks at the end.

In a quotation consisting of several paragraphs, quotation marks are placed at the beginning of each paragraph but not at the end of any of the paragraphs except the last one.

Use quotation marks to enclose titles of relatively short literary works, such as short stories, short poems, short plays, chapters from books, essays, articles, songs, and speeches. (The titles of longer works are italicized or underlined; see below.) Examples:

correct: "To an Athlete Dying Young" is one of Housman's best poems.
correct: The one-act play "Schizoid" was a success.
correct: The ninth chapter of *Candide* is entitled "The Old Woman's Story."
correct: Did you read Barbara Tuchman's article "History as Mirror" in the current *Atlantic?*

Words used as words and not for their meaning may be enclosed in quotation marks or underlined (see below). Example:

correct: I thought he was using "tomato" as a slang term.

Words or phrases used in an ironical or unusual sense are usually enclosed in quotation marks. Example:

Lucius is so "literary" that I can't stand his company.

The writer means that he doesn't approve of the kind of literary affectation that Lucius exhibits or that Lucius only thinks he is a literary person but really is not.

Short definitions of terms are usually enclosed in quotation marks. Example:

correct: The word *irony* comes from a Greek word meaning "feigned ignorance."

Do **not** use quotation marks to enclose a title standing at the head of a composition, though a part of the title might necessarily need to be enclosed in quotation marks. Example:

title as heading: An Analysis of the Imagery in Keats's "Ode to a Nightingale"

If this title were mentioned within a paragraph, double and single quotation marks would be needed. Also do **not** enclose a slang word in quotation marks as an apology for using it.

In typewriting or longhand, underlining is used where italics would be used in print. Underline the titles of books, long plays, long poems, magazines, newspapers, musical compositions (except song titles), and works of art. Also the names of ships and aircraft are usually underlined. Examples:

correct: Hemingway's first novel was The Sun Also Rises.

correct: All My Sons is one of Arthur Miller's best plays.

correct: Scientific American is my favorite magazine.

correct: The Mona Lisa is on loan to Japan.

Words used as words may be underlined; in fact, most writers prefer to underline such constituents rather than to put them in quotation marks. Example:

correct: There were too many but's and if's in his proposal.

Also foreign words and phrases that are not yet anglicized should be underlined. Example:

correct: The theme of "The Rubaiyat of Omar Khayyam" is carpé diem.

Carpé diem, a Latin phrase, means "seize the day," or simply "enjoy life while you can."

EXERCISE 32. Rewrite the following sentences, inserting quotation marks and underlining where appropriate and adding any needed commas.

1. Professor Snowl said explicitly: Read Herman Melville's short story Bartleby the Scrivener.

2. The current issue of The New Yorker contains a poem entitled Demon in the White House.

3. The sine qua non of palmism is ambiguous generalizations.

4. The twenty-fourth chapter of Moby Dick is entitled The Advocate.

5. Did John say, You shouldn't be married?

6. Bowlbee's article Guru in Trouble is in the July issue of Harper's.

7. Shakespeare's funniest comedy Twelfth Night contains the song Come Away, Come Away, Death.

8. Milton's Paradise Lost consists of twelve books, space enough for him To justify the ways of God to man.

9. In has last lecture Professor Longueil said, I like Shakespeare's lyric Fear No More the Heat of the Sun, which comes from Cymbeline, better than any other.

10. The title of my term paper will be "A Study of Pope's 'The Rape of the Lock.'"

_____

_____

11. If you use <u>consequently</u> in one more sentence, I will require you to read all of Ariosto's <u>Orlando Furioso.</u>

_____

_____

12. Wordsworth's best lyric, "The Intimations Ode," contains the line "Trailing clouds of glory do we come."

_____

_____

13. A <u>non sequitur</u> is a conclusion that does not follow from the **reasoning** given to support it, such as saying that since it is about suicide Thomas Hood's poem The Bridge of Sighs is of poor quality.

_____

_____

_____

14. Sara asked, "Are you reading Maugham's novel <u>Of Human Bondage</u>?"

_____

_____

15. "No," I answered. "I am reading his play <u>The Circle.</u>"

_____

_____

CHAPTER 33

PARAGRAPH UNITY AND COHERENCE

Paragraphs should have both **unity** and **coherence,** qualities which are very closely related but which are not exactly the same. Unity, of course, means oneness, and a paragraph in the kind of writing we are studying is unified when all the material in it pertains to the one main point that the paragraph is supposed to develop. When some of the material in a paragraph does *not* pertain to the main point expressed in the topic sentence, the paragraph is disunified and thus loses much of its effect. Most commonly, **disunity** in student writing is due to the inclusion of more than one main point in one paragraph.

Here is an example of paragraph disunity:

It's been said that money is the root of all evil, but it is really lack of money that is the root of most evil. Schoolboys, drug addicts, winos — all sorts of people — steal because they lack money. Certainly stealing is evil. I've read that a burglary is committed every two seconds, and usually because someone needs money. Often it is not just an individual who needs money but a family. Where there is never enough money, many wives seek divorces. Many people think divorces are evil.

The writer of this paragraph did not plan his basic organization well and thus carelessly put two main points — the lack of money as the cause of stealing and its lack as the cause of divorce — into one paragraph, producing disunity. If you will prepare a good basic organization of main points and will faithfully develop only one main point in each paragraph,[1] you will avoid the weakness of disunity. Well-expressed topic sentences greatly help a writer maintain paragraph unity.

A paragraph is unified when all of its material pertains to its one main point, which is usually stated in a topic sentence in the kind of writing we are studying. A paragraph is *coherent* when all of its sentences (and large constituents in long sentences) are closely linked together. Naturally, unity and coherence go together, but unity can be present with coherence absent. Here, from student work, is an example of this fact:

> Some teenagers assume that parents exist solely to be exploited. Teenagers owe many obligations to their parents.

The two sentences belong together and thus do not exhibit disunity, but coherence between them is lacking. Note how much more smoothly the two ideas read when a means of linking them — that is, of making them coherent — is added:

> Some teenagers assume that parents exist solely to be exploited, *but in actuality* teenagers owe many obligations to their parents.

The italicized connective phrase *expresses* the relationship between the two independent clauses and thus provides coherence. The unity that was at least partially concealed is now made fully evident. Thus we can say that a paragraph is coherent when *in some way* each sentence (or clause) is clearly related to the previous or a previous sentence (or clause). Coherence is a quality that helps make writing clear, smooth, and intelligible. It might be likened to glue that holds articles together or to stitching thread that binds pieces of cloth together.

The most easily recognizable method of achieving coherence in paragraphs is the use of **coordinating transitional words and phrases,** which serve as connectives between sentences and between independent clauses in compound sentences. (The subordinating connectives, such as *because, though, if,* and so on, show a relationship only between parts of a complex sentence, never between sentences or independent clauses.) Few aspects of informative and persuasive writing affect its clarity as much as the adeptness with which its author uses his connectives. Among the most frequently used coordinating connectives are the coordinating conjunctions, such as *and, but,* and *or,* and the conjunctive adverbs, such as *however, therefore,* and *moreover.* We also use enumerators, such as *first, second, next,* and *finally.* In addition, our language has many transitional phrases that are in effect connectives, such as *in addition, on the other hand, on the contrary, in conclusion,* and so on.

---

[1] In compositions of more than 400-500 words, sometimes one main point may call for two or more paragraphs of development. This is because it is customary nowadays in informative writing to have a new paragraph indentation for every 100 to 200 words even though the same point may still be under discussion.

In general, students do not use coordinating connectives in their writing nearly as much as they should. Seldom is such a connective awkward or out of place, and usually it contributes to coherence and thus to clarity. To understand better the importance of connectives, first read this paragraph, which has no coordinating connectives:

Most people believe that there is only one reality and that they understand what it is. Anthropological studies are showing that what a person thinks is reality depends entirely on the kind of culture he is reared in and the experiences he has had. A person educated in modern science believes that reality consists of the operation of immutable natural laws on the material substance of the universe. Shamans in many tribes are known to have defied so-called natural law. The languages of some tribes do not have the tenses to distinguish past from future, showing that they interpret the world far differently from the way we do. Some anthropologists now believe that different cultures hold different world views and that these views are all relative with no one necessarily being true or false.

Though a reader can make some sense of this paragraph, he certainly feels that the sentences are isolated and not bound closely together by the glue of coherence.

Now read the paragraph with connectives entered into it:

Most people believe that there is only one reality and that they understand what it is. *But* anthropological studies are showing that what a person thinks is reality depends entirely on the kind of culture he is reared in and the experiences he has had. *For example*, a person educated in modern science believes that reality consists of the operation of immutable natural laws on the material substance of the universe. *Yet* shamans in many tribes are known to have defied so-called natural law. *Or, for another example*, the languages of some tribes do not have tenses to distinguish past from future, showing that they interpret the world far differently from the way we do. *Thus* some anthropologists now believe that different cultures hold different world views and that these views are all relative with no one necessarily being true or false.

Now the paragraph is smooth and clear because its unity is made evident by the verbal expression of the relationships that exist between its sentences. This verbal expression provides coherence.

A second important method of achieving coherence is the **repetition** in one sentence **of an important word** from the previous or a previous sentence. The repetition of the word helps bind the sentences together. Here is an example from student writing:

Most people think of pigs as dirty, repulsive animals, for they have seen them only in pig pens with muddy wallows. *Pigs*, however, may not only be raised in clean surroundings but can actually be easily trained as house pets. One woman in Illinois kept an 800-pound *pig* — or hog — in her house as a *pet.* Junior, as this *pig* was known, was actually housebroken and never caused one bit of trouble. But *pig*-haters in the community forced the woman to get rid of her *pet.* Oddly enough, the reason *pigs* make such good *pets* is that they are very intelligent. Neither dogs, cats, nor horses can learn to solve problems or perform tricks as quickly as *pigs* can. So the next time you see a *pig* in a muddy wallow, realize that you are watching an *animal* that could become a desirable companion for man.

The repetition of the words *pig, pet,* and *animal* in this paragraph is its chief source of coherence. The repetition helps keep the reader's mind in a smooth groove as he reads the paragraph. He does not feel any disjointedness in the writing.

Now note how failure to repeat a key word *weakens* coherence between these two sentences:

> The physiology of chimpanzees is almost identical to that of humans. Every organ is similar to and in the same place as the equivalent human organ.

Unity is present, but the reader feels a disjointedness or vagueness as he moves from sentence one to sentence two. Now note how repetition of a key word eliminates the disjointedness and provides coherence:

> The physiology of chimpanzees is almost identical to that of humans. Every organ in a *chimpanzee* is similar to and in the same place as the equivalent human organ.

With the repetition of *chimpanzee,* the sentences are closely bound together and coherence is perfect.

A third method of achieving coherence is to use a **pronoun** in one sentence to refer to a noun or idea in the previous or a previous sentence. Here is an example from student writing:

> Football is more than a sport. *It* is an acting out of aggressive tendencies in man, and watchers of the game can work off their aggressive tendencies just as the players can. *This* means that pro football is important socially, for *it* decreases the number of arguments and fights that a fan might get into if he did not have games to watch. *It* might even become a substitute for war. Those people who condemn *it* have not given the matter any thought. *They* just want to criticize people who don't like the same things *they* do. If *they* watched some football *they* might get rid of *their* aggressive tendencies towards football fans.

The italicized pronouns in this paragraph provide the chief verbal glue that gives the paragraph coherence. They act as signals to keep a reader's mind focused on a train of thought.

Now note how absence of such pronoun reference can destroy coherence:

The professor accused the student of dishonesty. Instances of cheating were cited.

Again, the reader feels a jar as he passes from sentence one to sentence two, for coherence (though not unity) is lacking. Now note how pronoun reference provides coherence:

The professor accused the student of dishonesty. He cited several instances of the student having been caught cheating.

The *he*, as well as the repetition of *student*, provides full coherence.

Coherence may also be effected through **parallelism of ideas** and parallelism of sentence structure. Here is an example:

The world, it seems, has always been going to hell. There have been few years since the dawn of civilization in which no war was being fought. Revolutions occur regularly. Pollution of the environment is as old as man. Natural disasters, such as earthquakes, floods, droughts, and epidemics, occur regularly and wreak havoc. Tyranny is always at hand in more than half the countries of the world. Civilizations rise and fall as though they follow some natural law. The "good old days," in fact, have never existed.

The coherence of this paragraph is provided by the close relationship of each sentence to the topic sentence. There is no progression of ideas — just a parallelism of ideas — and thus connectives, word repetition, and pronoun reference are not needed. Also parallelism of sentence structure contributes to the coherence of the paragraph.

We should say, however, that such paragraphs are rare and that, in general, coherence in your writing will depend mostly on your use of the three verbal means of achieving coherence: **connectives, word repetition, and pronoun reference.** As you write, always keep your previous sentence in mind so that you can bind the next sentence to it.

EXERCISES

In the following paragraphs underline the connectives, repeated key words, and pronouns that make the paragraphs coherent.

1. The returns on these investments are real enough. But they are imponderable and deferred. Values created by the schools in educating the next generation, by public works to preserve the fertility of the soil, do not have a market price and would, therefore, not be undertaken by ordinary private enterprise. This is the realm of investment by public authority which does not have to pay its way and show returns measured in money within a short span of time. For the most farsighted private investment cannot look much beyond one generation; only the exceptionally prudent plant trees for their children. But a society, as Burke so eloquently said, comprehends the dead, the living, and the unborn. And as the living in-

herited the national estate from their ancestors so they must transmit it to their posterity. This carries with it the obligation to plough back some portion of the current income into the foundations of the social economy.

— from *The Good Society* by Walter Lippman

2.   First, natural law theory does not pretend to do more than it can, which is to give a philosophical account of the moral experience of humanity and to lay down a charter of humanism. It does not show the way to sainthood but only to manhood. It does not promise to transform society into the City of God on earth, but only to prescribe, for the purposes of law and social custom, that minimum of morality which must be observed by the members of a society, if the social environment is to be human and habitable. At that, for a man to be reasonably human, and for a society to be truly civil — these are no mean achievements. They carry man and society to the limits of the obligatory. This moral horizon lies at sufficient distance from the inertness and perversity which are part of the human stuff; it sets for man a goal that is not ignoble.

— from "Natural Law and Public Consensus"
by John Courtney Murray, S.J.

3.   Prejudice is sometimes distinguished by psychologists and sociologists from discrimination. Prejudice is an antipathetic feeling or attitude against some person or group not rationally justified by objective evidence. Discrimination is a pattern of behavior in which one acts against others by excluding them from opportunities commonly enjoyed. At the moment it is experienced, one can't help feeling prejudiced. But one *can* help discriminating unless under some compulsion. No one chooses to be prejudiced. But one chooses to discriminate. And because one does, one's choice can be inhibited or influenced by many things besides his prejudice. In a sense, everyone has a right to his thoughts or feelings. But not everyone has a right to discriminate. Neither the state by law nor society by custom has a moral right to discriminate prejudicially against individuals and groups in public life. Such a pattern of discriminaton is segregation.

— from *Political Power and Personal Freedom*
by Sidney Hook

USAGE
LESSON
33

MISPLACED
MODIFIERS

Most mature, well-formed sentences consist of a sentence nucleus of subject-verb-complement (though a complement, such as a direct object, may not be present, and in a request sentence, such as "Shut the door," no subject is present) plus various large and small constituents called **modifiers.** For a sentence to be immediately clear and smooth, modifiers must be carefully placed. A **misplaced modifier** will at the very least cause a reader to pause unnecessarily to think out the word relationships; it might confuse him. For example, consider this sentence from a newspaper:

> *misplaced modifier:* Father Kaufman scolded her every time she distributed her poisoned candy severely, and eventually she stopped the practice.

A reader must pause to understand the intended meaning. But with the misplaced modifier *severely* placed properly, the reader need not needlessly pause:

> *properly placed modifier:* Father Kaufman scolded her severely every time she distributed her poisoned candy, and eventually she stopped the practice.

Now the modifier *severely* is clearly placed.
  Here is another example, taken from a magazine:

> *misplaced modifier:* Frank Sinatra celebrated the birth of his grandchild at Brentwood's Gatsby's Restaurant.

At first the reader thinks the grandchild was born in Gatsby's Restaurant.

properly placed modifier: Frank Sinatra celebrated at Brentwood's Gatsby's Restaurant the birth of his grandchild.

You must *think* about the structure of your sentences in order to avoid misplaced modifiers. Remember that what seems clear to you may not be immediately clear to your reader.

EXERCISE 33.   Rewrite the following sentences so that all modifiers in them are properly placed.

1. Nearly a third of all owners of guns have had some sort of accident with them in this country.

2. Disc brakes can be relined by anyone who has been trained at the factory in about an hour.

3. A father is concerned about his son's plans for a career for his own satisfaction.

4. People are affected by their government from birth to **death in many** ways.

5. The news about Agnew's resigning on television startled my father greatly.

6. I became aware that many basically honest people can at times be dishonest suddenly.

7. She was not just sure which of the two she would marry at first.

8. I decided that I would major in anthropology the next day.

_____

_____

9. I picked up the rifle and began to run quickly.

_____

_____

10. People tend to dream towards the end of their night's sleep about the previous day's events.

_____

_____

11. People sit and talk about many things around the dinner table.

_____

_____

12. All students are not lazy.

_____

_____

13. Professor Rolfe lectured about the sinking of the Titanic in an interesting way.

_____

_____

14. At last I saw the course that my life would take clearly.

_____

_____

15. We decided that we would not be able to raise the money we needed by the end of the first day of the fund-raising campaign.

_____

_____

_____

CHAPTER
34

ACHIEVING GOOD STYLE AND VARIETY IN SENTENCES

Proper organization of the whole composition and development of unified, coherent paragraphs are certainly two of the basics of good informative and persuasive writing. But just as fundamental to good writing are mature, well-formed sentences. Look again at the quotation from James Michener in Chapter 25; there is truth in what he says. Furthermore, we can say in truth that anyone who can write really good sentences can easily learn the other important basics of writing. Most sentences in good informative writing will be composed of more than just one basic statement, will read smoothly, will possess clarity and simplicity (not to be confused with simpleness), and will exhibit variety in structure.

A composition written only in simple, childish sentences cannot be considered good even if it has no errors in usage and expresses some good ideas. For example, here is a passage from a theme written as part of a classification test given to entering freshmen:

> I think that victimless crimes should be punished. Then people will stop hurting themselves and others. Drunkenness often leads to accidents. People may even be killed. Gambling is not a big thing, but it may get out of hand. Then people can be hurt. Possession of a little marijuana might not hurt anybody. However, heroin addicts started out on marijuana. So even these so-called victimless crimes are harmful.

Aside from the fact that this student did not plan a good basic organization (the rest of his paper mostly just repeated what he had already said), the sentences in this passage are over-simple and do not have the characteristics of good sentences mentioned in the first paragraph of this chapter. Occasional short, simple sentences can be effectively used, but mature writing calls for mature sentence structure, and that means that most sentences in a paragraph will contain more than one basic idea. For example, the above paragraph with its monotonous simple sentences would be far more effective with such mature sentence structure as is exemplified in this revision:

Those who commit so-called victimless crimes should be punished rather than just given citations, for in fact such crimes are not victimless. In committing such crimes, people almost always hurt themselves and often hurt other people too. Drunkenness, for example, frequently leads to traffic accidents, with many resulting deaths. Gambling might seem innocent enough, but when a family man gambles too much his family often suffers, perhaps even to the point of being impoverished. Possession and use of small quantities of marijuana usually is not harmful, but far too often users of pot go on to hard drugs, such as heroin. Thus the so-called victimless crimes are usually harmful, which means that those who commit them should be punished in order to diminish the number of such crimes.

The chief difference between this revised paragraph and the original (we won't say anything about the content) is that each sentence in the revision contains more than one simple statement. The purpose of this chapter will be to show you some of the techniques of composing such mature, well-formed sentences.

To understand the aspects of sentence composition that we are about to discuss, first imagine that a writer has in his mind fifty separate bits of information that he is going to combine into one paragraph composed of just a few sentences. What happens in his mind? The answer is that his mind **generates** complex sentences out of what are called kernel sentences, that is, sentences that are the simplest, most basic possible. For example, two of the fifty bits of information that our theoretical writer is to put into his paragraph might be these:

The president was guilty.
The president resigned.

Through a generative — or transformational — process, his mind would likely produce

The guilty president resigned,

which, though apparently a simple sentence, is in a sense complex because it contains two ideas or bits of information. The writer's other forty-eight bits of information would similarly be transformed into more and more complex structures so that his finished paragraph might consist of just four or five structures that we call sentences.

Just how basic transformations are produced in the mind is not well understood, and we will not be concerned with elemental generation of sentences just above the kernel level. Instead, we will see how moderately complex sentences traditionally called simple can be transformed into large sentence constituents to produce an immense variety of mature, well-formed sentences. Our intent is to improve your ability to compose sentences that experienced readers will recognize as "good" and not "childish." For example, we will be discussing such transformational processes as this one:

The millions of neurons connecting the two hemispheres of an epileptic's brain are sometimes severed to cure his disease.

Then the former epipeptic's right hand may literally not know what his left hand is doing.

Through a transformation we can convert the first simple sentence into a large sentence constituent and compose one complex sentence:

After the millions of neurons connecting the two hemispheres of an epileptic's brain are severed to cure his disease, the former epileptic's right hand may literally not know what his left hand is doing.

Helping you improve your sentence style in this way is the purpose of this chapter.

In describing several kinds of transformational processes we will need to use some grammatical terms, such as *adverb clause* for the large sentence constituent in the example sentence just given. However, you need not be concerned with the grammatical labels but only with the basic fact that composers of good sentences use various large sentence constituents rather than just writing many short, simple sentences to deliver their information. The large constituents should be composed and placed so that the resulting sentences are smooth, clear, and pleasing in their variety.

A simple **deletion transformation** may be used to generate compound constituents. Example:

The dictator Amin Borodo imposed martial law.
The dictator Amin Borodo imprisoned many of his political opponents.
The dictator Amin Borodo ordered most aliens to leave his country.

By deleting the subjects of the second two sentences, we get a compound predicate (italicized):

The dictator Amin Borodo *imposed martial law, imprisoned many of his political opponents,* and *ordered most aliens to leave his country.*

This is a simple generative process that you use frequently, but probably not frequently enough. As you compose your sentences, *think* about their structure and watch for opportunities to reduce excess wordage and improve your style.

A deletion transformation also produces the appositive phrase as a large sentence constituent. Example:

> A neutron star is the remnant of a supernova explosion.
> A neutron star is so dense that just a handful of one would weigh millions of tons.

By deletion we get

> A neutron star, *the remnant of a supernova explosion*, is so dense that just a handful of one would weigh millions of tons.

The italicized appositive contains the full information of a sentence and allows for improved sentence style. In general, students do not use appositives nearly as frequently as they should. You can improve your command of sentence composition considerably by cultivating the appositive construction.

Another general kind of deletion transformation produces verb phrases as large sentence constituents. Example:

> The vice president engaged in plea bargaining.
> The vice president was allowed to pay a small fine and not go to prison.

Through deletion and verb-change transformations we get

> The vice president, *having engaged in plea bargaining*, was allowed to pay a small fine and not go to prison.

Another example:

> The president wanted to avoid impeachment.
> The president employed delaying tactics in turning over his tapes to the Judiciary Committee.

Through deletion we get

> *To avoid impeachment*, the president employed delaying tactics in turning over his tapes to the Judiciary Committee.

These italicized verb phrases are just two of a considerable variety that can be used as large sentence constituents carrying the information of a full statement. The use of such verb phrases, and not a knowledge of their names, is most important to a writer.

Also a deletion transformation can produce an adjective phrase for use as a large sentence constituent. Example:

> The judge was not sober enough to understand the testimony against the alcoholic.
> The judge dismissed the case.

Through deletion we get

> The judge, *not sober enough to understand the testimony against the alcoholic,* dismissed the case.

As is sometimes the case, the italicized large sentence constituent here is longer than the basic independent clause. In fact, as you will learn in the exercises for this chapter, the basic independent clause of a sentence often carries only a small part of the information in the whole sentence.

A deletion transformation also may produce a large-constituent prepositional or adverbial phrase which functions as a sentence modifier. Example:

> Mr. Imbiber did not pay the least attention to his wife's directions.
> Mr. Imbiber carelessly took the wrong freeway exit and wound up fifty miles from home.

Through deletion plus verb change and addition of a preposition we get

> *Without paying the least attention to his wife's directions,* Mr. Imbiber carelessly took the wrong freeway exit and wound up fifty miles from home.

A considerable variety of large-constituent phrases such as the italicized one here are available in our language. Most students need practice in using them.

Adjective clauses are introduced by the relative pronouns *who, whom, whose, which,* and *that.* A **substitution transformation** allows a simple sentence to be converted into an adjective clause, which then serves as a large sentence constituent. Example:

> The last scientific expedition to Anarctica was organized to explore for possible fossil fuels on that continent.
>
> The last scientific expedition to Anarctica found, deep under the ice cap, bacteria perhaps a million years old.

Through substitution we get

> The last scientific expedition to Anarctica, *which was organized to explore for possible fossil fuels on that continent,* found, deep under the ice cap, bacteria perhaps a million years old.

Use of the italicized adjective clause helps produce mature, pleasing sentence structure.

Finally, **addition transformations** produce adverb clauses, which are introduced by such subordinating conjunctions as *because, since, so that, though, while, if, as, as if, before, when, after,* and so on. Example:

Kubec was considered a revisionist.

Kubek was expelled from the Communist Party.

Through addition of a subordinating conjunction we get

Because he was considered a revisionist, Kubek was expelled from the Communist Party.

Students probably use adverb clauses more effectively than any of the other large sentence constituents we have illustrated. The reason for this is that the subordinating conjunctions express a logical relationship — such as cause-and-result, contrast, condition, method or manner, time, comparison, and so on — between the adverb clause and another part of the sentence, and thus the writer often must use an adverb clause if he wants to make his meaning clear. Still, it will be worthwhile for you to work with adverb clauses in the exercises for this chapter.

Of course these various kinds of large sentence constituents, each carrying the meaning of a full statement, may be combined in countless ways to produce good sentences. For example, here is a series of statements that one writer put into two well-phrased sentences by using the processes discussed above:

Telestar is an experimental communication satellite.
It is remarkably successful.
It was sponsored by the Bell System.
It was launched on July 10.
It is an impressive demonstration of the electronics art.
This art has depth.
This art has facility.
The satellite weighs 170 pounds.
It was built by Bell Telephone Laboratories.
It is 34½ inches in diameter.
It occupies an orbit.
The orbit is inclined 45 degrees to the Equator.
The Orbit's altitude ranges from 529 to 3454 miles.
This altitude is within 50 miles of the intended orbit.

The writer combined all these statements into these two sentences:

Telestar, the remarkably successful experimental communication satellite sponsored by the Bell System and launched on July 10, is an impressive demonstration of the depth and facility of the electronics art. The 170-pound satellite, built by Bell Telephone Laboratories, is 34½ inches in diameter and occupies an orbit inclined 45 degrees to the Equator, ranging in altitude from 579 to 3454 miles (within 50 miles of the intended orbit). — *Scientific American*

This writer did not think about grammatical labels as he composed, but he knew how to use large sentence constituents well. You too can learn to use them more adeptly.

We should emphasize again, however, that often short, simple sentences are effective and desirable. Also we should reemphasize that in moderately long, complex sentences the large constituents must be artfully combined; otherwise an ineffective "stringy" sentence will result. Example:

ineffective stringy sentence: Telestar is an experimental communications satellite that is remarkably successful and that was sponsored by the Bell System and launched on July 10 and demonstrates impressively the depth and facility of the electronics art.

This sentence is stringy and almost formless; compare it with the effective sentence above and you will see that the effective sentence is well composed — that is, has its large constituents properly related to each other.

EXERCISES

1. Using any of the large sentence constituents illustrated in this chapter, and without being concerned about grammatical labels, combine each of the following sets of short simple sentences into one mature, well-formed sentence. Be concerned about clarity and smoothness of style. Here is an example of how to perform this exercise:

A. 1. Cepheid variable stars were discovered.
   2. Then astronomers were able to determine the distance to many other stars.
   3. The Cepheids have regular periods of pulsation.
   4. The periods of pulsation can be used to guage the absolute brightness of other stars.

After the discovery of Cepheid variable stars, astronomers were able to determine the distance to many other stars, since the Cepheids have regular periods of pulsation to guage the absolute brightness of other stars by.

1. a. The Titanic had supposedly been built to be unsinkable.
   b. The Titanic sank in 1913.
   c. The Titanic hit an iceberg.
   d. The Titanic carried more than 1000 people to their death.

2. a. Samuel Taylor Coleridge wrote the famous "Rime of the Ancient Mariner."
   b. He had trouble as an alcoholic.
   c. He had trouble as an opium addict.
   d. This trouble was so much that his literary production was very irregular.

3. a. A. E. Housman had written what he thought was his last poem.
   b. He entitled his second volume of poems *Last Poems*.
   c. Two later volumes appeared under his name.
   d. They were *More Poems* and *Additional Poems*.

4. a. Professor Snouty was too young to retire.
   b. He was too sick to teach.
   c. He was a world-renowned author.
   d. He had to live off the royalties from his books.

5. a. Harvard College was founded in 1636 to train ministers.
   b. It grew slowly.
   c. Now it is world famous.
   d. It has the largest endowment of any university in the world.

6. a. The U.S. Senate is composed of one-hundred members.
   b. It has more power than any other legislative body in the world.
   c. It is the upper house of the most powerful country in the world.

7. a. The blue whale is the largest animal now living.
   b. It deserves worldwide legal protection.
   c. It is now near extinction.

8. a. Fat Bertha had no visible means of support.
   b. She aroused the suspicions of the police chief.
   c. The police chief assigned plainclothesmen to watch her twenty-four hours a day.

9. a. Thomas Hardy was as good a novelist as England has produced.
   b. He gave up writing novels.
   c. He began writing poetry again.
   d. The critics viciously attacked his last novel.
   e. His last novel was *Jude the Obscure*.

10. a. John Donne was one of the greatest clergymen in the history of the Church of England.
    b. He wrote in his younger years some obscene poetry.
    c. In his later life he tried to have the obscene poetry destroyed.

2. Choose some complex sentences from any good piece of informative writing, break each down into several short, simple sentences, put those short sentences aside for at least a day without referring to them, and then try to reconstruct the original sentences. After you have reconstructed the sentences, compare your versions with the originals.

USAGE
LESSON
34

DANGLING
MODIFIERS

One common kind of error in sentence structure is known as a **dangling modifier.** In its most common form, a dangling modifier is an introductory sentence constituent which expresses an action or state of being and which is supposed to be, but is not, followed immediately by the **person or thing** (which will be the subject of the sentence) performing the action or existing in the state of being. For example, this might be an introductory sentence constituent:

Having been cleared of the charge of perjury

The reader naturally expects next to learn who has been cleared of the charge. But suppose the sentence continues in this way:

Having been cleared of the charge of perjury, the charge of obstruction of justice was still to be faced.

The italicized modifier dangles because it has nothing to modify. The sentence can be corrected if the name of the person who was cleared comes after the modifier (that is, becomes the subject of the sentence):

Having been cleared of the charge of perjury, Mr. Mitchell now faced the charge of obstruction of justice.

Now the modifier does not dangle, and the meaning is crystal clear.
Here is another example of a dangler:
When depressed, the church is a good place to go.

The sentence seems to say that the church is depressed. Such **danglers can** be corrected in several ways. Here is one:

When you are depressed, the church is a good place to go.

Now the phrase does not dangle because the person depressed has been put in the phrase (now a clause) itself so that the subject of the sentence does not have to be the person depressed.

EXERCISE 34. Rewrite each of the following sentences so as to eliminate any dangling modifiers.

1. By refusing to turn over the tapes, the scandal was just drawn out many more months.

    _____

    _____

2. Knowing that I was completely trustworthy, his billfold was always available to me.

    _____

    _____

3. Unlike Texas, no ranch hands were needed.

    _____

    _____

4. Although at times cranky and stubborn, cooperation could usually be counted upon.

    _____

    _____

5. By studying long hours, a high GPA was easy to achieve.

    _____

    _____

6. Not aware of the danger, more firewood was brought into the cabin.

    _____

    _____

7. No solution to the problem seemed possible, not having realized that there was a gadget on the market that would help.

    _____

    _____

8. Besides lowering the purchasing power of people on fixed incomes, the stock market also suffers when there is inflation.

_____

_____

9. With a well-thought-out program for teaching students the evils of Communism, all the other programs seemed to be successful too.

_____

_____

10. By letting high school students do just independent study, I think a very poor education is offered there.

_____

_____

11. When very intelligent, a private school is often better than a public one.

_____

_____

12. After settling the argument over voting rights, another one broke out about qualifications for being a candidate.

_____

_____

13. The pot party was especially exciting, not having had such an experience before.

_____

_____

14. Besides being quite entertaining, most people also learn a lot from the TV series "Nine Lives."

_____

_____

15. Although encouraged by my math teacher, English still seemed to be the hardest course.

_____

_____

CHAPTER 35

AVOIDING WORDINESS IN SENTENCES

'

The fine edge of good style may be blunted by any number of undesirable characteristics: errors in usage (see all chapters in this book), inappropriate or inexact word choice (see the next chapter), immature sentence structure (see the precedng chapter), awkwardness of phrasing, and so on. But one of the most common enemies of good style is **wordiness.** Sometimes wordiness is due to a roundabout rather than a direct way of phrasing a statement. For example, compare these two sentences:

Irony can be said to be a kind of language usage in which what a person says is not what he means but is just directly the opposite of what he means.

Irony is language whose intended meaning is the opposite of its literal meaning.

The first sentence, though meaningful, is so rambling and roundabout as to be devoid of any vestige of pleasing style. The revision, though not sparkling, is concise and in a full paragraph would contribute to pleasing style.

Wordiness can also be due to the use of a long sentence constituent when a shorter one would deliver the same meaning. Compare these two sentences:

William Faulkner, who was a Southern novelist, created a whole human world out of Yoknapatawpha County, Mississippi.

> William Faulkner, a Southern novelist, created a whole human world out of Yoknapa-
> tawpha County, Mississippi.

The second version, by using an appositive phrase instead of an adjective clause, eliminates two words, the consequent increase in terseness producing a better stylistic effect.

Or wordiness may be due to **redundancy,** which means expressing the same meaning twice. Such wordiness is also called **deadwood,** since revision calls not for rephrasing of the sentence but just for omission of useless (or "dead") words. The italicized words in the following constructions are redundant:

> a *new* innovation
> biographical information *about his life*
> Repeat that *again.* (meaning just one repetition)
> a figure of speech *that is not literal*
> audible *to the ear*
> will always be true *forever*

Such deadwood is also known as tautology and pleonasm, though *redundancy* is the most common term applied to it.

True wordiness is of course a flaw in style, but a striving for brevity should not be taken to extremes. First be sure you have said all you want to say and have said it clearly; then be concerned that you haven't been wordy. Mark Twain once cautioned:

> But tautology cannot scare me anyway. Conversation would be intolerably stiff and formal without it; and a mild form of it can limber up even printed matter without doing it serious damage. Some folks are so afraid of a little repetition that they make their meaning vague, when they could just as well make it clear, if only their ogre were out of the way.

That is a sensible comment.

But true wordiness is common, and you should form the habit of listening to and examining your sentences to avoid it. As you compose your sentences you can give considerable attention to avoiding wordiness, but to produce a finished composition that is not wordy you must revise. For illustration, we will show you how professionals might revise to eliminate wordiness. In each case, *a* is the wordy version and *b* the revision. Where possible, italics show the elimination of wordiness.

1. a. The word *convention is used* to mean a custom that a particular *society or* group of people have *figuratively come together to* accept as proper and correct for them.
   b. The word *convention* means a custom that a particular group of people have accepted as proper and correct for them.

2. a. Conventions in usage are arbitrary linguistic structures that particular segments of our society agree are the proper ones, *even though the agreement may be completely unconscious on the part of many or most members of a particular group.*

   b. Conventions in usage are arbitrary linguistic structures that particular segments of our society tacitly agree are proper.

3. a. Must such errors occur in writing; *people don't make many errors in sentence structure or idioms* in their conversation.

   b. Such errors occur more frequently in writing than in conversation.

4. a But since *in over 99 percent of the cases this rule involves* only *able* or *ous*, we have entered *only them* in the rule for simplicity's sake.

   b. Since that usage is so rare, we have, for simplicity's sake, entered only *able* and *ous* in the rule.

5. a. Sometimes a really careless writer will use a pronoun without even an adjective or closely related noun to show what the implied antecedent is. Examples:

   b. Here are two other examples of pronouns having only implied antecedents:

6. a. Many people, *in their colloquial usage at least,* use modifier forms forms once thought wholly incorrect.

   b. Many people use, colloquially at least, modifier forms once thought wholly incorrect.

7. a. Mixed sentence structure is usually due to faulty sentence sense *on the part of the writer.*

   b. Mixed sentence structure is usually due to the writer's faulty sentence sense.

8. a. *Each of* the following four chapters discusses in detail the characteristics *of one* of these four forms of discourse.

   b. The following four chapters discuss in detail the characteristics of these four forms of discourse.

9. a. Language is so complex that *it is almost literally true that an infinity of* styles *of writing* is possible.

   b. Language is so complex that innumerable styles are possible.

10. a. An original figure of speech *is no more out of place in* exposition than *it is in* description.

    b. An original figure of speech can enliven exposition as much as description.

These examples show how much a writer can tighten his style *after* he thinks he has written well. Note that in example 2 one word — *tacitly* — does the work of twenty words in the faulty sentence. Remember, as you write and as you revise, watch for roundabout phrasing, uselessly long constituents, and redundancy, or deadwood.

EXERCISES

Rewrite the following sentences to eliminate wordiness and achieve conciseness.

1. One of the most important factors pertaining to the subject of politics is the fact that many unqualified people who don't understand the issues which are involved vote even though they don't know what they are voting for or against.
2. Teachers who teach in elementary schools should be trained in a way that is different from the way that teachers who teach in high school are trained.
3. The process of becoming college educated is a far more complicated process than it is thought to be by those college students who are just beginning the process of becoming educated.
4. Modern medical doctors nowadays who specialize in treating just certain parts of the body have to take a great deal more specialized training to become specialists than similar specialists had to take twenty-five or thirty years ago in the 1950's.
6. In my opinion, I believe that no matter what a person wants to do in life, he can do whatever he wants to do if he tries hard enough to do it and firmly and fully believes that he can do whatever he wants to do.
7. Running the hundred-yard dash in a track meet is one of the most grueling and strenuous track meet events that a track man can run in the entire field of track sports.
8. Drunken drivers when they are behind the wheel of a car are more likely to cause accidents that shouldn't happen than sober drivers who are behind the wheel of a car.
9. Not very many modern people today know much about the subject of astronomy on account of the fact that the subject of astronomy is very complicated and therefore it is very difficult for people to understand very much about it.
10. On account of the fact that we are now entering the first initial stage of a political era of time, we should be very careful to analyze the issues before going to the polls to vote.

USAGE
LESSON
35

FAULTY
PARALLELISM

Two or more sentence constituents in a series (see Chapter 25 for punctuation of them) are said to be in parallel structure because they are grammatically similar (or equal in rank) and function identically in the sentence. Almost any kind of sentence constituent can be used in a series of two or more. Example:

> *correct:* *Realizing the danger* but *not wanting to alarm my mother*, I crept very quietly along the ledge.

The italicized constituents both are verb phrases of the same kind, are functioning identically, and are joined by a coordinating conjunction; thus they are in parallel structure, or exhibit proper parallelism.

When two or more constituents in a series are not grammatically similar (with the qualification noted below), they are said to be in **faulty parallelism.** The error is one in sentence structure and is serious. Examples:

> *wrong:* *Realizing the danger* but *I did not want to alarm my mother*, I crept very quietly along the ledge.

The two constituents are a verb phrase and an independent clause and are faulty in parallelism.

> *wrong:* The committee *discussed the proposal for three hours* but *not agreeing whether to accept it.*

The two constituents are one kind of verb phrase (the sentence predicate) and a different kind and are thus in faulty parallelism.

> *wrong:* She knew *that I was married* and *I was lying to her.*

Here a noun clause and an independent clause are in faulty parallelism.

The foregoing three example sentences can be corrected by making the two constituents in a series grammatically similar. The first correct example sentence above is a proper version of the first faulty example sentence. Here are correct versions of the other two:

correct: The committee *discussed the proposal for three hours* but *did not agree whether to accept it.*

Now two similar verb phrases (sentence predicates) are in parallel structure.

correct: She knew *that I was married* and *that I was lying to her.*

Now two noun clauses are in parallel structure.

To be correct, constituents in a series must always function identically, but sometimes they do not have to be identical grammatical structures. Examples:

correct: Laurie was *angry* and *in no mood to cooperate.*

The two italicized constituents — an adjective and a prepositional phrase — are not grammatically similar but they function identically as adjectivals and thus are in proper parallel structure.

correct: *Printed beautifully* but *full of typographical errors*, the book provoked laughter.

The two italicized constituents are a verb phrase and an adjective phrase and thus are not identical grammatical structures; but they both function identically as adjectivals and thus are in proper parallelism.

You do not need to know grammatical labels to recognize and correct faulty parallelism. If you will listen to your sentences with your mind's ear, any faulty parallelism will usually become apparent, for the sentence will just sound wrong.

EXERCISE 35. Rewrite the following sentences to eliminate faulty parallelism and establish proper parallel structure.

1. After studying the principle of uncertainty for an hour but I did not understand it, I closed the book and opened the whisky.

   _____

   _____

2. Professor Snooty neither enjoyed his classes and he did not like to give students extra help.

   _____

   _____

3. The jury knew that Halderk was guilty and he was perjurying himself.

   _____

   _____

4. Silver Belle increased her speed but not catching up with the front runner.

   _____

   _____

5. To obey the ten commandments and following Christ's injunctions in The Sermon on the Mount will ensure a happy life.

   _____

   _____

6. The host suggested parlor games and that we begin with charades.

   _____

   _____

7. This text is well-edited, comprehensive, and can be resold at a high price.

   _____

   _____

8. When you achieve fame, monetary success, and are not egotistical, you will have many friends.

   _____

   _____

9. We want a boycott of table grapes, to prevent non-union labor from entering the vineyards, and voting secretly on a new contract.

   _____

   _____

10. I use my car not only for commuting to school but let my sister use it on some weekends.

    _____

    _____

11. The poem begins with a chipmunk gathering food and is so busy he doesn't see the eagle coming.

    _____

    _____

12. The athletes at our college are academically equal to the nonathletes, none of them failing and many make high grades.

    _____

    _____

13. This course teaches young ladies poise, charm, and to have the qualifications to become models.

    _____

    _____

14. Professor Schnear said that I was his best student and I should plan to go to medical school.

    _____

    _____

15. There are two ways to avoid losing money in the stock market: One is never to buy any stock and second don't ever sell any stock that you own.

    _____

    _____

CHAPTER 36

CHOOSING EFFECTIVE WORDS

Organization, paragraphing, sentence compostion — all are important in most kinds of writing. Choice of words is also important and is the final basic of compostion that we will discuss. The term **diction** is used to mean word choice, and we will use it in that sense in this chapter. We will discuss **appropriateness** and **exactness** of word choice, or diction.

Just as there are levels of behavior in society — say the differences in behavior of a businessman at a stag party for his cronies and at a formal banquet for highly important executives —, there are **levels of diction.** For example, in a friendly letter to your best friend you probably would not hesitate to write "That's a lot of bunk"; but if the letter were to your minister, you probably would write "That's a lot of nonsense." That levels of diction exist and that we choose words according to the nature or importance of the writing (or speaking) situation cannot be denied.

Experts do not fully agree on the labels to apply to particular levels of diction, but we will use one suitable set of terms. **General-purpose words** are those appropriate for *any* writing situation. These include not only the structure words of our language, such as *of, not, many, and,* and so on, but also many common content words, such as *word, large, clothes, full, agree,* and on and on. **Standard diction** is used to mean all general-purpose words and all words suitable for informal and formal situations. **Nonstandard diction,** on the other hand, applies to words that most people of at least moderate education consider inappropriate for any use, such as *drownded* for the standard *drowned, learn me* for the standard *teach me,* and so on.

Formal and semiformal diction (which is used in conjunction with general-purpose words) can be combined into one category. Such words are not commonly used in casual conversation but are nevertheless useful and natural words for writing of some importance. Words in this category should not be considered pretentious (see below) nor the tools of snobbish people. Some examples are *callow* for *green* (meaning "inexperienced"), *vindicate* for *prove not guilty*, *discreet* for *careful about what he says*, *specious* for *not true*, *acquiesce* for *give in*, and so on. Words on this level will, when properly used, sound natural and suitable, not showy or pompous.

Below the formal or semiformal level is the **colloquial,** or **informal,** level. The word *colloquial* has nothing to do with *locality* but comes from a Latin word meaning "conversation." Thus a colloquialism is just an informal word or expression, such as *stuck up* for *conceited, cop* for *policeman, loony* for *insane, loose* for *promiscuous, mad* for *angry, bug* for *disease-producing microorganism,* and so on. Colloquialisms are in no way tainted but may sound out of place in semiformal or formal writing. You want your writing to sound natural and unaffected, and that means occasional colloquialisms are not out of place, but writing consisting *only* of colloquial phraseology seldom has a style pleasing to experienced readers. For example, compare these two sentences:

> The kids took out their beef on the teacher by cutting up and pooh-poohing at her.
> The children showed their displeasure by misbehaving and refusing to cooperate with the teacher.

Any one of the expressions in the first sentence might by itself be used effectively, but a *piling up* of just colloquial phrasing usually produces poor style.

A great many of our colloquial expressions are phrases with single-word equivalents on a higher level of diction. Here are some examples:

> do away with — abolish
> catch on to — comprehend *or* understand
> get going — depart *or* begin
> catch up with — overtake
> be in on it — participate

Usually, though not always, the single-word equivalent is stylistically superior to the colloquial phrase.

Slang (see Chapter 17) is a level of diction below the colloquial. In general, it should be avoided in semiformal writing, but an occasional racy, vigorous slang term can be used quite effectively in serious writing. For example, compare these two sentences:

Professor Shnall has a hang-up about students entering his classroom late.
Professor Shnall suffers emotional stress when students enter his classroom late.

Many knowledgeable readers would prefer the pungent slang term *hang-up* to the semiformal *emotional stress*. Even high-quality magazines such as *Harper's* occasionally use a slang term, such as *gift of gab* and *hot number*. But you should use slang in your compositions only sparingly and only when you think you will achieve a desirable stylistic effect.

Our final label for levels of diction is **pretentious diction,** which includes words that masquerade as semiformal or formal but which sound as though the writer is striving mightily to impress or overwhelm his readers. Pretentious diction lacks the naturalness and ease that formal or semiformal diction can achieve. It has much in common with jargon (see Chapter 19). Here is an example, from a textbook, of pretentious diction:

> In reworking the data, in addition to counterindicative matrices Gleason used another lexicostatistic subgrouping technique, one which tabulates a weighting of exclusively shared cognates.

It is not only the jargon but also the tone of this passage that puts it in the category of pretentious diction. Fortunately, students do not ofen write in pretentious diction.

For the most part, then, you should strive in your informative and persuasive writing to complement general-purpose words with words on a semiformal level, using colloquialisms and slang sparingly and only when they add desirable flavor to your style.

In addition to choosing appropriate words for your composition, you also want to choose words that say precisely what you mean. **Exactness of word choice** is perhaps even more important than appropriateness. For example, if you say that someone is *obtuse* when you really mean that he is *ignorant* (look the words up), you have used inexact or imprecise diction, which reflects poor thinking, creates poor style, and obscures meaning. Here are other examples of inexact diction taken from any essay exam on the poetry of Emily Dickinson:

> Her most common themes were those *surrounding* nature.
> She took *pride* in nature as an almost god-like force.
> To her, *partaking* of nature was an *enviable* experience.

Dickinson's themes did not *surround* nature but were simply *about* nature. She didn't take *pride* in nature, but *joy*. She didn't *partake* of nature but *communed* with nature. And her experience was not *enviable,* but *joyful* or *ecstatic.* Choice of words for exact meaning can greatly improve the style as well as the clarity of your writing.

EXERCISES

1. Suggest a single-word equivalent for each of the following colloquial phrases.

bring it off	get carried away
beat the rap	do him in
on the go	get your kicks
down in the mouth	make a go of it
up against it	give in
give up	join up
make a bundle	make it up to you
make it up	get on with it
get up out of	put up with
keep on	hang on to it
get stuck with	carry it out
make up for	play a big part in
get a hold of yourself	cut down on
on account of the fact that	get a kick out of
run into	put up a fuss
get down off of	go down into
get away from	run rings around
come up with	talk a lot about
make a hit with	come in contact with
find out about	leave out
be full of	go on with

2. Rewrite the following sentences to achieve a higher level of diction. The phrasing that should be changed is italicized. Here is an example of how you should perform this exercise.

    A. 1. When a student *gets in a hassle* with his girl friend, he usually *goofs off in* his homework.
        2. When a student quarrels with his girl friend, he usually disregards his homework.

1. I *am now going to talk about* how this prejudice *shows up* and *does bad things*.

2. I don't think it is *one bit fair* for an eighteen-year-old *to get put in jail* for drinking.

3. A teenager should *care enough about* his parents *to try and do things right*.

4. *Right now* if a teenager wants *to get hold of* alcoholic drinks *it is easy enough*.

5. Whatever you do, *you can bet* your child *will grow up doing it* too.

6. We must *educate ourselves more than ever to stay with the times.*

7. Our founding fathers *put first* the *individual person* as *being more important.*

8. Although I know I *want to take* certain subjects that *interest me best,* I don't know *just how far I want to go in* these subjects.

9. Whether you *try your hand at one thing or another,* it's good experience and sometimes *fun just to see if you can do it or not.*

10. The *part I enjoyed most* about my job was that *I got to work with* people.

USAGE
LESSON
36

CONFUSED
SENTENCE
STRUCTURE

Some kinds of faulty sentence structure appear over and over and have names: faulty shifts in number, person, tense, and voice; faulty comparisons; misplaced modifiers; dangling modifiers; and faulty parellelism. In other ways sentences sometimes are faulty because their structure is mixed or confused. Sometimes the flaw is due to the writer's starting out with one kind of structure in mind and then shifting to another, incompatible kind of structure. The resulting confused sentence structure is a serious error. Example:

> *confused structure:* Natural resources are only, and will only last as long as we make them.

It is not clear what structure the student intended as he began the sentence; perhaps he intended to say "are limited" but lost his way after *are*. At any rate, the incorrect structure "'are last as long . . ." is demanded by the grammatical structure of the whole, and thus the sentence structure is confused. Note, too, that the last part of the sentence is ambiguous.

Here is another example:

> *confused structure:* By containing Communism can assure the continued freedom of the free world.

Here the nature of the faulty shift structure is clearer. After "By containing Communism" the student must have intended to say "we can. . . ." But he evidently forgot the structure he began with and incorrectly tried to make the prepositional phrase serve as the subject of *can assure*. He either should have omitted *By* or should have inserted *we* after *Communism*; both resulting sentences would be correct.

Sometimes the structure of a sentence is faulty because logically its subject does not fit its predicate (that is, the subject might fit the predictae

grammatically, such as in "Green peas eat alligators," but not logically).
Here is an example wih a slash between the subject and predicate:

confused structure: The first step in learning to drive / is the clutch.

Since a car's clutch is not a step in learning to drive, the sentence subject does not logically fit its predicate, and thus the sentence structure is faulty. The student could have written

correct: The first step in learning to drive / is to learn to engage the clutch smoothly.

Now the subject logically fits the predicate, since to learn something can be a step in a process.
     Here is another example:

confused structure: One way to improve our environment / is trees.

Since trees themselves are not a "way," the sentence structure is faulty. The student could have written

correct: One way to improve our environment / is to plant more trees.

Now a real "way" is specified and the structure is correct. It is careless thinking that leads to the kind of faulty sentences we have illustrated. In writing, try to think clearly and reread your sentences carefully to see that they are correctly constructed.
     A special kind of faulty sentence structure occurs in *is when* and *is where* sentences when neither a time nor place is mentioned. Examples:

incorrect: Fraudulent advertising is when you suggest untruths about your product.

incorrect: Gourmet cooking is where you use exotic recipes that few people know about.

These *is when* and *is where* sentences are faulty in their structure because advertising is not a time and cooking is not a place. Avoid such constructions and instead write sentences like these:

correct: You are guilty of fraudulent advertising when you suggest untruths about your product.

correct: Gourmet cooking calls for the use of exotic recipes that few people know about.

Now the sentence subjects logically fit their predicates.

EXERCISE 36. Rewrite the following confused sentences so that correct structures are established.

1. This course teaches the value of a two-house system, such as the U.S. Congress is set up.

   _____

   _____

2. With most people there is a sort of language barrier between the child and his parents.

   _____

   _____

3. A constitution is when people govern themselves.

   _____

   _____

4. If aid is granted and would promote undemocratic policies is one which is very controversial.

   _____

   _____

5. By grouping all these superior students into one class could cause them to learn less.

   _____

   _____

6. The radio is coming back as an advertisement which appeals to young people.

   _____

   _____

7. The public's morals are being reduced to how high his financial status is.

   _____

   _____

8. Big surprises come in little packages is another way the advertisers hook the public.

_____

_____

9. Conservation is where we replant all the trees that have burned or been cut down.

_____

_____

10. Anything a foreigner does comes in contact with advertising.

_____

_____

11. In other ways, which offset the bad qualities, are the benefits we receive from student government.

_____

_____

12. Some rivers are being allowed good drinking water to go into the sea.

_____

_____

13. Through God's creations alone is the only concept of God that man has.

_____

_____

14. The first point of view is what if the United States should surrender.

_____

_____

15. I have known people in our community that if you make a comment on the news they always disagree.

_____

_____